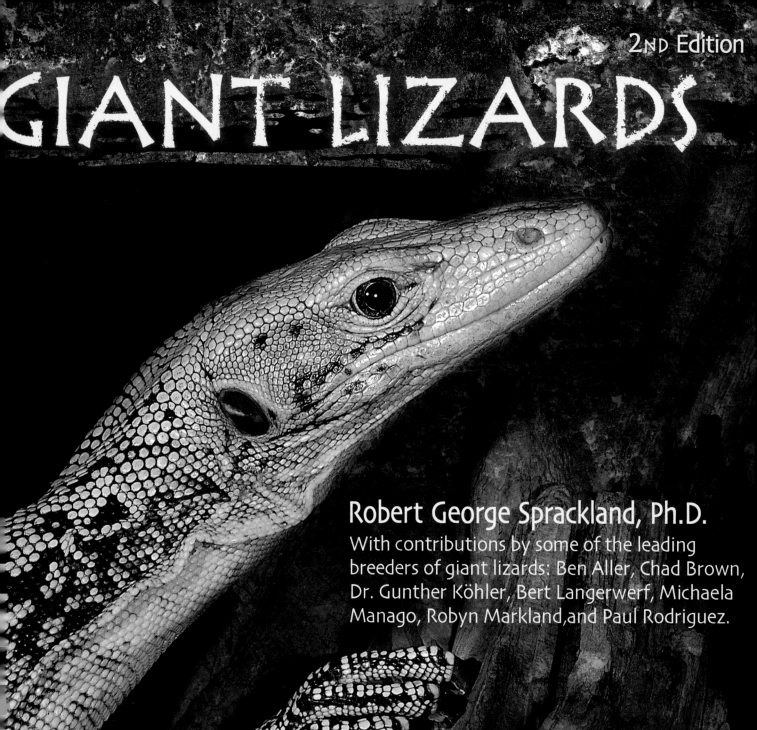

2ND Edition

GIANT LIZARDS

Robert George Sprackland, Ph.D.

With contributions by some of the leading breeders of giant lizards: Ben Aller, Chad Brown, Dr. Gunther Köhler, Bert Langerwerf, Michaela Manago, Robyn Markland, and Paul Rodriguez.

Dedication:
For George Albert Boulenger (1858-1937) who provided a professional inspiration,
And Teri Sprackland Beloved partner for life who knew she had to "love me, love my lizards," and did, and still does.

Project Team
Editor: Tom Mazorlig
Copy Editor: Stephanie Fornino
Indexer: Lucie Haskins
Design: Mary Ann Kahn

TFH Publications
President/CEO: Glen S. Axelrod
Executive Vice President: Mark E. Johnson
Publisher: Christopher T. Reggio
Production Manager: Kathy Bontz

T.F.H. Publications, Inc.
One TFH Plaza
Third and Union Avenues
Neptune City, NJ 07753

Printed and bound in China
09 10 11 12 13   1 3 5 7 9 8 6 4 2

Library of Congress Cataloging-in-Publication Data
Sprackland, Robert G.
  Giant lizards : the definitive guide to the natural history, care, and breeding of monitors, iguanas, and other large lizards / Robert G. Sprackland. -- 2nd ed.
      p. cm.
  Includes bibliographical references and index.
  ISBN 978-0-7938-0581-5 (alk. paper)
1. Captive lizards. 2. Lizards. 3. Monitor lizards. 4. Lizard culture. I. Title.
SF515.5.L58S65 2008
639.3'95--dc22
                                2008018345

This book has been published with the intent to provide accurate and authoritative information in regard to the subject matter within. While every reasonable precaution has been taken in preparation of this book, the author and publisher expressly disclaim responsibility for any errors, omissions, or adverse effects arising from the use or application of the information contained herein. The techniques and suggestions are used at the reader's discretion and are not to be considered a substitute for veterinary care. If you suspect a medical problem consult your veterinarian.

The Leader In Responsible Animal Care For Over 50 Years!®
www.tfh.com

CONTENTS

Basiliscus plumifrons

PREFACE

This is an unusual book. It deals with a totally artificial assemblage of animals, chosen on the arbitrary basis of size. But this is not the first time such a book has been published, being preceded by several decades by Pope's *Giant Snakes* and Minton's *Giant Reptiles*. Giant lizards are in vogue, have been since the late 1970s, and probably will be for years to come. Television and magazine articles have made them familiar, zoos have made them accessible, and animal dealers have made them available.

Many herpetoculturists have reservations about private individuals keeping such species as water monitors and adult iguanas. In response, I point out that much of our basic husbandry knowledge has come from the private sector, from people shelling out their own time, money, and space to learn something about these animals. Zoos only represent the tip of the iceberg when it comes to the husbandry of lizards. I strongly support zoos and the dedicated people who work for them. Zoo work is rarely glamorous—in fact, it's often tedious. Professional institutions have pioneered techniques of veterinary care, environmentally controlled terraria, nutrition, and captive breeding. They will remain the best major facilities for the housing and breeding of giant animals, a role that can only be enhanced by the care and cooperation of the private sector.

This book represents the culmination of notes accumulated over nearly 40 years of studies by the author and draws heavily upon the experiences of others, many of whom are listed in the bibliography. My interest in monitors goes back to 1969, and since then I have studied specimens in museums, zoos, private collections, and in the wild, from Papua New Guinea to Austria. I have also kept live monitors for more than 26 years. For much of that time, I was trying to learn how to improve husbandry techniques for these large

The black tegu has been one of the most available of the giant lizards for several decades.

Australia does not allow the exportation of its wildlife, so Mertens' monitor is rarely available to the private hobbyist.

making captive reproduction of animals a top priority. The literature available to help those people was either out of date, hard to find, or just plain nonexistent. Successful husbandry and breeding were often frustrating and expensive experiences. Still, many people persevered and succeeded in their efforts to better care for and breed exotic reptiles and amphibians. To these keepers a new term was created: herpetoculturists. Just as students of birds have been described as scientific ornithologists or bird-keeping aviculturists, and fish workers are either ichthyologists or aquarists, the world of amphibians and reptiles has its own natural division between herpetologists and herpetoculturists.

At the beginning of what would become the herpetocultural revolution, I took my own prior two decades' experience in studying the natural history and husbandry of large lizards and decided to compile a massive book that brought together much of the then-known information about the animals under one cover. Based on my firsthand experience with the animals, coupled with a broad professional knowledge of technical and foreign language reports on them, I wrote and T.F.H. Publications, Inc., published *Giant Lizards*. It quickly became a popular book in its field. Released in 1992, *Giant Lizards* went on to have an important influence on the keeping of large (and, I am told, small) lizards under captive conditions. Not surprisingly, though, herpetoculture has been extremely busy going much further with the acquisition of new species, improving husbandry, and breeding nearly every species covered in the

and often active animals. At no point, though, did my research focus on captive breeding, for which reason I have invited several of the most successful lizard breeders to contribute to this revised volume. When the first edition was written in 1989–1990, the number of successful captive breedings of large lizards was quite small and often restricted to one-time incidents in zoos. Since then, captive propagation has become much more common, and several businesses are based primarily on the sale of captive-bred stock.

In the early 1990s, there was a blossoming of interest in the keeping of exotic reptiles and amphibians as never seen before. Private keepers increased in number while zoos expended more time and effort on improving husbandry and

Most of the green iguanas in the pet trade are now from farms in Central America.

original volume. In large measure the discovery of new species has been driven by herpetoculture; of the many species of monitors described since 1990, nearly all came to light primarily through the herpetocultural trade. Others are currently awaiting description. It is therefore time to produce a completely new version of the 1992 book.

Herpetoculture now is far less divided into "professional" zookeeper and "amateur" dealer and breeder camps than it was back in the 1980s. The "Berlin Wall" that had long been a divide between those very dedicated but often exclusionary groups was also largely a remnant by the early 1990s. Today, many animals that form the breeding stock for commercial and private herpetoculture can trace their origins to offspring

from zoos that have been sold, traded, or loaned to the private sector. This melding of worlds is reflected in the contributions by the breeders who so kindly joined me in updating this book. These top breeders have done field research, worked at zoos, and collaborated with academics to achieve their noteworthy accomplishments. I trust that readers of this second edition will be as grateful as I for the contributions by Ben Aller, Chad Brown, Dr. Gunther Köhler, Bert Langerwerf, Michaela Manago, Robyn Markland, and Paul Rodriguez.

In the 19 years since I wrote the first edition of *Giant Lizards,* much has happened for me, too. I completed my Ph.D. studying monitors, made numerous field trips to Australasia to study the lizards in the wild, and logged thousands of hours and miles to visit the world's best zoos, museums, and private breeders to learn about the leading-edge research and "best practices" on giant lizard husbandry. The resulting new book, *Giant Lizards, 2nd Edition,* goes beyond the earlier work, to the point that it is now, quite literally, a different volume.

Among some of the suggestions I have incorporated in this edition is expanded coverage of natural history information, including more detailed habitat descriptions. To qualify for inclusion in *Giant Lizards*, a species must attain a typical total length of at least 3 feet (0.9 m). Species that do not meet that mark have been omitted, and therefore many species included in the first edition are not in the second.

Many friends and colleagues have provided ideas, reviewed the manuscript, allowed me access to materials, donated study specimens,

○○

Cooperation between the zoo and herp hobby communities continues to grow.

or helped in many other ways toward the completion of this second edition. I therefore extend my deepest thanks to Lynette Abra, Kraig Adler, Per Ahlberg, Nick Arnold, Michael Barnes, Richard Bartlett, Aaron Bauer, Peter Baverstock, Ilaiah Bigilale, John Binns, Wolfgang Böhme, Joanne Brodsky, Barry Clarke, Craig Clayton, David Coffee, Harold Cogger, Paul Cooper, Michael Cota, Patrick Couper, Tim Criswell, Daniel Diessner, Michael Dlooglach, Giuliano Doria, Gina Douglas, Bernd Eidenmüller, Kelsey Engel, Jeff Ettling, Susan Evans, Danté Fenolio, Jayna Fowler, Chaz Franklin, Maren Gaulke, Jacques Gauthier, Heinz Grillitch, Ulrich Gruber, Danny Gunalen, Rainer Günther, Gary Gyaki, Rae Lynn Haliday, Robert Hassur, David Heppell, Marinus Hoogmoed, Hans-Georg Horn, Raymond Hoser, Grant Husband, Terri Irwin, Hans Jacobs, Ronald Javitz, Chris van Kalken, Lori King, Gunther Köhler, Peter Krauss, Fred Kundert, Michael Lee, Alan Leviton, Chad Littlewood, Rob MacInnes, Elaine and Bob Mackin, Anita Malhotra, Larry Martin, Hyman Marx, Colin McCarthy, Andrew Milner, Mark O'Shea, Pierre Pfeffer, Hans-Dieter Phillippen, Barry Pomfret, Paul Rodriguez, Andrew Rowell, Udo Schweers, Ben Siegel, Frank Slavens, Chris Smeenck, Hobart Smith, Becky Speer, Pete Strimple, Gerry Swan, Geoffrey Swinney, Ann Sylph, John Tashjian, Rainer Thissen, Stella Thissen, Bertus van Tuijl, Harold Voris, Joe Wasilewski, John Weigel, Klaus Wesiak, David Williams, Andrew Wisniewski, John Wombley, Luke Yeoman, George Zug, and Richard Zweifel. Financial and logistical support for various research projects over the years has come from the Alexander Koenig Museum, Australia Zoo, Fitzroy Island Resort, Linnean Society of London, the National Museums of Scotland, the Natural History Museum London, Queensland Parks and Wildlife Service, San Diego Herpetological Society, Senckenberg Museum, the Shoestring Foundation, University College London, University of London Graduate Research Fund, and the Virtual Museum of Natural History.

This book discusses all the lizards that reach a length of 3 feet (0.9 m) or more, including the legless species, such as the sheltopusik.

Their support is gratefully acknowledged. Businesses that have donated study specimens are Ben Siegel Reptiles, California Zoological Supply, and Strictly Reptiles.

Once more I extend my special thanks to friends and colleagues who are no longer with us. I extend my sincere thanks to Wendy McKeown for allowing me to publish many of Sean's slides. Thanks also to these late herpetologists for their help at various times and in important ways: Walter Auffenberg, Mark Bayless, Paul Deraniyagala, Steve Irwin, Sean McKeown, Robert Mertens, H. G. Petzold, Joe Slowinski, Edward H. Taylor, and Garth Underwood.

Shortly before this book went to press we lost our colleague and contributor Bert Langerwerf. His kindness and dedication made him a pleasure to know, and many of us learned a great deal from his pioneering and enterprising efforts in lizard care and breeding. Herpetology has lost an important leader, and all of us who knew him lost a good friend. The author, editor, and contributors of *Giant Lizards, 2nd Edition* are grateful for Bert's involvement in the project.

Thanks to the institutions that have allowed me access to study their collections: American Museum of Natural History, Australian Museum, Australian Reptile Park, Australia Zoo, Denver

Zoo, Doria Museum of Natural History Genoa, Field Museum of Natural History, Florida State Museum, National Museum of Natural History Leiden, National Museum of Natural History Paris, Natural History Museum London, Papua New Guinea National Museum and Art Gallery, Queensland Museum, Royal Museum of Scotland, San Diego Natural History Society, San Diego Zoo, Sarawak Museum, United States National Museum of Natural History, University College London, University of Kansas Museum of Natural History, Woodland Park Zoo, Zoological Museum Amsterdam, Zoological Museum Berlin, and Zoological Museum Munich.

Special thanks to Dr. Chris Cannon for her critique of the veterinary chapter and the crash course in modern herpetological therapy. Rae Lynn Haliday did a similar edit of the section on laws affecting herpetoculture, for which I am grateful.

For the gracious loan of photographs I thank Michael Barnes, Aaron Bauer, John Binns, Craig Clayton, Michael Cota, Tim Criswell, Bernd Eidenmüller, Danté Fenolio, Danny Gunalen, and Bert Langerwerf.

I extend my thanks also to my longtime editor at T.F.H., Tom Mazorlig, with whom it has always been a pleasure to work.

I am most grateful to my wife, Teri Sprackland, for her detailed edits and syntactical corrections. My dear wife is also my longtime editor, and I thank her for ensuring that there is only the smallest gap between what I write and what I intended to write! Her support has spanned all the classic marriage vows—through sickness and health, richer (when??) and poorer, and so on—and she has been steadfast and encouraging from the academic halls of Britain through the great basements of Europe and into the bush of northeastern Australia. To Teri my deepest thanks.

Monitors and other large lizards are neither more nor less interesting than other reptiles, but they do present a special sense of the dramatic, if not the prehistoric, that smaller or less "dinosaurian" creatures cannot match. The primary difficulty in studying many of these species is their distribution in parts of the world that still recall the old mapmaker's words, "here be dragons." In reply, I would respond "aye, and so many!" It is of little consequence that there are still places to be explored and animal species to discover. We are unable to travel back to dinosaurian times, but in those difficult-to-reach places of today with their poorly known faunas, we still have great unknowns, the places where no scientist has gone before. As I was completing the fourth revision of this manuscript in February 2006, biologists announced a massive discovery of many new animal species from a part of West Papua (Indonesian New Guinea) that had never been previously explored.

An appreciation of giant lizards is perhaps as much about those exotic places from which they come as the animals themselves. If these animals can inspire us to conserve these wildernesses, then perhaps the benefits of our fascination aren't so one-way as it appears.

Robert George Sprackland, Ph.D.
Seattle, Washington
Cairns, Australia
May 2008

11

Tupinambis teguixin

INTRODUCTION

The beaded lizard (and its close relative, the Gila monster) appears as a motif in Native American art.

Because monitor lizards (such as the Nile monitor shown here) prey on crocodile eggs, it was a common belief that they warned of the presence of crocodiles.

You are reading this book because you have an interest in the fascinating world of lizards. This fascination is not new; mankind has long been enthralled with giant reptiles. Peoples as diverse as the Egyptians, Indians, and Australian Aboriginals mixed fear, respect, and reverence for the crocodiles they lived with, aware of the possibility of sudden death that could result from an unexpected encounter between human and reptile. That the creature could appear silently, without warning—indeed, without being seen as it approached from beneath mud-colored waters—added to the mystique.

Among these huge reptiles were smaller and equally dragon-like counterparts, creatures known as monitor lizards. The larger species were regular predators of crocodile eggs and young. They were also credited with magical properties, and while less obvious than crocodiles, formed an important part of myth and folklore. There is, for example, a good deal more monitor lizard than crocodile in the stylish, coiled dragon of Chinese legends. Nor did the Europeans who developed modern science doubt the existence of the mythical beasts. Linnaeus himself bestowed the name "*Draco*" to the small East Asian gliding agamas because, upon seeing their wings, he was convinced that they were the hatchlings of great dragons.

Until the mid-1990s, most keepers (and their pets) suffered from a lack of good information about reptile care. Then, interest mushroomed around the world. There were many herpetological magazines and scores of books filling gaps in reptile information. Internet

INFORMATION SOURCES

The successes in prolonging captive reptile life spans and getting specimens to breed are conspicuously underlined by the many outlets for reports on these accomplishments. We've come a long way since Raymond Ditmar's 1910 book, *Reptiles of the World.* As recently as 1988, such English language reports were largely restricted to the *International Zoo Yearbook, Herpetological Review,* and many regional herpetological societies such as those of Chicago, Philadelphia, San Diego, New York, and Maryland. Beginning in 1989, a whole new field of herpetological journalism blossomed, so that today we have glossy, professionally produced periodicals, including *Reptiles, Herpetological Natural History,* and *Reptilia.* Add to these the many herpetocultural books, care sheets, videos, workshops, and short courses, and you virtually eliminate the excuses of no information or information that is too difficult to obtain. The new problems are finding quality information and being able to afford it and still pay for reptile food, plus a movie ticket or two for you and your family!

sites spread. Steve Irwin became television's Crocodile Hunter, followed by venomous snake authority Mark O'Shea, filmmaker Nigel Marvin, and a seemingly endless cadre of hosts of reptile-based programs. Many were excellent resources, while many more were junk. Herpetology and herpetoculture had truly entered mainstream society.

The Rise of Herpetoculture

Appreciation of reptiles was never restricted to professionals. The ranks of private herpetoculturists are filled with people who spend their time, money, and living space to enjoy and learn about their animals. Through their efforts, more people are exposed to lizards in a positive way. Improvements in husbandry inevitably lead to captive breeding, and with that comes prestige. It takes a savvy keeper to raise his animals through their entire life cycle, and in so doing, herpetoculture has achieved the respectable status of aviculture and aquaculture.

The number of new discoveries has been important for the science of herpetology. We now know that several groups of nongeckos have voices and that incubation temperature determines the sex of hatchlings for many turtles and lizards. Depending on hemipenial structure, males of some species must use both hemipenes during mating if they are to fertilize both oviducts in the female. In other words, shortened matings could reduce clutch size by half.

Zoos and universities, meanwhile, may be buried in paperwork needed for even simple specimen acquisitions or transfers. As a case in

Captive breeding of the giant lizards is becoming more commonplace. These are hatching Argus monitors.

point, it took me eight months to get a CITES permit from the United States to export a preserved lizard from California to London! The British government gave me a permit in just ten days. The paperwork makes humorous and frustrating reading, and if it affected more people, would warrant a Michael Moore documentary. I don't even want to start talking about the quagmires involved in transporting live reptiles abroad. And if you want to see a zoo curator become schizophrenic, ask about the paperwork needed to transfer San Francisco garter snakes (an endangered domestic species) from one zoo to another within the United States.

Captive Breeding

The big break for herpetoculture came with the rather sudden flow of repeatable captive breedings that began in the early 1990s. Wonderful boons occurred as better hiding facilities (along with, admittedly, many other factors) were provided. It was quite a breakthrough when pioneers such as Dr. Richard Ross published detailed information on natural habitats. This information on habitats resulted in keeping herps at more appropriate temperatures, including following the natural cycles of warm and cool temperatures most of these animals experience in nature.

It was also something of an innovation to increase the feedings for lizards to daily or

More and more hobbyists are traveling to see herps in their natural habitat. The Galápagos Islands—home of the marine iguana and other notable herps—are a popular destination.

alternate-daily offerings. Prior to the 1980s, books left readers with the impression that if snakes needed to eat only once a month, so did lizards; it doesn't take a physiological ecologist to figure out that starving animals have diminished sex drives.

Today, captive breeders provide many animals to zoos, and zoos often provide surplus animals to breeders and experienced private persons. These networks help ensure varied gene pools while also providing an informal but essential exchange of husbandry information. Such exchanges are going to become more important as biodiversity and preservation programs gain greater interest and funding over the coming years.

Communications

The evolution of North American herpetoculture has expanded to embrace all manner of herpetologically inclined people. America's working model is approaching that of the Germans, who, in 1963, formed a major herpetological society as a bridge among academic, zoo, and private workers. Founded largely through the efforts of Prof. Dr. Robert Mertens, one of the most respected herpetologists of the 20th century, the melding of the three spheres was reflected in their name: the German Society of Herpetology and Terrarium-keeping (the DGHT). The DGHT publishes one of the finest

17

The water monitor is still abundant, but local peoples harvest many thousands for leather each year.

herpetology journals in the world, *Salamandra*, along with the shorter *Elaphe* and the special issues of *Mertensiella*.

It is amazing to review the literature for many reptile groups and see how much life-history data are generated from observing specimens in captivity. Furthermore, all societies now host conferences to exchange information. The "Big Three" American professional academic societies (American Society of Ichthyologists and Herpetologists [ASIH], Herpetologists' League [HL], and Society for the Study of Amphibians and Reptiles [SSAR]) are now joined by the National Reptiles Breeders Expo (NRBE), the International Herpetological Symposia (IHS), and many regional meetings focusing on captive breeding and husbandry. These links among academics, zoological parks, and private keepers are to be commended, encouraged, and expanded. The information exchanged benefits herpetology and the animals it studies. One largely untapped resource for academic studies is the donation of dead reptiles to local museums and universities. Too many species that are common in the hobby are represented by very few museum specimens.

One benefit of these exchanges is that they sometimes lead to discovery or rediscovery of species that would otherwise remain unknown. A downside is that species of little interest to collectors, which may be quite common, will remain poorly known and uncollected. As with all human interests, profit must be a factor at some level in the process before any animal group will get further attention. I agree with the

NRBE's organizer, Wayne Hill: Profit is not a dirty word, and there are many benefits to herpetology through reasonable and responsibly operated commercial ventures. Is the sale of captive-bred animals to fund further research really that much different from the professional hat-in-hand routine called grant writing? Is it really different from the mass breeding of rodents or fruit flies for laboratory research?

Many species, unfortunately, will ease into extinction. Beasts like the Cape Verde skink (*Macroscincus coctei*) are now to be seen only as preserved museum specimens. Many species have tiny ranges, some on extremely beautiful and costly property. Laws may protect a species, but million-dollar homes are still built on their habitats. Will it be possible to save those species through captive breeding? Will we be allowed to try?

Restrictive laws, local legislation, corrupt wildlife officers, political unresponsiveness, and habitat destruction are the major impediments to further advances in herpetology. As herpetoculturists and herpetologists unite in their largely common goals, these impediments may yield a bit. In 2003, Western Australia finally relaxed some of the most draconian laws (no reptiles could be kept privately) to allow licensed people to keep and breed herpetofauna. Perhaps, just perhaps, we can halt a few imminent extinctions while also making sure that there are herptiles available to live with our next generation. For now, we watch the animals and wait for each success.

And wait...

Varanus varius

PART
1

LIZARD
BIOLOGY
AND
HUSBANDRY

Varanus albigularis

OVERVIEW OF LIZARD ANATOMY, PHYSIOLOGY, AND TAXONOMY

Despite being closely related, lizards–even legless species such as the sheltopusik–are physiologically different from snakes.

The reductionist approach to biology is to learn about an organism such as a lizard by reducing the subject to its smallest components. This philosophy is about as valid as claiming that one can fully understand an automobile only when one fully understands every wire, nut, and liquid that makes up the full object. Of course you will have a greater degree of understanding this way, but few would argue that understanding the full scope of the auto–or lizard–would be revealed. Cars and organisms are more than merely the sum of their parts.

Long before one reaches the reductionist's ultimate level of study, there is a more essential interrelatedness that is relevant. Simply knowing about the types of cells that compose the heart will not yield knowledge of its function. Reductionism may loosely be equated with anatomical study, while knowledge of function falls under the domain of physiology.

Herpetoculturists have long used hit and miss techniques to devise methods for proper care of their lizards. In many cases, a better understanding of physiology could have been

24

QUEEN ANATOMY

Anatomy has long been called the Queen of Biological Science because it is almost impossible to garner any valuable understanding of an organism without knowing how it is assembled. In the 1980s, Scotsman James Hutton transformed geology into a modern science by declaring that "the present is the key to the past," meaning that the same processes of erosion, earthquakes, and flooding (among others) that shaped modern landscapes would also account for land shaping in the prehistoric past. A few decades later, the French Baron Georges Cuvier would similarly exclaim that comparing the anatomies of different species could shed light on the natural histories of poorly known–and prehistoric–creatures. Comparative anatomy remains a central block in the larger scientific structure of understanding nature and the actions and interrelationships among organisms. From the study of comparative anatomy we find important similarities among species that further allow us to develop classification systems.

invaluable. For example, how many lizards were lost in the pre-1980s because the prevailing belief was, in essence, that lizards are just snakes with legs and therefore need only occasional meals? We now know that most lizards eat almost daily, sometimes more than once per day, and that the old "snake diet" regime is simply a sentence of death by starvation for lizards.

The intent of this chapter is to provide a thumbnail overview of important anatomical and physiological topics that bear directly on proper herpetoculture. Each section begins with a survey of one aspect of gross anatomy and then moves into the relevant physiological and metabolic processes that a keeper may find useful.

Basic Lizard Anatomy

Herpetologists use several shorthand terms when discussing reptilian anatomy. Among the most commonly used are those referring to metrics, or morphometric characters. Morphometrics are features that have a range of possible conditions, such as length, weight, and scale counts. Because many lizards may lose their tails to predators or accidents, the standard metric for length is the snout-vent length, abbreviated SVL. SVL is measured along the ventral (belly) surface, from the middle tip of the chin (mental scale) to the front edge of the vent, or cloaca. Total length, abbreviated TL, is used when the tail is intact and includes the snout-vent length and tail length

With but a few exceptions, lizards have visible ear openings, shown here on a water monitor.

(SVL + Tail = TL). Measurements usually are given in millimeters (mm); there are 25.4 mm to 1 inch.

Defining Lizards

The definition of "lizard" has been considerably modified since the 1780s with the advances made from new methods of evolutionary analyses. Snakes are now considered to be part of the saurian branch of the reptile tree–hence the old terms for the suborders Lacertilia and Serpentes are no longer in general usage. Additionally, tuatara are now also placed on the same stout branch of relatives as both "snakes" and "lizards."

Even features that are considered signatures of snakes are not universal among serpents. Many sea snakes (family Laticaudidae) and thread snakes (family Leptotyphlopidae) lack enlarged belly scales, while thread snakes have lower jawbones that do not unhinge and are instead firmly fixed together. Most (but not all) snakes have tails that are much shorter than the SVL. The bifid ("forked") tongue seen in snakes is found among several lizard groups (tegus and monitors), none of which are close to being limbless. Universally, however, snakes lack moveable eyelids, and some have the eye concealed under opaque scales–as do many lizards. Finally, it was long held that only lizards– and only some lizards–had the ability to break off and then regenerate the tail, an ability known as autotomy. Many lizards lack this ability (including the majority of giant lizards), as do the vast majority of snakes, but at least some neotropical snakes in the genus *Scaphiodontophis* possess autotomy (Slowinski and Savage, 1995). The lines between the groups are not nearly as well drawn as many have supposed.

What, then, is a lizard? Lizards and other reptiles are animals that possess a flexible bony spine and a dorsal hollow nerve tube; breathe with lungs instead of gills or the skin; have a body at least partially covered in keratinous

26

LIST OF CHARACTERS TRADITIONALLY USED TO DISTINGUISH LIZARDS FROM SNAKES AND EXAMPLES OF EXCEPTIONS

"LIZARD" CHARACTER	EXCEPTION
anterior lower jaw tips firmly articulated	some flap-footed lizards (*Lialis*)
well-developed limbs present	many limbless species among the skinks, flap-footed lizards, anguids, dibamids, etc.
external ear opening present	earless lizards (*Cophotis, Lanthanotus, Cophosaurus*, etc.)
moveable eyelids present	most geckos, flap-footed lizards, night lizards, many skinks, dibamids, amphisbaenids, etc.
tail longer than SVL	some geckos, skinks, chameleons, and flap-footed lizards

scales; have a single occipital condyle that joins the skull to the vertebral column at the atlas (mammals and amphibians have two condyles); reproduce via embryos protected by membranes called the amnion and allantois; and produce young that do not undergo a metamorphosis from a larval stage but that more or less resemble miniature versions of the adults. (For more on these topics, see Chapter 3: Reproduction.)

Within the reptiles are the Diapsida, to which belong those creatures with two openings (foramina) in the skull in the temple region. Presently some debate exists about whether the turtles represent part of the Diapsida whose skeletal elements have been misinterpreted, leading to the belief that they are anapsids rather than diapsids with roofed-over foramina. (See section "The Skull".) Lizards and snakes are diapsids. In any event, the lizard-snake clade is united by the presence of paired male copulatory organs (called hemipenes); a transverse cloacal slit called the vent; acrodont or pleurodont (but never thecodont) teeth (see "Tooth Types" sidebar); and a three-chambered heart (two atria, one ventricle).

The following sections provide a gross overview of important aspects of lizard anatomy. For more detailed accounts, consult references such as Bellairs (1970), Kardong (1995), Romer (1956), or Romer and Parsons (1986).

Skulls of *Varanus rudicollis*, *Basiliscus plumifrons*, and *Ctenosaura acanthura* (left to right) showing the large opening in the skull behind the eye, a feature typical of lizards.

Skull

For a zoologist, no part of a vertebrate's anatomy tells more than the skull. Lizards and other reptiles have more skeletal elements in their skulls than do mammals and fewer than many amphibians. The reptilian skull, in general, tends to be stronger and lighter than that of most amphibians, and it is considerably more complex than that of mammals. For example, reptiles have several bones in each half of the lower jaw, while mammals have but one. Lizards also possess a pair of large openings in the skull behind each eye, one above the other. The bordering bones form arches, and the holes are called **fenestrae** (singular = fenestra, from the Latin word meaning "window"). Because lizards, snakes, crocodilians, dinosaurs (including birds), and their relatives have two such temporal fenestrae on each side of the skull, this large group of reptiles has been given the Greek name Diapsida (δι, di-, two, plus πσ, aps, opening). Diapsids represent the largest number of terrestrial backboned animal species on Earth. In the same way that snakes and many lizards have lost their legs through evolutionary modification over time, these two groups have also lost the lower bony arch of the skull. The loss has given the skull considerable elasticity, while diapsids that retain a lower bony brace have a considerably more restricted gape. Several anatomical features serve to separate the very lizard-like tuatara of New Zealand from other diapsids, including its retention of the lower temporal arch. (Additionally, tuatara differ from lizards in having abdominal ribs and a longitudinal vent and in lacking a male copulatory organ.)

BONES FOUND IN LIZARD SKULLS

	FOUND IN LIZARDS	ALSO FOUND IN HUMANS
UPPER SKULL	basioccipital	basioccipital
	basisphenoid	basisphenoid
	ectopterygoid	
	epipterygoid	
	exoccipital	
	frontal	frontal
	jugal	
	lacrimal	lacrimal
	maxilla	maxilla
	nasal	nasal
	occipital	occipital
	parietal	parietal
	postfrontal	
	prefrontal	
	premaxilla	
	proötic	
	pterygoid	
	quadrate	
	septomaxilla	septomaxilla
	squamosal	
	stapes (columella)	stapes (columella)
	supraoccipital	
	tabular	
	vomer	vomer
JAW	angular	
	articular	
	coronoid	
	dentary	dentary
	prearticular	
	splenial	
	surangular	

When one bone attaches to another, they are said to be **articulated**. In a solid articulation, or suture joint, there is very little or no movement possible between the bones. Where a joint exists and some movement can occur, there is loose articulation. In a ball-and-socket-type joint, the bony part that resembles the ball is called a **condyle**. In measuring a skull, a straight-line measure is taken from the most anterior part of the premaxilla to the most posterior part of the occipital bone. (The point where it attaches with the first vertebra, called the **atlas**, is the **occipital condyle**.) The width of the skull is usually measured across the postorbital region, which in most species is the widest point. The skull of male lizards is often wider than that of females.

Upper Skull

The upper skull of lizards generally contains premaxillary, maxillary, nasal, frontal, jugal, lacrimal, parietal, palatine, pterygoid, squamosal, tabular, vomer, occipital, columella, basioccipital, and quadrate bones. The maxilla and premaxilla are the primary tooth-bearing bones, but smaller teeth may be present on the vomers, pterygoids, and palatines. Other bones may be present, and their presence or absence is diagnostic for some groups. For example, the jugal bone (beneath and behind the eyeball)

29

The details of the bones of the skull are useful tools for taxonomists. In the African monitors, these details helped determine that *Varanus albigularis*, *V. exanthematicus*, and *V. ocellatus* were separate species.

Premaxillary bones lie at the very tip of the snout and may extend back as far as the eyes. (Left) The thin, knife-like premaxillary seen in *Varanus albigularis*. (Right) The broad, flat-topped structure found in *Varanus exanthematicus*.

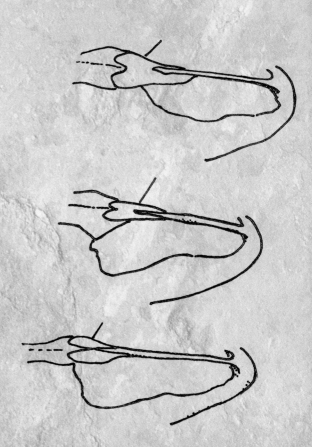

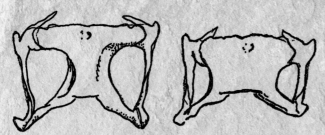

Dorsal view of the rear of the skull showing differences between *V. albigularis* (left) and *V. exanthematicus* (right). From Bayless and Sprackland, 2000a.

The structure of nasal bones is often important in identifying monitors and establishing hypotheses of relationships among species. (Top) The long single nasal bone of *Varanus albigularis*. (Center) The small single nasal of *V. exanthematicus*. (Bottom) The smaller paired nasals of *V. ocellatus*. From Bayless and Sprackland, 2000.

is either greatly reduced or absent in the Gekkota but present in most other lizards. Diurnal lizards typically possess a small aperture in the parietal bone called the pineal foramen, which is the socket for the pineal eye. Most nocturnal species and snakes lack this structure.

The rearmost fully lateral bone is the quadrate, which in reptiles represents the hinge point for the jaw. It is to the quadrate that the main muscles attach lower jaw to upper. In tuatara the quadrate is rigid because it is attached to the lower temporal bony arch. However, lizards and snakes lack that arch, giving the quadrate the ability to move like a pendulum, and it is for this reason that the gape of snakes and many lizards is so substantial.

Most lizards have a very poor bony housing for the brain. The anterior and inferior portions of a lizard's brain are generally protected by a variety of elastic connective tissue, quite unlike the solidly encased mammalian brain. Consequently, as lizards eat, food presses against the braincase. More highly derived lizards, including the monitors, have most of the brain encased in bone. Because this condition parallels that seen in snakes, it is one bit of evidence that has long been used to hypothetically link monitors to the ancestral relatives of the snakes.

Ear

The reptilian ear is considerably simpler in structure than that of mammals, containing a single rod of bone, the columella. Mammals, though, have three inner ear bones. Through evolutionary modification that may be tracked by

TOOTH TYPES

Placement of teeth in vertebrates falls into one of three categories. Teeth that fit into sockets are termed **thecodont**, seen in mammals, dinosaurs, and crocodilians. Teeth that sit along the ridge of the tooth-bearing bones are called **acrodont** and are seen in agamids and chameleons (and tuatara). The vast majority of living reptiles possess teeth that lie attached to the inner (lingual) surface of the jawbones, a condition known as **pleurodont**.

studying developing embryos, we have learned that the reptilian columella gets twisted into the mammalian stapes ("stirrup" bone), and the quadrate becomes the incus ("anvil" bone). The small bone (articular) that attached the lower jaw to the upper at the quadrate evolved into the malleus ("hammer" bone). Although the mammalian ear is capable of discerning a broad range of sounds, there is question as to how well reptiles can hear.

Teeth and Jaws

Teeth in reptiles are unspecialized; that is, we do not see distinct dental types such as incisors, canines, and molars in any single species. Reptile teeth tend to be uniform in structure within a species, but this structure is subject to considerable variability. Iguanas have teeth that resemble tiny maple leaves with serrated edges. Carnivorous lizards generally have peg-like or slightly recurved

The sailfin lizards have broad scales on their toes, an adaptation that aids in swimming.

coronoid represents the rear edge of the mouth in the living lizard.

Limbs

The majority of lizards possess four limbs that end in clawed digits. The major limb bones are the same as seen in other limbed vertebrates: the arm comprises a single upper bone, the **humerus**, and two lower arm bones, the **ulna** and **radius**. Similarly, the rear leg comprises the single upper thighbone (**femur**) and the two lower bones, the **tibia** and **fibula**. The femur may fit into a distinct socket of the hip called the **acetabulum**, where the ilium, ischium, and pubis articulate. In lizards with reduced or no limbs, the corresponding bones may similarly be reduced or absent.

Lizards generally have small and limited muscles in the digits, so they cannot display any great independent movement of the digits. One

and conical teeth. The giant monitor *Varanus salvadorii* of New Guinea has unique compressed dagger-like teeth. Teeth may be simple pegs of bone, as seen in geckos, or have complex infolding of the dentine and enamel, as seen in monitors. Lizard teeth are often shed and replaced throughout life, at least until extreme old age. In some larger species, tooth morphology changes with age. South American caiman lizards (genus *Dracaena*) and several monitors develop blunt, broad teeth in the posterior part of the jaws as the lizards reach maturity. The modification allows them to crush the shells of adult prey–crabs, snails, and crayfishes–but is not actually structurally distinct enough to warrant being called molars.

The lower jaw comprises several elements, but only the dentary bone bears teeth. The coronoid is the crest on the upper surface of the jaw to which muscles attach. The position of the

SHOT THROUGH THE HEART

Any murder mystery aficionado knows that a stab to the heart is fatal. That's true for all mammals but not necessarily true for reptiles. Clinical extraction of blood by cardiac puncture is a standard procedure in the veterinary care of reptiles; it is often the only way to get enough blood from animals with such tiny blood vessels.

Lizards' tails have adapted to serve various purposes. The laterally compressed tail of the water monitor functions as a rudder, aquatic propulsion, and weapon.

exception is seen in geckos, which are equipped with strong upper digital muscles, allowing them to coil the extremities upward, disengaging the sticky lower surfaces (called **lamellae**) from substrate. Chameleons also possess well-developed digit muscles, giving them both incredible dexterity and a strong grip. Aquatic lizards lack webbing on the digits, although the Asiatic sailfin lizards (*Hydrosaurus*) have broad toes with expanded flat lateral surfaces.

Tail

The tail is a complex appendage, capable of some combinations of functions, including distraction of predators, threat display and offense, grasping, balance, fat storage, housing and protection of male genitalia, and aquatic locomotion.

Many smaller species of lizards have the ability to break off and later regrow a replacement tail, an attribute lost by most of the giants. Similarly, many smaller lizard species–particularly among the Scincomorpha–may possess brightly colored tails, which serve to distract a potential predator's attention away from the more essential head and body. If the tail is seized, it is easily broken off, or the lizard may voluntarily detach part of the organ–hence the term "autotomy," meaning "self-cutting." Equipped with nerves and muscles, a severed tail may wriggle violently for many minutes and will often respond by jerking if stimulated as much as an hour after autotomizing.

Instead, large lizards tend to have muscular and at least somewhat prehensile tails that are readily used in threat displays and defense. A tail held erect and slowly waved, recalling a similar behavior performed by cats, is a standard warning of many large lizards toward perceived threats. Monitors, iguanas, and some agamids are able to whip the tail with considerable speed at an attacker. This living leather weapon may cause considerable pain, and even a medium-sized iguana or monitor might rip skin and leave a nasty abrasion on human skin.

MARTIAN SKINKS?

The only terrestrial vertebrates that do not have red blood are the New Guinea green-blooded skinks in the genus *Prasinohaema*, and some vipers, where the green color is a product of extremely high bile pigment concentrations. The red blood cells are, however, still red. Several marine Arctic and Antarctic ice fishes have clear, colorless blood, but all other vertebrates have red blood.

Monitors and a few other species may also have tails with considerable grasping ability, which facilitates mobility in trees. Semiaquatic lizards also use the tail to scull through the water, precisely in the fashion of crocodilians. For the lizards that run bipedally–basilisks and frilled lizards–the tail is an essential balancing rod. None of these lizards have autotomy (which means that the lizard cannot voluntarily drop its tail) and will only lose a tail to a determined predator or some significant accident.

The tail is capable of storing fat reserves to varying degrees, depending on the species. Semiaquatic monitors tend to store little fat, while beaded lizards can increase tail mass considerably with fat reserves. Stored fat is a source of slow-burning, high-calorie nutrition during times when food is scarce. Lizards that are starving will show a loss of caudal fat reserves, visible to a keeper when the upper surfaces of the hip bones (ilia) are visible above the vent.

Circulatory System and Blood

The heart, blood, lungs, and kidneys of lizards differ considerably from their mammalian counterparts. The heart is technically a three-chambered organ containing left and right **atria** and a single posterior **ventricle**. A muscular ridge in the ventricle functionally subdivides that chamber into three further chambers. Blood entering the heart from the body arrives in the right atrium, then passes the right atrioventricular valve into the cavum venosum ("chamber of the veins") of the ventricle. The blood flows over the muscular ridge to fill the cavum pulmonale ("chamber of the lungs"). When the ventricle contracts, most of the blood in the cavum pulmonale is ejected into the pulmonary artery and heads toward the lungs. At the same time, blood returning from the lungs that has entered the left atrium enters the ventricle's cavum arteriosum ("chamber of the arteries"). When the ventricle contracts, blood from the cavum arteriosum exits the heart via paired aortae. This differs from the mammalian condition, in which blood leaves the heart via a common and broad aorta and then is subdivided into various systemic trunks. In lizards and snakes, the aortae are paired vessels that differ little from the blood vessels that carry blood to major body regions (via large arteries called **systemic arches**).

The ventricular wall, a muscle that generates the pressure to move blood through the arteries, is the thickest portion of the heart. Because there is only one ventricle, both **oxygenated** (returning from the lungs and high in oxygen, O_2) and **deoxygenated** (coming from the body

and high in carbon dioxide, CO_2) blood enter the common chamber. However, the flow of the blood is more efficient at staying segregated than one might think, and mixing of oxygenated and deoxygenated blood is limited. Lizards do not become exhausted as quickly as would be the case if the ventricular blood were fully mixed, and in species such as monitors, which can breathe while running, the oxygen transport capacity is remarkably similar to that seen in mammals. Thus, a monitor can exert effort without becoming exhausted for a much longer time than can most other lizards.

As in other vertebrates, blood from the body enters the heart through a large vein called the **vena cava** and leaves to supply the

body from a large aorta. Blood carried away from the heart travels in arteries, and blood travels back via veins. The only artery to carry predominantly deoxygenated blood is the pulmonary artery (which takes CO_2-rich blood to the lungs), and the only vein that carries oxygen-rich blood is the pulmonary vein.

The **erythrocytes** (from Greek, meaning "red cells"–they are the red blood cells) of reptiles differ from those of mammals in that the reptilian blood cell retains its nucleus and genetic material after the cell matures. That means that a reptilian erythrocyte is generally larger than its mammalian equivalent. As in almost all other vertebrates,

Cyclura and the other iguanas possess salt-excreting glands in their nasal passages.

lizard blood is bright red when oxygenated and maroon when deoxygenated.

Lizard erythrocytes, like those in all other animals, contain the iron-bearing protein hemoglobin. It is to **hemoglobin** that both oxygen and carbon dioxide molecules attach in the bloodstream. Because blood is rich in proteins and available oxygen, it is an excellent environment for many microscopic bacteria and parasites. In the event that blood is contaminated by certain body fluids (such as when an ulcer perforates an organ or tissues die and become gangrenous), the condition is known as **septicemia** (from Greek, meaning "sewer blood"). There is little that can be done medically for an animal with septicemia.

All blood contains both solid and liquid portions. Solids include the various blood cells that include red blood cells, a variety of white blood cells (leucocytes)–most make up the immune system–and proteins, including clotting factor and substances such as **complement**. Complement attaches to and punctures the membranes of pathogens, causing them to burst. The chemical structure of complement is highly specific to each species. If complement from different species is mixed, an observable and measurable reaction takes place, and the intensity of the reaction may be used to calculate the degree of relatedness between species. Formally known as microcomplement fixation, or MCF, the technique has been widely used to produce **phylograms**–trees showing purported degrees of relatedness and biochemical similarity–among many different groups of animals, including apes,

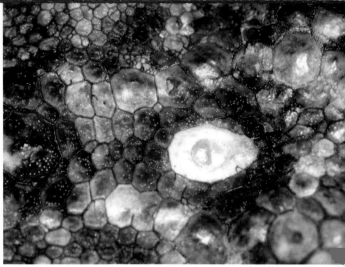

Many lizards have a light-sensing organ on top of their head–shown here on *Cyclura nubila*–that helps regulate basking and other behaviors.

snakes, monitors, and even different populations of humans.

Lungs

Lizard and mammal lungs are similar, consisting of a pair of spongy sacs lined with microscopic spheres called **alveoli**. No diaphragm exists in reptiles. Reptile lungs are less dense than mammalian lungs; the latter look much like soft sponge when dissected. It is within the thousands of alveoli that oxygen enters the blood and the waste product carbon dioxide leaves the blood, entering the air spaces of the lungs to be eliminated by exhaling. The process is called a **countercurrent exchange** because as the current of alveolar air and its high O_2 content pass the CO_2-rich capillary blood, CO_2 diffuses

off hemoglobin and out of the blood, while O_2 diffuses out of alveoli and into blood and onto hemoglobin.

The diffusion of gases can only occur across a moist surface, and alveoli are lined with a combination of water and a fatty lubricant known as **surfactant**. Surfactant keeps the walls of alveoli from sticking shut when the lungs exhale air. Maintenance of pulmonary moisture is in part a function of humidity, which is why species from the humid tropics may quickly succumb if kept in dry, low-humidity terrariums.

Reptiles do not perspire, so cutaneous water loss–which occurs–is of far less importance to them than it is to mammals. As lizards become warmer, their most significant route of water loss is from the open eyes (which is why many lizards bask with their eyes closed) and secondarily from exhaled air. Overheated reptiles will move to cooler locations to control temperature, and if unable to do so, will begin panting. Because panting rapidly ventilates warm air from the lungs, water loss increases dramatically. If

Lizards (brown water dragon shown here) have lungs similar to those of mammals but lack a diaphragm.

terrarium specimens are observed panting, it may be indicative of an enclosure with no cool retreat for the inhabitants.

Kidneys

Kidneys are organs of water reclamation, toxin excretion, and ion regulation. When foods are broken down at the molecular level, the proteins are fragmented into their component amino acids (NH_2), which rapidly form into the lethal molecule ammonia (NH_3). As cells excrete ammonia, it diffuses into the blood and is transported to the liver. The liver then converts this and other metabolic toxins into somewhat less potent chemicals, predominantly uric acid, that will then be collected and excreted from the body by the kidneys.

Because of their relatively small sizes and residence in warm habitats, reptiles are prone to rapid water loss and dehydration and so cannot afford to generate water-rich urine. Mammals have resolved this difficulty by producing a specialized kidney tube, the loop of Henle, which allows considerable reuptake of metabolic water into the blood before excreting wastes as urine. Reptiles evolved a simple kidney that excretes wastes with a minimum of water loss. Unlike the water-rich urine passed by amphibians and mammals, reptiles (including birds) excrete a pasty white liquid called uric acid, which quickly dries into a crusty

powder when exposed to air. The dried residue is also called guano. Dehydrated reptiles lack sufficient water to pass the relatively dry uric acid, which leads to kidney disease, failure, and death.

The functional kidney units are microscopic **nephrons.** As blood enters a nephron, it is diffused into a collecting area called the Bowman's capsule. Excepting blood cells and plasma, almost everything else in the blood is secreted in the capsule as filtrate, the vast majority of which (85 to 95 percent) will be returned by the nephrons back into the blood. The remaining substances, including uric acid, urea, ammonium, sodium, and water, will eventually be converted into uric acid and excreted into the bladder or its equivalent. Many critical modifications to blood occur in nephrons, including control of blood pressure (by controlling the water content of blood), removing toxins and used drugs, regulating blood sugar levels, and regulating blood ion content (called electrolytes) of sodium, calcium, potassium, phosphorus, and chloride. Consequently, damage to the nephrons causes serious illness and may lead to death.

In legless lizards (and snakes), one of a pair of organs tends to be elongated and the other greatly reduced. The heart and liver tend to be elongated as well.

Glands

Although they have far fewer types and quantities of glands than do amphibians or mammals, lizards have several different types of glands in or under the skin. Maintaining appropriate salt levels

Eye of a Komodo dragon. All the giant lizards have well-developed eyes and eyelids.

in the body is accomplished by both the kidneys, and in some species, special salt-secreting glands. These glands are usually situated in the nasal or suborbital cavity and extract excess salt from the blood. Salt is then mixed with small quantities of water for excretion, usually at the nostril, but also as flaky white tears that run from the eye. As water evaporates, the dry salty crust dries and is blown or wiped away. The glands are found in species that live near salt or brackish water and in

deserts. Giant lizards that posses nasal salt glands include all the iguanas (Hazard, 2004), blue-tongued skinks, and most monitors, including water, spiny-tailed, Gould's, Argus, golden, heath, desert, mangrove, and the perentie.

Femoral glands form a single line along the lower surface of the thigh in many lizard species. In males, the femoral glands exude waxy cones that may be important in cuing females to be receptive to mating. The glands are common in all lizard groups except the Anguimorpha. Preanal pores are typically represented by two to six tiny openings that are situated just anterior to the vent; they are larger in males than females. Although not universal, they are present among all major lizard groups and are especially conspicuous in geckos and iguanians. Postanal glands are similar to preanal pores, but they are situated just posterior to the vent. They are most typically seen in geckos.

Femoral pores on a male iguana. These pores are used in mating and territorial behavior.

Parietal Eye and Behavioral Control

Most diurnal lizards possess a parietal organ, sometimes called the third eye. The organ fits into a round aperture in the parietal bone (**parietal foramen**) and is rooted by a parietal nerve to the brain. Although a true eye–with lens, cornea, retina, and optic nerve–the lens is opaque, covered by a scale, and not capable of focusing a visual image on the retina. However, there is considerable experimental evidence showing that the pineal eye is sensitive to ultraviolet light and acts as a photoreceptor to signal lizards when to seek the sun and when to seek shelter. Lizards that have been experimentally treated so that the eye

is covered tend to stay exposed to sunlight much longer–and to the point of reaching a dangerous body temperature–than normal lizards (Kavaliers et al., 1984; Larson and Summers, 2001; Packard and Packard, 1972; Solessio and Engbretson, 1999; Summers and Greenberg, 1995). The organ is absent in geckos, tegus, and most nocturnal and burrowing species, as well as all snakes.

There has been a range of research focused on the parietal organ in lizards and other vertebrates, including humans. A direct cause-and-effect system has been discovered in which the activity of the pineal directs the conversion of the hormone melatonin from serotonin in response to exposure to sunlight or artificially produced UV light. Melatonin and serotonin are known to have important effects on appetite, mood, and behavior in humans–clinical

Examples of head pattern diversity among monitors from central Indonesia. From left to right: *Varanus indicus*; *Varanus indicus* (juvenile, paratype for *Varanus indicus rouxi*); and *Varanus salvator togianus*. From Sprackland, 1995.

depression and seasonal affective disorders are linked to their imbalance–and on the normal seasonal, behavioral, and reproductive cycles of creatures such as lizards. There are many stories, for example, of docile captive reptiles such as Komodo dragons and Gila monsters that became suddenly aggressive when exposed to sunlight (Bogert and Del Campo, 1960; Ditmars, 1933). Docile lizards would suddenly lash at their keepers when exposed to sunlight. Ditmars wrote about the abrupt change in temperament of some large water monitors (*Varanus salvator*) at the Bronx Zoo:

On the day following the placing of the monitors in their new enclosure, Keeper Snyder entered with their food. He was surprised to hear a loud hiss from his big pet... and behold that burly reptile puff up in angry fashion, then make a movement as if to deal a blow with the tail. Snyder dodged, but not quick enough... Returning later... Snyder was attacked by the big fellow... and with a wonderfully quick blow of the tail struck the man on the arm, inflicting as severe a welt as if dealt with a whip.

(Ditmars, 1933: 93)

The hapless Keeper Snyder was a victim of learning about the difference a few active hormones can make in animal behavior. It is largely because of the hormonal functions that either natural sunlight or decent artificial UV sources are important in maintaining the health of captive animals. Reproductive cycles and aspects such as spermogenesis (sperm formation) and oogenesis (egg formation) may be severely impacted in lizards

denied adequate UV radiation as captives. The pineal gland converts serotonin into melatonin during daylight and releases melatonin into the brain at night. High melatonin levels inhibit gamete (sperm and eggs) development. Therefore, when spring arrives, bringing longer days, the amount of melatonin produced drops considerably, allowing gametes to develop.

Eyes and Vision

Lizards have spherical eyeballs with a clear lens, cornea, retina, sclera, and an anterior chamber; the eyes are filled with a gelatinous vitreous humor. The retina and cornea are supported by a series of tiny bony structures called scleral ossicles (absent in mammals), and there may be up to three eyelids (upper, lower, and nictitating). The majority of lizards have good eyesight, and their retinas are lined with both rods and as many as four types of cones. Rods are specialized nerve cells that respond to light intensity, while cones are sensitive to different bands of wavelengths (= colors) of light. As far as is known, all diurnal lizards have good color vision (Underwood, pers. comm.).

Most diurnal lizards have a moveable lower eyelid that can cover and protect the visual organ. Chameleons have the most unusual eyelids, which are formed from a cone of skin into concentric rings that can close at the ends. Geckos, many skinks, and a variety of other small lizards may have the eye covered by a spectacle that is, as in snakes, a clear scale that completely covers the eye and is shed as a single monocle. Finally, there are many legless lizards that lack a visible external

Like snakes, monitors, tegus, and heloderms have forked tongues that aid in detecting scents. A Komodo dragon and its tongue are shown here.

eye at all. In such species–none included among the giants–the eye is merely covered by an opaque or nearly opaque scale and has no significant function. Diurnal species generally have round pupils, while many nocturnal lizards have elliptical pupils.

Ears and Hearing

The lizard ear is rudimentary compared with that of a bird or mammal. The tympanic membrane, or eardrum, may lie near the body surface or deep in a recess. It may further be naked and semitransparent or thickly covered by scales. In the latter case, lizards are called "earless," when in fact the ear is merely concealed.

Instead of having three middle ear bones to conduct vibrations, as is typical in mammals, the

VENOM GLANDS

A report published in 2005 by an international team of biologists provided evidence for the presence of venom glands in iguanian and varanid lizards (Fry, Bryan; N. Vidal, J. Norman, F. Vonk, H. Ramjan, S. Kuruppu, K. Fong, S. Hedges, M. Richardson, W. Hodgson, V. Ignjatovic, R. Summerh, and E. Kochva., 2005; Tennesen, 2006). Iguanians, such as the bearded dragon group (genus *Pogona*), have ancestral glands and delivery systems that are incapable of delivering a dangerous bite to anything as large as a human. Although Dr. Bryan Fry and his team took venom proteins from iguanians, the amount of venom and its low level of toxicity make the lizards harmless to all but, potentially, very small prey. Varanids, however, possess mandibular glands that secrete venom proteins into the tooth bases of the lower jaw. Toxicity and quantity of delivery varies—just as it does in venomous snakes—from harmless (to humans) to dangerous (as in Komodo dragons). Fry was quick to add that lizard owners should not be unduly concerned by the findings. The relative harmlessness of bearded dragons, iguanas, and most monitors to humans has been long established. "We don't want people to suddenly be afraid of their pets," Fry told Reuters News, "nor do we want any silly laws being passed against the keeping of these lizards."

There are broad evolutionary implications of the study by Fry et al., for they claim that the presence of venom delivery systems across so many more taxa than previously thought supports the hypothesis that venom mechanisms developed once in squamates, and the system evolved along different lines subsequently.

lizard ear has but one—the slender columella, or **stapes**. This bone is a thin cylinder that attaches to the eardrum and the membrane-covered oval window deep inside the skull. The inner ear cavity contains a complex snail-like cochlear duct and semicircular canals, which are primary organs for hearing and maintaining balance, respectively. In structure and function, the reptilian cochlea does not differ greatly from that of "higher" tetrapods, including humans.

Some uncertainty exists about the extent to which lizards can hear airborne sounds. Geckos, lacertids and some skinks certainly produce true vocalizations, and presumably they convey **intraspecific** information to other lizards. Many other lizards, including monitors and tegus, seem

oblivious to airborne sounds, including the loud clapping of hands by a nearby herpetologist. They are unquestionably able to detect ground-borne vibrations. Lizard auditory capability is thus a viable field for research.

Tongue and Smell

All lizards possess a tongue, and the vast majority can extend the tongue at least a short distance outside the mouth. At the extreme are true chameleons, capable of extending their cylindrical tongues with considerable force at nearby prey to a length equal to or greater than their snout-vent length. Monitors, while not nearly as lingually spectacular, can often extrude their bifid tongues a distance greater than their head length. Tegus may have a similar extension.

Tongue morphology varies tremendously among lizards, from the short, blunt, and barely nicked iguanine tongue to the broad, leaf-shaped blue organ of some skinks. Gekkotans may use the tongue to wipe the eye spectacle as well as to manipulate prey in the mouth. Most broad-tongued species use the tongue to manipulate food and as part of agonistic displays. Tegus, monitors, and several other groups use long forked tongues principally to detect the scent of potential prey, mates, and rivals. Tongue flicking in these species becomes quite intense in the proximity of food or a conspecific. In monitor lizards, tongue color is species specific, so it is often possible to distinguish among similar species by tongue color.

Although lizard tongues generally contain taste buds, the numbers and kinds vary among

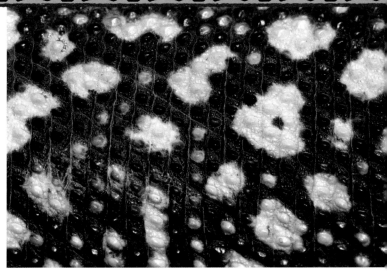

Close-up view of the scales of a beaded lizard, showing the granular scale texture.

major groups. In all cases, though, the primary sensory mechanism for discriminating odor and possibly taste is the **vomeronasal**, or Jacobson's organ. Located in a postnasal cavity above the septomaxillary bones, the paired organs have direct openings into the upper mouth. Particles of air brought in by the tongue are then analyzed by the highly innervated cells lining Jacobson's organ, and the resulting data are interpreted in the brain as food, a potential mate, a potential rival, an enemy, or a home burrow.

Brain

The lizard brain is structurally simple compared to that of birds or mammals (Greenberg and MacLean, 1978). Most species have good vision, and there is a correspondingly large cerebral occipital region. Images from the eyes are formed in this posterior

TYPES OF SCALES

Lizard scales come in a variety of sizes, shapes, and textures. There are some standard terms that describe some of these variations, and knowing the terms can be very useful when using diagnostic keys. The terms and their meanings are:

- carinate: keeled, having a raised longitudinal ridge along the length of the scale (example: ctenosaur tail)

- granular: scales that are small, convex, and do not overlap (example: *Heloderma*)

- imbricate: when the rear edge of one scale overlaps the front edge of the next (example: *Trachydosaurus*)

- rugose: a scale with a rough or pitted surface (example: *Sceloporus*)

- smooth: scales that are flat and shiny (example: tegu)

- striated: having parallel lines etched in the scale; often visible only under magnification (example: *Mabuya* or *Gerrhosaurus*)

area. Lizards also have enlarged olfactory regions in the brain that are related to the extremely sensitive sense of smell. The nearly smooth cerebral cortex is almost unrecognizable compared to its mammalian counterpart. Like birds and mammals, reptiles have 12 pairs of cranial nerves.

Skin and Scales

Scales and leathery skin are among the most distinguishing characters that mark the reptiles from other creatures. Each scale is a bit of folded skin on a broad and contiguous fabric of integument. Whether it is the soft and pliable skin of a gecko or the tough spine on a mastigure's tail, the visible surface of the lizard's body is made of dead keratinized material that is both defensive and protective in nature.

The epidermis is considerably more watertight than the underlying live dermis, and it thereby reduces the rate of evaporative water loss through the skin. Because it is made of dead cells, the epidermis does not grow, and the lizard must occasionally shed the older outermost layer, called the stratum corneum, through a process called **ecdysis**, or shedding. The skin revealed after a shed has been bathed in fluids that helped separate the old and new layers, and it is closer to the live cells containing pigments beneath. The result is that freshly shed reptiles appear brighter and cleaner than those near shedding. Production of the separating fluid is impaired when a specimen is dehydrated, and the result may be a patchy or incomplete shed. Lizards that are having difficulty shedding because of water loss may be soaked in water to soften and loosen skin.

HOMOLOGOUS PARTS

The human hand, bat's wing, and whale's fin are all made from the same groups of bones and muscles and so are homologous. The wing of an insect, however, is derived from different tissues in the back, and so it is not homologous to the wing of a bird or bat. In other words, the insect and bat wings are analogous, meaning they serve the same function but are derived from a different source.

The lizards will almost always drink the water in which they soak, which will also help them restore normal internal water concentrations.

Within the living dermal cells may be pigment-containing structures called **melanophores**. Melanin is a brown protein-based pigment that is stored in melanophores in either a permanent form or as an expandable form. In the latter case, the melanin may be highly compacted, at which time the reflective and prismatic properties of the skin cells (along with the properties of other chemicals in those cells, such as guanine) may give the lizard a light appearance, with colors in the yellow, green, or tan range. As melanin expands due to temperature or hormonal control, the cells become brown in appearance. Depending on the number of cells engaged and the degree to which the melanin is compressed or expanded, the lizard skin will appear darker, from brown to dark red to black.

Although the color and pattern of any group of reptiles are largely genetically constrained, there is considerable variation in the specific manifestation of that pattern. Just as human skin and hair color is controlled by a suite of several different genes, so too are reptilian color and pattern. So while all beaded lizards from a particular population may be black and yellow, the specific patterns of how that yellow is distributed is probably as unique to each individual as fingerprints are to humans. Similarly, the failure of a majority of one type of color-coding genes may result in unusual color patterns and colors–such as blue-green tree monitors or unpatterned Duméril's monitors. Albinism, which is the total absence of any pigment-producing cells, results in pale animals with red eyes, the red and pink hues being blood vessels visible through the colorless skin and eyes.

It has long been part of the physiological dogma of vertebrate zoology that the reptilian scale largely lies behind the secret of tetrapods "conquering" life on land. This is because the reptilian scale is presumed to be highly water retardant, tremendously reducing evaporation of body moisture to the environment. It is this very attribute that makes reptilian leather such a highly sought consumer good. With the production of scaleless snakes to study, it has since been demonstrated that it is not so much the scale that contributes to water retention as it is the structure of reptilian skin itself (Licht and Bennett, 1972). Reptiles do not perspire, so primary water loss in lizards is through moist membranes–mouth, eyes, nostrils, and cloaca–that are routinely exposed to the external environment. Humidity may enhance or retard water loss, which is why the herpetoculturist

WHY ARE GIANT LIZARDS SO RARE IN TEMPERATE PLACES?

Very few large lizards make their way into the temperate regions of the Earth, but those that do—such as red tegus and lace and heath monitors—beg the question of why they are exceptions. There are two essential factors that govern the size and temperature tolerance of lizards: thermal physiology and diet.

A large body tends to heat up or cool down slower than a small body. For example, an unheated swimming pool will still be quite warm even several days after an extreme cold snap, but a glass of water will chill or possibly freeze much more quickly. Similarly, a large tegu facing a sudden change in temperature will generally remain warm enough as temperatures start to drop to find adequate shelter before it becomes seriously threatened. But when temperatures rise again, it will take that tegu a long time to warm up to activity levels. During basking that lizard is sluggish, unable to hunt and very vulnerable to warm-blooded predators. This is why the few cold-tolerant large species of lizards are found where there are few of their predators. Even so, the large species cannot survive in places where cold weather lasts for more than two or three months.

Diet is the second limiting factor. Giant lizards of temperate areas are all carnivorous. Digestion of proteins (flesh) is physiologically much simpler than digestion of plant matter (consider the multiple stomachs and gut bacteria needed by ruminants such as cows, for example), and so a meat-eating animal can obtain nutrients from food much more quickly than a plant eater. Because of their size, large herbivorous lizards in a temperate climate would not have sufficient warm periods to thrive. The more stable the environment, the better for plant eaters' physiology, which explains why all the largest herbivorous lizards are tropical and subtropical species, and none reach the temperate regions. By the same token, for a large predator to survive in temperate areas, there must be adequate prey; an adult red tegu could not be successful if it fed only on insects because it would take more energy to catch the insects than the lizard could recover by eating them. They require medium-sized rodents, birds, and birds' eggs, all of which also become seasonally less plentiful in environments that experience longer, cold winters.

must regulate terrarium moisture with the same dedication as one controls the heat.

Lizard scales may contain microscopic sense organs that are capable of distinguishing texture. Monitor lizards will routinely prod a potential food item with the snout, possibly to ascertain if it is indeed a prey item (Sprackland, 1989d). When viewed under magnification, the scales on monitor lizards are seen to have a small round pit and an extremely tiny hair-like structure protruding.

Taxonomy

A lot has happened in taxonomy since the 1980s. The term "lizard" has become much more inclusive than it once was, now embracing all the squamate reptiles. The squamates of then are the lepidosaurs of now. Just as birds have been subsumed as a subgroup within the larger Dinosauria, snakes and worm lizards are now considered branches–admittedly quite unusual branches–of the larger lizard tree. This genealogical reshuffling is the result of the prevailing paradigm of assessing relationships using methods known as **phylogenetics**. A zoologist employing phylogenetic methods is expanding upon the rules of comparative anatomy to produce a stick diagram that purports to show the most likely path taken by evolution. This diagram is called a cladogram, for which reason phylogenetics is more commonly known as "cladistics." To really understand why taxonomy changes, it is essential to understand the methods used and assumptions made by the scientists doing the taxonomy.

Today's evolutionary biologists are largely, if not predominantly, followers of the **phylogenetic species concept (PSC)**. Following on Darwin's observation that an understanding of evolution would eventually allow us to construct lineage trees for all organisms based on modification with descent, a phylogenetic analysis is first and foremost a hypothesis of

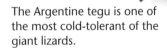

The Argentine tegu is one of the most cold-tolerant of the giant lizards.

47

relatedness between and among organisms. Unlike the traditional Biological Species Concept (BSC) that is predicated upon a physiological function (reproduction), the PSC is based on comparison of homologous features–those that are derived from common parts. Thus, the hand of humans, bats, and whales tells us something about their relatedness because the bones are similar, located in the same relative positions, and derive from the same embryonic tissues. It doesn't matter that hands, wings, and flippers do different tasks; what matters is that they originated from a common source of anatomical parts.

This gives the PSC both empirical and objective criteria upon which to make species decisions. For example, do all the members of a particular group share a structure or structures that derive from a common ancestor? The degree to which one can say yes helps determine the rank, or grade, of the decision. For example, having a five-fingered hand unites the bat, whale, and human among the tetrapods. Additional features, such as lung structure, red blood cells that lack nuclei, presence of a four-chambered heart, presence of a single lower jawbone, possession of mammary glands, and the presence of body hair further unite them all as mammals. The distinctions in the forms and functions of those features help distinguish species.

Phylogenetic analysis was greatly advanced by the methods of German zoologist Willi Hennig. His methods, now referred to as cladistics, formalize the way biologists record and evaluate data about an organism's body parts–including protein structure and the sequence of nucleotides that make up RNA and DNA molecules–to produce a tree of relationships called a cladogram. Naturally enough for a system devised by a brilliant German scientist, cladistics has a very formal and formidable jargon, including such important terms as "synapomorphy" and "plesiomorphous." A synapomorphy is a trait that is shared among a group of organisms (the hair of the human, bat, and whale), while an apomorphy is a special trait found only in a single group (i.e., only bats, among mammals, have wings). In contrast, a plesiomorphy is a trait commonly found among members of a group (such as the five fingers found in most mammals, reptiles, and amphibians) but absent from other groups.

Deleted, too, are the old terms "primitive" and "advanced" for describing anatomical traits. Instead, systematists now refer to traits found early in a group's lineage as "ancestral," while those that appear later in the evolutionary record are called "derived." The important thing to remember is that cladistics finally gives biologists a mathematically precise model for testing evolutionary hypotheses and even for determining the statistical likelihood of any hypothesis being correct. Yes, it has certain limitations and methodological problems (many of which I addressed elsewhere–see Sprackland, 1995), but its array of positive and testable features makes it the preferred mode of evolutionary analysis among contemporary biologists.

One important rule of both phylogenetics and good comparative anatomy research is to consider characters in proper context. Not only must the zoologist be sure that homologous characters

are being compared, but he must also remember that the absence of evidence is not evidence of absence. Snakes, for example, are not "lizards" without limbs; instead, they represent lizards that have lost their limbs. Eels, though, are limbless fishes, for their ancestors never had legs that could later be lost. The essential implication (supported by the presence of vestigial limbs in pythons and boas, the discovery of fossil snakes with limbs, and the fact that numerous lizard lineages have reduced or lost their limbs) is that snakes derived from limbed ancestors. For the practicing taxonomist, this means that we may not properly define a group by features it does not have. Thus, we cannot include in our definition of the lizard/snake clade such comments as "lacks abdominal ribs," "lacks a longitudinal cloaca," or similar negative information statements.

Contemporary Lizard Taxonomy

Taxonomy, as you can see, is not really a precise science, and the result is that taxonomists must labor under rather unusual circumstances. This leads to the fairly common business of having to revise taxonomic accounts by changing names, rearranging genealogies, and revising hypotheses of relatedness. Some of these revisions may remain for decades or centuries, while others may remain in constant dispute for some time. In the end, little of the taxonomic effort affects herpetoculture–although I shall enumerate those places where it has definitely been a factor.

Lizards have long been divided into four large groups termed either infraorders or superfamilies, depending on the authority. These groups are the **Gekkota**, **Iguania**, **Scincomorpha**, and **Anguimorpha**. To these are now added the Amphisbaenia and Serpentes, but neither is included in this book. Among the recent modifications to saurian family level taxonomy are these:

Gekkota–Gekkonidae, Eublepharidae, Diplodactylidae
Gekkonidae: Divided into three groups during the 18th and 19th centuries (Gekkonidae, Uroplatidae, and Eublepharidae), most of the 20th century united all geckos into the Gekkonidae. At present, though, geckos are classified in three families: the Diplodactylidae (including the limbless "pygopodids" of Australia and New Guinea), Gekkonidae, and Eublepharidae. Only the latter possesses moveable eyelids, and eublepharids also lack adhesive toe pads.

Iguania–Iguanidae, Agamidae, Chamaeleonidae
Iguanidae: This group has been fragmented into eight smaller families by Frost and Etheridge (1989), and their system has generally been used among academic herpetologists. However, some have argued against the scheme, and many people from both academic and herpetocultural camps retain the more inclusive use of "Iguanidae."
Agamidae: Frost and Etheridge also considered the agamids to be part of the chameleon family, such that their Chamaeleonidae includes subfamilies for Agaminae, Chamaeleoninae, and Leiolepidinae.

Undoubtedly, many so-called subspecies are actually valid species in their own right. *Varanus albigularis* was once considered a subspecies of *V. exanthematicus*.

Scincomorpha–Scincidae, Gerrhosauridae, Cordylidae, Gymnophthalmidae, Teiidae, Lacertidae, Xantusiidae, Amphisbaenidae

Teiidae: There has been considerable consensus among herpetologists in dividing these lizards into two groups. For many years, teiids have informally been described as being either "microteiids" or "macroteiids," and the new taxonomy simply reflects that division formally. Small teiids are now classified in the tongue-twisting family Gymnophthalmidae (pronounced, if you must, as: Gim-no-fah-THAL-muh-day), while macroteiids, including the tegus and caiman lizards, remain in the Teiidae (Presch, 1973, 1983).

Anguimorpha–Anguidae, Anniellidae, Xenosauridae, Shinisauridae, Helodermatidae, Lanthanotidae, Varanidae

Many herpetologists subdivide this group into the smaller Anguines for the first four families, and Platynota or Varanoidea for the latter three. Depending on the author, the Anniellidae may be included in the Anguidae. Shinisaurids were separated from xenosaurids and there is little resistance to that move. Most authors have accepted the placement of the Lanthanotidae within the Varanidae, but this is not universal.

Subspecies and Variation

In 1639, Englishman John Ray introduced the term "species" to biologists (who, incidentally, were not called biologists at the time; the term "biologist" wasn't coined until the early 1800s). Since then, scientists have heatedly debated just how to define species, and all definitions have, so far, been shown to have exceptions. In practice, species are usually described on the basis of individuals that form part of a recognizable, self-perpetuating group. Problems arise when one sees the range of variation within such groups. Remembering that species are constantly in the process of evolving, such gradients are to be expected. Difficulty in being able to make a clean species identification has resulted in many of these variant groups being termed "subspecies" and dubbed with a third Latinized name.

I have witnessed some intense arguments about the nature and reality of subspecies. People seem to be either strong believers or dedicated debunkers, and in fairness I should state that I fall in the latter category. To the best of my knowledge–and I specialize in studying variation–any detailed scrutiny into so-called subspecies has resulted in either a) the recognition that more than one species is involved, b) the recognition that the degree of variation was simply unknown prior to detailed study, or c) both of these situations.

Considerable disagreement exists among zoologists as to what, precisely, a subspecies might be. Is it merely a geographical variant or a population that is moving toward becoming a new species? While most people who only know about the definitions of species from one or two biology classes think that we have this problem neatly wrapped up, the fact is that there is still no universal or near universal consensus as to what species are! We know that there are species–compare a tiger and a tiger snake and you can readily tell that they are very different creatures–but when we start looking among similar species, the lines of demarcation become quite fuzzy. It follows, then, that if we cannot yet agree on how to define "species," the whole point of "subspecies" is a bit of an irrelevance.

In some cases, a subspecies name is used for reasons of outright ignorance, such as when white-throated monitors (*Varanus albigularis*) were considered to be subspecies of savanna monitors (*Varanus exanthematicus*). That classification was predicated largely on

OUR INDEFINITE DEFINITIONS

It is not that we have no useful definitions for "species"; rather, we have several good ideas that work for some groups of organisms but not others. This is not an uncommon problem in science, though, for we often lack really solid definitions for the most basic terms. We are still far from universal agreement on defining life, energy, and time, among others.

comparisons of external characteristics and geographical distribution. Further studies using a variety of approaches have clearly shown the two animals to be distinct species.

Even a cursory review of the reptile price lists over any five-year spread will show how certain "subspecies" carry a higher price tag than others. I certainly would not deny an ethical animal dealer the right to make an honest living, and if there is something distinct about particular specimens, it should be so noted and an appropriate fee attached. But as we do not see anyone claiming that albino or unusually patterned specimens are new subspecies, neither should we invent or retain subspecies names purely as a matter of commercial facility. The use of terms such as "Ionides-phase white-throated monitor" should supercede "*Varanus albigularis ionidesi*," (see species account for *V. albigularis*) eliminating an improper term from use and still maintaining the information content desired.

Physignathus cocincinus

2
AQUISITION AND CARE

Giant lizards start out small; be prepared for the adult size before you acquire one. A hatchling sailfin lizard is shown

If you are a novice intent on keeping large lizard species, prepare yourself properly. There is no excuse for shoddy husbandry today, given both the diminishing populations of wild animals and the myriad terrariums and equipment available commercially. First and foremost, be prepared to make a major space commitment, for it is unfair to an animal to cram it into an artificial environment in which it will always be stressed. Even lizards need privacy, so a shelter within the terrarium must be large enough to completely conceal the animal. It must be accessible for thorough cleaning–be assured that cleaning up after large lizards is a time-consuming chore.

Be advised also that these lizards eat considerably more than a few crickets now and then. Monitors and tegus require large quantities of meat, plus vitamin and mineral supplements. Some individuals can be fed weekly, while others eat three or four times per week. Meat prices vary, with beef sometimes costing less per pound (kg) than rodents, but this is a fluctuating factor you must consider: Can you *afford* to feed a large lizard?

Then there are "practical" considerations. Does your landlord allow pets? If so, does he allow big lizards? Does your city? Local ordinances are unpredictable, but fines can be stiff, and confiscation of the animals–including smaller, legally held ones–is a distinct possibility.

Do you have children or pets such as dogs or cats? If so, be sure that your lizard cages are secure. You do not want mammalian predators or children's fingers to encounter your reptiles. If you are keeping really big (4.25 feet/1.3 meters or more) lizards, keep the cages locked. Ideally, cage maintenance should be done early in the morning, before the inhabitants have warmed up enough to be overly active. Remember that even if the specimen cannot hurt you, it may hurt itself trying to avoid you.

Captive-bred black rough-necked monitor. Captive-bred lizards are almost always healthier than wild-caught ones.

One other consideration: breeding potential. More than ever, the cultivation of healthy, viable gene pools of captive animals is necessary, both to reduce the strain of collecting from wild populations and to ensure the survival of many critically reduced species. For the private herpetoculturist, room may not be available to permit breeding of even moderately sized giants. However, the availability of your animals to zoos and other breeders, on loan, can be a valuable service. If you plan to go this route, check with zoos to see if they have the species you keep and if they would be interested in breeding loans. Additional information on such programs can be obtained from the websites listed in the bibliography. They can provide information on major herpetological collections and suggest appropriate curators who share an interest in your species.

Although each species of lizard, giant or otherwise, has particular characteristics and needs peculiar to that species, there are nevertheless considerable areas of overlap when it comes to the captive maintenance of lizards. Specimens are much more likely to be acquired through purchase from a dealer than from the keeper collecting his own animals from the field. There are a limited number of preferred substrates to use in the terrarium of a giant lizard. All the species described in this book prefer the warmer habitats within tropical and subtropical climes, and all need considerable legroom in either the horizontal or vertical planes–sometimes both! All these lizards require individual hiding spaces, a reliable heat source, clean drinking water, and frequent feedings. The diets, amount of available water (both as liquid water and as ambient humidity), and materials for climbing, perching, or burrowing are among the most conspicuous variables.

Obtaining Lizards

The Romans had a phrase that has lost none of its relevance some 1,700 years after their empire

Frilled lizards were rarely captive bred before the late 1990s. Now, most of those available are from captive stock.

faded into history: *caveat emptor*, let the buyer beware. You want to obtain a specimen of a giant lizard? There will be plenty of people willing to provide you with an animal. Many dealers will be honest and sincere in helping you get a healthy animal that will fully satisfy your requirements. Some among these will have no way of knowing if a particular animal is suffering from an illness or injury, though, because many reptiles do not manifest symptoms until weeks or even months after an illness has set in. Is the eventual deceased lizard, then, the fault and responsibility of such a dealer? The answer must generally be no.

But other sellers will offer wild-caught animals, some in better condition than others. If you are personally handpicking an animal, your odds of obtaining a sound lizard can be quite high. On the other hand, if you are buying blind via mail order, your chances of getting a problem animal increase. It is always in your best interest to obtain specimens from a reliable source, one with whom you have had successful dealings with earlier or one who comes recommended by a collector whose animals are in good health. Among the people you might approach regarding reliable reptile suppliers are zoo curators and members of regional herpetological societies.

WHAT TO LOOK FOR IN A HEALTHY LIZARD

Choosing a new lizard is similar to choosing a new puppy: Don't feel sorry for the scrawny, listless, wet-eyed animal and think that you can bring it back to health. Chances are that a creature, especially a reptile, that looks ill is already extremely ill and probably beyond all but the most heroic efforts to revitalize. Remember that reptilian physiology is considerably slower that that of a mammal such as ourselves. By the time many lizards show any recognizable symptoms, it may already be too late for treatment. At the risk of sounding callous, enter the business of purchasing a lizard the same way you would a used car: Don't take on someone else's insurmountable problems. If you obtain a lizard that is or appears to be healthy and then discover problems, you should first see if the supplier will offer a replacement. Failing that, refer to Chapter 4: Veterinary Care.

When obtaining a new lizard, look for the general signs of good health. Unless the animal has been handled frequently, it should be alert and respond as you approach. It may move away from you, display, open the mouth, lunge, or just follow your motion with a noticeable turning of its head.

The mouth and nostrils should be clean, clear of objects or liquids, and without blood or any type of crust. (Iguanas and some other species secrete salt out of their nostrils, so salt deposits in this area are normal.) The rear of the head should be robust; you should not be able to clearly see the outline of the skull arches. The base of the tail should also be well formed, without bony protrusions. The cloaca should be clean–although, if handled, a healthy lizard may very well empty its cloacal contents for (at) you.

Healthy lizards do not generally have the entire ventral surface in contact with substrate; the head is usually raised, and the front legs often hold the lizard in a push-up posture. If you lift a lethargic-looking specimen and then release it, it should stand in such a posture (or run away or bite). If it returns to the fully flattened posture, it is probably not a healthy animal.

Beginning giant lizard keepers would be wise to avoid keeping those species with a reputation for aggression, such as Nile monitors.

By the mid 1990s, most of the species represented in this book were being successfully captive bred with some regularity, and by 2001, many could be obtained at reasonable prices from a fairly large number of both private and commercial breeders. There are significant advantages to obtaining captive-bred animals. First, captive-raised lizards are generally in better condition, without scars, missing toes, or "nicks" that are almost inevitable in wild-caught specimens. This means that you will acquire a better-looking animal for display. Second, captive-raised lizards will not be carrying the various parasites and microbes–notably disease-causing microbes–that wild-caught animals may be carrying. This is not to say that a captive-bred lizard is going to be parasite free, but it does

mean that it is less likely to have parasites and much less likely to be carrying exotic parasites that may be hard to eradicate. The third potential advantage is an ethical issue that will vary depending on myriad circumstances. By purchasing captive-bred lizards, you will reduce demand for the harvesting of animals from wild populations. On the face of it, this seems a noble justification in and of itself.

However, the matter is not as clear cut as some well-intentioned conservationists might wish. If the actual (and ideal) result is to leave the lizards alone in the wild so that their populations remain strong and the species survive in nature, there could hardly be an objection. In reality, though, most animals, including reptiles, are in danger less from collectors than from habitat loss. In some cases, the strongest argument at the local level for maintaining a habitat is that it yields commercially valuable animals and plants. In places such as Madagascar, herpetologists may explore an area and come away with several to dozens of new species, only to find that on later trips, the entire habitat has been leveled into farmland or to satiate the timber industry (Goodman and Benstead, 2004). There are many recently described species from across the world that are now only to be seen in a few museum collection jars. Climate change and its global warming effects have already begun taking its toll on wildlife, from corals to cloud-forest frogs (Thomas et al., 2004). It may well be that many species will survive the 21st century only in captivity. Despite the best-stated intentions to the contrary, the best argument for obtaining captive-

Walk-in enclosures are the best housing option for many species of giant lizards. This is an outdoor enclosure housing rock iguanas, *Cyclura* sp.

bred animals is that you are much more likely to be getting good-looking, defect-free, healthy animals than you would if you bought a wild-caught lizard.

The better dealers may try to steer you away from one species toward another. This is not necessarily an attempt to steer you toward a higher-priced specimen. Rather, some species may be better suited to your herpetocultural skill level, resources to provide long-term care, or the space available to maintain your lizards. If you were looking for a reliable large lizard you could safely handle, then you would generally be better served by passing on a Nile monitor and considering instead a savanna or Duméril's monitor. Listen to the pros and weigh their advice. With the help of this book, you might decide to follow their advice, or you may have the information at hand to make a different decision.

Terrarium Considerations

Keepers of giant lizards are not usually herpetocultural novices, so I shall assume that you have at least some solid reptile husbandry experience that has come from keeping a variety of more modest-sized animals. Many of the same principles that apply to smaller lizards also apply to their giant cousins. Among the common factors they all require are these:

- adequate space (rule of thumb: a terrarium is never too large)
- enough cover for each specimen
- proper heating, lighting, and humidity
- proper diet and dietary schedule

Size

When considering space, try to think in terms of both leg and tail room. Captive lizards should easily be able to stretch out their entire length

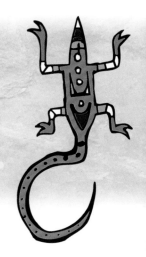

An appropriate terrarium for a pair of white-throated monitors includes basking sites, hiding places, a large water container, and a safe substrate.

in a straight line, with at least two more total lengths available. Terrestrial species need lots of ground room and may do well in a terrarium that is not very tall, while arboreal species and those that climb will need much taller facilities. To the requirements for the ground dwellers add proper substrate–sand mixed with clay is a good choice–that is deep enough to allow the lizards to burrow. Monitors, tegus, and mastigures are all known to excavate extremely long burrows that may extend many feet down and several yards (meters) long. A terrarium doesn't have to offer that much space, but the subterranean needs of captives should be taken into account. Most breeding successes with giant lizards come once keepers recognize the importance of burrows to egg laying and provide adequate substrate.

Keepers of giant lizards will generally neither care to nor be able to provide a terrarium that accurately reflects the lizard's natural habitat. Not only would the needed cage size be prohibitively large, it would also be unlikely to stay clean. Large lizards excavate, shred bark, tear plants, and mess water to the extent that it is simply not feasible or healthy to try to mimic a natural habitat. Even zoos equipped with considerable facilities limit the degree to which they recreate a piece of Komodo or the forest of the Aru Islands.

However, it is important to know something about the habitat and climatic conditions from which a lizard comes. Seasonal variations of temperature, humidity, and light cycle can have a major impact on colonies you wish to breed. An excellent source of information about the weather for any spot on the globe is www.wunderground.com.

No matter how big the lizard, it still needs hiding areas to relieve stress. This young Komodo dragon has an artificial burrow for shelter.

Substrate

The question of what substrate to use is common and often yields surprisingly heated discussions. Terrarium substrate is material used to cover the floor space and ranges from simple materials to naturalistic ones. Some herpetoculturists vigorously reject the use of any such materials, while others provide enough sand or soil to allow animals to excavate deep and extensive burrows. As in many cases, the use and choice of substrates are based as much on personal and functional preferences as anything else.

For enclosures that are kept off public display, a bare floor made of solid wood, concrete (although only as a temporary substrate), plastic, or glass is adequate and easy to clean. Loose substrate materials, such as sand, soil, or wood chips, will continuously be shifted by the lizards and produce what humans would consider a mess. If you choose to use wood shavings or chips, cork bark, orchid bark, and cypress mulch are okay, but cedar is deadly toxic. Other safe, if less than appealing, substrates include shredded newspaper and rabbit food pellets (alfalfa). Matting moss has been used as a substrate for arboreal lizards with some success because it looks natural and may hold moisture. However, it also easily harbors mites and may remove moisture from the terrarium air, reducing humidity if not misted frequently. For the same reasons, AstroTurf should be avoided. Sphagnum moss may be a better–albeit more expensive–alternative.

One of the aesthetic problems with all loose substrates is that they will be moved by the lizards, destroying whatever naturalistic look they were intended to provide. All giant lizards will dig–even sheltopusiks–so seeing them

61

Most giant lizards require high temperatures, usually provided by using heat lamps. This is a rhinoceros iguana under her heat lamp.

plow through substrate is the rule. Many loose substrates, such as gravel and corncob, can be accidentally swallowed by lizards and may cause lethal internal impactions. It is also a difficult task to clean a cage with loose substrate.

Alternately, newspaper, paper towels, and brown butcher paper make effective substrate materials that are analogous to paper at the bottom of a birdcage. They are easy to place and remove, can generally contain all the trash that must be periodically removed, and are cheap, readily available materials. For the standard glass terrarium, these are the substrates that will be the least difficult to handle. However, they will also be the most quickly shredded and turned into an ugly mess. The use of paper substrate is generally reserved for terrariums housing young lizards or primarily arboreal species.

Calcium-based terrarium "sand" has recently been introduced and can be purchased at many pet shops. This material is nontoxic, possibly of some nutrient value, and comes in a variety of colors. It has been used with success for varanids in smaller terrariums (20 to 50-gallon [75.7 to 189.3-l] aquarium size) and other moderately sized terrestrial species, especially when aesthetics are important.

Territory and Shelter

A great many reptiles, including a number of the giants, are territorial animals that will not, or barely, tolerate intrusions into their territory by other lizards, particularly members of the

HEAT ROCKS

When should a lizard keeper use heat rocks in the terrarium? The best use of a heat rock comes when it is associated with lizards that detect temperature through skin receptors instead of measuring ultraviolet light intensity. In other words, nocturnal lizards and species without a parietal eye–such as geckos and beaded lizards–are most likely to benefit from a heat source that comes from the substrate. Diurnal species such as monitors, tegus, and iguanians, however, often have very bad experiences with hot rocks. Because these lizards gauge heat by measuring ultraviolet intensity via the eyes or parietal eye on top of their heads, they may sit on a heat rock and–literally–stay there as they start cooking themselves. Their cue to get out of the heat is not in the belly, so the lizard may get severely burned to the extent that veterinary care is required or even until they die from heat and burns.

In no circumstance should a heat rock be the only or primary heat source in a terrarium. These devices are useful for supplemental heating only.

same species. Most often it is the males that will engage in agonistic behaviors, initially trying to intimidate an interloper into leaving. The behaviors may involve arm circling, head and neck bobbing, drastic color change, holding the body erect, or swelling the trunk or any crests, frills, or dewlaps. If that fails, combat may follow, and serious injuries to both parties may result. By the same token, some of these same species will do fine in groups containing just a single adult male, several adult females, and a number of immature animals of both sexes. An important consideration for the herpetoculturist, then, is to know to which of these categories a given species belongs *before* acquiring specimens.

Humidity, Water, and Moisture in General

It is a common error to assume that the ambient humidity is a minor factor in the care of captive reptiles. Anyone who has done field studies in areas where a humid forest abuts dry grasslands has seen a marked inhibition of many species to cross lines. This is not merely a restriction based on the vegetation content; an open grassy area on a humid mountain may harbor many specimens of a "forest" species, but the same species will avoid the drier habitat because of the humidity difference. The proper function of lungs is affected greatly by the amount of moisture they contain, and organisms have evolved so that they maintain

Green iguanas and most other rainforest species require high humidity levels in their enclosure.

a proper balance of water in the lungs. Putting an animal from a high-humidity environment into a dry one may cause difficulty in breathing because with each exhalation, the lizard loses more water than can be replaced from the body. There is a physiological link involved, and it extends to other aspects of reptilian life as well. Desert animals that are kept too moist may develop large blisters, while forest dwellers kept too dry may have considerable difficulty when it comes time to shed their skins. Because humidity levels are important to lizards, all terraria should have a working humidity gauge.

Temperature and Heating

Herpetoculturists may do a great many things that are not in the best interests of their animals, and still the creatures may survive. I have

known keepers who fed their iguanas nothing but cooked pasta and iceberg lettuce, put large monitors in painfully small terrariums, and allowed tegus to have free run of the house, and yet these animals–somehow–survived for many years. But one thing no reptile seems able to survive is life in an improper temperature range. On the one hand, tropical animals naturally need to be exposed to temperatures considerably warmer than what most humans would find comfortable; on the other hand, even the tropics get a bit cold at times. Many metabolic processes in reptiles, such as those activating hunting and mating, require heat. In contrast, digestion and sleep are often triggered or aided by a reduction of temperature. A terrarium must provide the thermal regime needed by the intended residents, and in most cases, the temperature must be allowed to vary to a degree that lets the normal hormonal activities in the lizards take place.

Thermal gradients are essential to the proper long-term husbandry of healthy animals. Lizards are not going to keep a constant body temperature. Diurnal lizards will be cool in the early morning and look for a basking site that will let them absorb sunlight and warm up. When they become warm enough to increase activity, they may hunt or seek water or a mate. When they get too warm, they will look for an escape from the heat. A thermal gradient is an environment that offers a variety of areas of different temperatures, allowing a lizard in a terrarium to seek out the place with a suitable temperature for a given activity.

Temperature ranges provided in the species accounts reflect what the prevailing terrarium air temperature should be to keep the animals healthy. In addition, though, many species will require a basking site where the temperature will be considerably higher. Such sites, necessary for monitors, iguanids, and agamids, must be localized so that a single rock or log receives the intense heat. Such areas should be allowed to reach 120 to 140°F (49 to 60°C). (Check the requirements of the exact species with which you are working.) Yes, these temperatures are lethal to animals if there is no escape to cooler temperatures, which underlines again why giant lizards must be kept in large terrariums. One innovative way to handle this thermal requirement is to build a stack of hide boxes–a saurian apartment complex–so that the uppermost level is under a small high-intensity heat lamp and the lowest levels are progressively cooler. In this complex, lizards can simply move from story to story to modify their temperature while also being able to stay concealed from view.

A variety of devices are available at reasonable prices, making control and monitoring of animal and terrarium temperatures simple. Heat tapes, ceramic heat emitters, and halogen and infrared heat lamps are all useful and reliable for providing proper temperatures. A series of different heating lamps can be regulated from specially designed thermostats and rheostats. Spot temperature readings, useful to record preferred body and basking site temperatures throughout the day, can be monitored with unobtrusive temperature probes, such as temperature guns or the probes of digital thermometers.

Proper housing setup for juvenile white-throated monitors; it includes both heat lamps and ultraviolet lights.

Ultraviolet Light

Although the precise importance of ultraviolet light to diurnal reptiles is not well known, experimental data show that the presence of full-spectrum lighting does correlate with increased blood calcium levels. Because calcium is essential for structural repair and many physiological processes–such as muscle contractions and generating nerve impulses–experienced herpetoculturists generally opt to use full-spectrum lighting for captive diurnal animals.

A considerable variety of UV-producing light products are available, ranging from fluorescent tubes most often used with indoor plants to more sophisticated incandescent bulbs and tubes. Among the options available to the herpetoculturist now are the following:

65

Fluorescent tubes are the most common method for supplying ultraviolet light to captive reptiles.

Mercury Vapor Lamps

These lights emit high-intensity UVB/UVA and full-spectrum light. Lamps are rated for from 12 inches (30.5 cm) to about 6.5 feet (2 m) above the substrate. They also emit a fair amount of heat, more than incandescent bulbs of comparable wattage.

Fluorescent Tubes

There are many different types of these on the market. Here, we are discussing those specifically manufactured for providing light to reptiles. These emit UVB, some UVA, and full-spectrum light with very little heat. Fluorescent tubes should be used with an incandescent light/heat source to create a thermal gradient. All lamps are rated for use at distances from 10 to 12 inches (25.4 to 30.5 cm). The optimum distance is 6 to 10 inches (15.2 to 25.4 cm) from the tube.

Incandescent Lightbulbs

These range from household screw-in bulbs to spotlight heat lamps. Depending on the brand and type, they can provide full-spectrum light, some UVA, and heat. Flood lamps create a larger heated area, and spot bulbs create a more concentrated heated area. Examples include daylight blue bulbs, available at most stores that carry lightbulbs.

Incandescent Night Bulbs

These blue or red bulbs provide limited visible light in both flood and spot lamps but generate considerable heat. Theoretically, this color of light does not disturb the normal sleeping behavior of reptiles. This may be false, as most lizards see red wavelengths quite well.

Foods and Feeding

With apologies for offering an old cliché, remember that you are what you eat, and the same premise applies to lizards. If you eat a diet high in fats and sugars, you should not be surprised if you become overweight, lethargic, and diabetic. If you feed lizards an inappropriate diet, do not be surprised if they decline in health or die. Although there are many physiological differences between humans and lizards (and for that matter, among different kinds of lizards), certain biochemical constants do apply. Most important is that all reptiles require some combination of proteins, carbohydrates, and

Most carnivorous giant lizards, such as this red tegu, will feed eagerly on rodents.

fats in their diets. The reason is simply because all living animal cells require all three chemical groups in their structure. The accompanying Chart of Nutrients, Sources, and Biological Functions shows the major nutritive chemical groups, their occurrence in the body, some functions, and some dietary sources high in concentration for each group.

A proper diet is important for captive animals because they cannot supplement missing components by foraging elsewhere. It is also almost completely unknown for a captive animal to be fed even a significant percentage of its natural food items while in captivity. Large carnivorous lizards typically consume prey that includes crabs, scorpions, "exotic" grasshoppers and kin, millipedes, and snails. Few

herpetoculturists can or will be able to supply such a costly diet. As a result, the conscientious keeper will give serious thought to the nature and sources of available foods offered to captive animals. For example, which prey will really be better for a breeding group of frilled lizards: crickets fresh from a pet shop that have been feeding on their dead kin and kept in their own filth, or crickets given a diet of cereals and fruit along with clean drinking water in a cage from which dead crickets are routinely removed? Today it is not just the most experienced keeper who provides charges with so-called "gut-loaded" foods; rather, it is only the most uninformed novice who does not.

The key to successful gut-loading of prey animals is to provide them with a decent diet until they are fed to your reptiles. Crickets and roaches thrive on soft green leafy vegetables, fruits, finely ground cereals, and cornmeal. Rodents should be fed rodent chow and not allowed to become so hungry that they eat newspaper, their own droppings, or other cage detritus.

Obtaining healthy live foods is important year-round but may pose special challenges during the colder months. The serious giant lizard keeper will want to ensure that he has adequate live foods and may choose to place orders with reputable suppliers. Keepers with large collections of reptiles may find it economical to breed their own lizard food.

It was once relatively safe to offer carnivorous lizards such food items as raw meat, fish, and eggs. The incidence of salmonellosis and other bacterial diseases, plus the possibility of parasitic threats, make the offering of these foods risky. As strange

as it sounds, uncooked meat intended for human consumption may actually be more dangerous to animals than rotting carrion in the wild.

Many canned dog foods can be used to supplement captive diets but should not form the bulk of the menu. If eggs are to be offered, they should be thoroughly cooked. Tegus, monitors, and even some iguanas will eat hard-boiled or scrambled eggs. In place of raw meats, herpetoculturists have sometimes utilized sausages. These may be custom sausages, including cooked and ground meats from poultry or beef, or cooked commercially available varieties. There are now also a variety of canned and packaged foods specifically marketed for reptiles, both carnivorous and herbivorous. Some contain adequate vitamins and minerals, but there are also several good commercially available supplements for reptiles on the market.

It was also common for reptile keepers to spend the warm months of the year harvesting a variety of insects for their lizards. Most agricultural and suburban areas, though, are now routinely sprayed with pesticides, making it chancy to feed wild-caught insects to a collection of herpetofauna.

A still-common failure for many herpetoculturists occurs when the amount of food offered is inadequate. This may be because some keepers erroneously think that large lizards, like large snakes, need not feed more than a few times per year. Lizards are generally more active than snakes, for lizards must generally forage or hunt, while snakes are often ambush predators. The energy requirements of each strategy differ enormously, and lizard keepers should assume that lizards will need to be fed at least weekly (for larger specimens taking large food items), while most need food daily or on alternate days.

Although carnivorous giant lizards will eat almost any prey they can subdue, studies reveal that invertebrates make up the majority of the diets of most species. Several commercially available large invertebrates make suitable prey for these lizards, and the hobbyist can culture many of these. Some examples include (left to right): silkworms, giant African millipedes, giant cave cockroaches, and Madagascar hissing roaches.

Terrarium and Animal Cleaning

Terrariums will occasionally need to be completely taken apart and cleaned, like after a cage inhabitant has suffered a fatal illness or after an infestation by a seemingly invincible colony of mites. If a terrarium must be completely revitalized, do not attempt to save any of the old substrate, be it oak bark chips, sand, or paper. Substrate is an excellent place for the smallest organisms to thrive, so just toss it away. Clean the cage with appropriate disinfectants, such as white vinegar, isopropyl alcohol, or one of the commercially available terrarium disinfectants. Allow the cage and props to dry before reconstructing the habitat, and be sure to give each item a close inspection before considering it clean. Mites can hide in the smallest places, so clean things thoroughly.

Avoid the use of certain toxic chemicals such as formaldehyde and full-strength chlorine bleach, as their residues can be dangerous to reptiles. A weak bleach solution (10 percent bleach to 90 percent water) may be used to clean terrariums and props made of glass, but it should not be used on wood, porous rock (such as sandstone or pumice), or plastics. Rinse all bleached materials thoroughly in clean fresh water and allow to dry before reintroducing them to the terrarium or its inhabitants.

Animals that require bathing–if they are covered in dried uric acid or mites, for example–can be immersed in warm water 82 to 90°F (27.8 to 32.2°C). Mites will drown quickly and may start migrating toward the lizard's head. Wipe these off as you see them, and periodically wipe the lizard

NUTRIENTS, SOURCES, AND BIOLOGICAL FUNCTIONS

BIOCHEMICAL GROUP	OCCURRENCE IN BODY	FUNCTIONS	DIETARY SOURCES	CAUTIONARY NOTES
proteins	cytoplasm (cytosol); parts of cell membrane; makes muscles, nerves, blood, bones	produces cell receptors, hormones, neurotransmitters, immunity cells	animal products (muscle meats, eggs); soybeans	excess may lead to: weight gain, gout, kidney damage
carbohydrates	stored in cells, especially in liver	rapid energy source for cells (as ATP), roughage cleans guts	fruits and vegetables	excess may lead to: weight gain, diarrhea
fats	cell membranes; fat deposits	long-term, slow-burning energy source; insulation; hormones	animal fats; vegetable oils	excess may lead to: weight gain, circulatory disease, coronary disease, lethargy, apathy
minerals/ions	almost everywhere	structure of bones, eggshells, blood, chemical activities, hormone structure	most foods, but captive animals often need supplements	deficiency may lead to: lethargy, poor immunity, loss of appetite, trouble shedding or healing
vitamins	in physiologically active tissues	used as substrates on which some structures are assembled; important to start and maintain many biochemical processes	most foods, but captive animals often need supplements	excess of fat-soluble (A, B, E) may lead to: liver failure, toxicity, neurological damage, death

Crocodile monitor feeding on a mixture of ground turkey and boiled eggs. Giant lizards are healthiest when fed a variety of foods.

Some of the giant lizards, such as *Cyclura* species, are primarily herbivorous and require daily feedings of leafy greens, vegetables, and fruit.

with a clean paper towel to remove obstinate parasites. Be sure to completely flush bathwater, and if the infestation was pronounced, provide a second bath immediately. Keep your lizards so cleaned in simple dry terrariums for two or three days, and return them to more complex terrariums only if there are no further signs of mites.

A Note on Natural Habitats

More and more people are taking excursions into the exotic worlds of giant lizards. With such travels, education about the true nature of tropical and subtropical locales is making better keepers of many herpetoculturists. Slowly fading are the ideas that deserts and rain forests are uniformly hot and consistent environments. These places,

in fact, can get quite cold at night or during the winter, and it is important for herpetoculturists to acknowledge that not only can their charges usually withstand far greater swings in temperature than they think but also a wider range of seasonal variation. For example, many equatorial rainforests may drop in temperature by as much as 27°F (15°C) at night, with equal or greater drops in many deserts. Similarly, the rainforest in the monsoon season is downright wet–swamps expand, rivers flood, and often the only "land" above water is to be found in the trees. During the dry season, rivers may dry up, land turn to mud, and no rain may fall for two or three months.

71

Tupinambis sp., albino

REPRODUCTION

Even though breeders are producing more giant lizards than ever before, some of the common species, such as green iguanas, are rarely captive bred.

Providing the conditions that induce animals to reproduce in captivity is one of the most important roles filled by a serious herpetoculturist. Success in this endeavor is a sure sign that terrarium conditions are satisfactory because distressed animals are essentially impossible to breed. Although captive breeding has exploded since about 1980, our knowledge of how to get lizards to breed is still far from complete. Some species almost follow a step-by-step formula, while others reproduce under seemingly inexplicable circumstances. If you are going to breed lizards, keep good notes on how you proceed, and share that information by publishing it in a magazine, journal, or website.

Sexing Giant Lizards

Unlike many mammals and birds, reptiles are not generally sexually dimorphic–meaning that there is no easily observable character that serves to distinguish males from females. Among the giant lizards, males typically grow to a greater length and have broader and more muscular heads, but a comparative feature is difficult to discern unless you have both sexes at hand to compare. In species that possess preanal or femoral pores, the structures are more pronounced in males; the femoral pores in males also exude waxy plugs that are most conspicuous during the mating season. Some disagreement still exists about the function of the femoral excretions, but it is likely that they serve as both olfactory/gustatory and tactile sexual cues for the female lizard.

Among iguanian lizards, it is common for the males to conspicuously differ from females in color (males tend to be more colorful) and have

Unlike monitors, most iguanas are visually sexually dimorphic. Male green iguanas develop larger crests, jowls, and dewlaps than the females.

larger crests. This is particularly noticeable among basilisks, where males have large sails on the head, back, and tail, but females have little or no crest on the head and reduced or absent dorsal and caudal crests. Males of many chameleon species have pronounced horns or nasal appendages; in females, these are much smaller or absent. Among the larger iguanians and tegus, healthy males grow enlarged jowls that may extend from the rear of the lower jaw to the middle of the neck.

Male lizards possess paired reproductive organs (see section "The Reptilian Egg and Embryo"), but many females possess similar paired organs. Again, the organs in females are considerably shorter than their male counterparts, but in the absence of a male's genitalia for comparison, it is difficult to ascertain sex. Many male lizards contain a tiny penile bone or cartilage called a

hemibaculum, which is absent in females of the same species. The hemibaculum is only visible by X-ray or ultrasound examination.

Like all other animals, reptiles carry their DNA on distinctive chromosomes. Just as humans have sex chromosomes–males are termed XY and females XX–many lizards have a similar chromosomal sex determination. Males of many monitors are of the so-called ZZ type and females of the ZW type. (That is, in contrast to the human condition, the monitor females are heterogametic, while the males are homogametic.) In many other species, sex is determined by hormone activity driven by the incubation temperature of eggs. Thus, any given clutch may turn out 100 percent a single sex. Blood tests will provide the materials for both sex chromosome and sex hormone level examinations.

Male monitors will sometimes evert their hemipenes (circled) when they defecate, as this savanna monitor is doing.

Parthenogenetic Lizards

There are three distinct modes of reproducing among living things: asexual, sexual, and unisexual. Asexual organisms, such as most microorganisms, reproduce by self-dividing one cell into two daughter cells. Each daughter cell starts life as half of the parent and grows until it, too, is large enough to divide again. In these cases where there is no exchange of genetic material (DNA) from one individual to another, there are no sexes– thus, the reproduction is asexual. Sexually reproducing creatures, including most animals and plants, have male and female sexes, in which males contribute DNA to a receptive female, who then keeps the developing fertilized zygote for a set period. The third major division includes animal populations made entirely of females. These females contain an unusual number of chromosome sets so that they can produce eggs that already contain the equivalent of paternal DNA, which is needed as the trigger to start developing an embryo. Such species are neither asexual nor sexless but are simple all-female. Because no mating is ever required for producing offspring, the females are self-replicating virgins, and these species are called parthenogenetic (from the Greek words παρθενο, meaning "virgin" and γενς, meaning "generate" or "produce"). Young produced via parthenogenesis receive only the DNA of their mother, making genetic novelties or new combinations extremely rare; offspring are clones.

Among vertebrates, parthenogenesis is not common, but there are many species of fishes

In some monitor species, the males have a group of enlarged scales (postcloacal tuft) at the base of the tail (circled).

in which it is observed. A few snake species have been reported as parthenogenetic, and some 30 species of lizards use this mode of reproduction, including members of the genera *Aspidoscelis, Cnemidophorus, Lepidophyma, Gymnophthalmus, Gehyra, Lacerta*, and others. However, parthenogenesis has only recently been documented among any of the giant lizards. The first to be so noted was the Argus monitor (*Varanus panoptes*), a broadly ranging generalist from Australia and New Guinea. In this case, the female that reproduced prior to ever mating with a male was later observed to mate successfully and reproduce offspring (Lenk et al., 2005), which means that this species of monitor is a facultative parthenogenetic species. (It has the ability to reproduce both sexually and unisexually.)

More famous, though, have been the parthenogenetic events of long-term captive Komodo dragons (*Varanus komodoensis*) because the unusual biology of these well-known and highly publicized animals caught the attention of the international press (Watts et al., 2006). As of this writing in 2008, Komodo dragons have reproduced parthenogenetically at London, Chester, and Sedgwick County Zoos. All offspring were male. This is possible because monitor sex is determined by the ZW chromosomal sex-determination system, not the mammalian XY system. The eggs were haploid (having only one set of chromosomes) and later doubled their chromosome number (became diploid), which is necessary for embryo development to occur. When a female monitor (having the ZW sex chromosome set) reproduces parthenogenetically, she gives the zygote only one chromosome from each pair of chromosomes, including only one of her two sex chromosomes–either a Z or a W.

The single sex chromosome is then duplicated in the parthenogenetically developing egg. Just as mammalian sex chromosomes may combine to form a female (XX) or a male (XY) with no YY option, monitor eggs receiving a Z chromosome become male (ZZ); those receiving a W chromosome become WW, which is unable to develop into a live embryo. Neither can a monitor produce a ZW combination parthenogenetically, for which reason there are no female offspring in the absence of a female-male copulation event.

The Reptilian Egg and Embryo

A characteristic of the class Reptilia is that its members are capable of reproducing their young on land without recourse to either water-immersed eggs or young that undergo a larval stage of development. This is a formidable leap from the amphibian or fish modes of embryological development.

All animal embryos, including those of the creatures reading this book, must develop to a considerable degree while immersed in water. Amphibians generally lay their eggs in the water or in a very moist microhabitat (such as inside a rotting log), and the young often go through a tadpole stage. Even for those amphibians that forgo free-living larval stages, the developing embryo transforms from a gill-bearing form to a miniature adult while still in the egg (or throat or stomach of the parent). As amphibians became more and more terrestrial, they were faced with increasingly inhospitable places to reproduce. Even before they have young, eggs must be

SIZE DOES MATTER

Determining the sex of a lizard often includes examination to see if hemipenes are present. One difficulty with this method is that females of many monitor species have hemipenes-like structures termed hemiclitorises. If equally sized representatives of each sex are available for comparison, the hemipenes will be considerably longer in the male. If you only have one specimen to examine, however, this method can be difficult to use because varanid hemiclitorises can be quite long and easily mistaken for hemipenes.

fertilized, and the majority of amphibians exercise external fertilization. Successful reproduction meant that the animal must either return to the water to fertilize and/or deposit eggs or find a way to bring the water farther inland. All the "higher" vertebrates–reptiles, birds, and mammals–evolved from an ancestor that managed to solve that problem; they brought the water with them.

All reptiles fertilize their eggs internally. Males produce sperm that are mixed with a viscous fluid and then inseminated directly into the female's reproductive tract via the cloaca. In the case of male lizards, there are two copulatory organs, rather inaccurately termed hemipenes. During mating, the male lizard may use either hemipenis or use them both sequentially. Hemipenes

EVEN EMBRYOS EAT

Blackburn (2000) has proposed that the terms "oviparity" and "viviparity" be augmented with terms that reflect the nutrient mechanism of the embryo. The term "lecithotrophy" is used for species in which nutrients are supplied from a yolk sac, while species that utilize "matrotrophy" are fed by the mother while the embryo is in the female's body. Under this classification scheme, the vast majority of reptiles are oviparous lecithotrophs, about 20 percent of squamates are viviparous lecithotrophs, and three skink clades fall under the viviparous matrotrophy category

are remarkably complex bits of anatomy that usually lie inverted at the base of the tail, facing posteriorly on either side of the vent. When in use, they are inflated and everted–turned right-side out–and can be seen to have a very wide range of shapes, relative sizes, and ornamentation. This ornamentation is characteristic for each species, such that hemipenial morphology is a major identification tool for most species. Once sperm has been introduced through the cloaca, it moves upward through the oviducts and fertilizes the eggs. But what of the developing embryos? How do they get immersed in a watery environment?

The solution has been to create something of an aquarium in which embryos may undergo early development. This aquarium is a membranous fluid-filled sac called an amnion. The developing embryos of all higher tetrapods form within an amnion, giving the group comprising reptiles, birds, and mammals the technical label of amniotes. Egg-laying amniotes, the truly oviparous species, produce a calcium-shelled egg, which greatly reduces water loss while also providing structural integrity for the egg's contents. Additional embryonic sacs include the yolk (which provides a high-fat source of nutrition) and allantois (from the French word meaning "sewer," which collects waste matter produced by the embryo), and these are surrounded by a tough chorion. Alternative modes of embryological development include retention of the eggs inside of the mother's body until the time of hatching–there is no shell, and the young appear to an external observer as live delivery (this mode is called ovoviparity); and complete development inside the mother, with food coming from a placenta instead of a yolk sac (called viviparity). Few large lizards are viviparous, with the Solomons skink being an exception. The rest are oviparous.

Mating sailfin lizards (*Hydrosaurus amboinensis*), a species rarely bred in captivity.

Mating

Lizards may be induced into mating either seasonally or year round. In the former category are lizards with ranges in regions with distinct seasonal cycles or in species with particularly long gestation times. Seasonal variations that may affect mating and egg laying (parturition) may include variations in length of daylight period, daily temperature, rainfall, and food abundance. In most cases, increasing periods of daylight increase hormonal activity under control of the pineal gland and parietal eye. Several studies link proper gonadal development and activity with the reception of adequate amounts of ultraviolet light. If prey species, such as insects, are abundant, lizards tend to feed actively and then seek a mate.

Mating is initiated with the male trying to gain proximity to a receptive female. This may involve assuming intense colors, performing head bobbing and other displays, or wrestling with rival males. If a female is receptive to copulation, she generally becomes submissive, allowing the male to approach from the rear and initiate mating. The actual process may take many seconds to a few hours, depending on the species and circumstances.

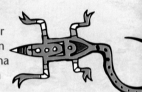

A homemade incubator made from a Styrofoam box. These green iguana eggs are incubating on vermiculite.

Most reptile species are indiscriminate in mating, and copulation among many individuals is possible. Some of the larger skinks, such as in the genus *Tiliqua*, have been observed to form lifelong mate pairs, while females of other species may refuse males that season after having had a successful mating.

Once mating has taken place, eggs may be laid in a matter of days or weeks. Oviparous females typically find a place to dig a nest in the soil in which to lay eggs. In the case of many giant lizards, the nests may be at the end of long and deep burrows. The herpetoculturist interested in breeding giant lizards is advised to provide the facilities for female lizards to make or use such burrows.

Incubation and Hatching

In the wild, there are some generally applicable parameters that coincide with reptilian reproduction. Mating takes place after a period of adequate feeding, meaning the spring for species in strongly seasonal locations. Once insects emerge and thrive, lizards can feed and bulk up, which in turn allows sex hormones to be produced in quantities sufficient to induce mating behaviors. Well-fed females will produce young or eggs; in the event of poor food supplies, the embryos or eggs may be reabsorbed by the mother's body or passed in an incomplete stage. Hatching or birth takes place when food supplies for the young are plentiful. The hatching is also

PREFERRED HATCHING TIME

By Bert Langerwerf

In nature, the incubation temperature will follow a nearly sinoid curve, with the lowest temperature in the early morning and the highest in the afternoon. For Australian water dragons, I have found that if incubated this natural way, babies all hatch when the temperature reaches this lowest level or shortly thereafter. I made a similar test for *Tupinambis merianae*, the Argentine tegu, and found that all babies would hatch when the incubation temperature rose, mostly between 10 a.m. and noontime. I have coined the phrase preferred hatching time (PHT) as a term for the phenomena of all the eggs in a clutch hatching at roughly the same time of day.

Breeders often incubate lizard eggs at a constant temperature, which is why PHT has been overlooked. It can be very useful for their survival if babies hatch at one certain time of the day. It is likely that PHT is much more widespread among reptiles, and I would urge people to incubate the eggs the natural way to obtain data like this. It is even possible that hatching success is increased this way, as lizards may wait for the best moment to hatch, and that moment never comes while incubating at a constant temperature.

timed so that the young have enough time and food to store sufficient fat reserves to survive the winter or dry season. There is still a considerable realm of research to attract herpetologists concerning these topics, but herpetoculturists are ideally situated to make useful observations regarding all aspects of reptilian reproduction and juvenile development and biology.

Viviparous lizards will bring young to full term inside the mother. The majority of giant lizard species, though, are oviparous and will lay one or more clutches of a few to many eggs per season. Most lizards will excavate at least a crude hole in the soil into which eggs are deposited and then covered. Others will excavate long burrows or find hollows in trees to serve as incubation sites. In virtually every case, the mother seeks a place where temperature and humidity levels will stay nearly constant through hatching.

In captivity, it is normal for the keeper to incubate lizard eggs artificially. Once laid, eggs should be carefully removed and placed in a

ALL ABOUT VERMICULITE

Vermiculite is a naturally occurring mineral that resembles mica. Most vermiculite is mined from preCambrian and older geological layers, but one Triassic mine in Montana was contaminated by a secondary diopside deposit, which is a source of asbestos. Because of the considerable press coverage about asbestos-laced vermiculite, all vermiculite products have, at least temporarily, become more difficult to obtain.

container that includes a mix of vermiculite or perlite and water. The exact ratio of the materials is determined by volume, not weight, and will vary depending on the species being incubated and its habitat preferences. Desert species may require a substrate-to-water ratio of 3:2, while rainforest lizards might fare better at 2:1. Details for several species are provided in the text, but with other lizards, there is still room for experimentation. It has also become clear that since the mid-1990s, both the frequency and likelihood of successfully breeding giant lizards in captivity is increasing. Excellent starter species include spiny-tailed and Duméril's monitors, as well as the water dragons.

Some breeders prefer to incubate their eggs on perlite instead of vermiculate. These are beaded lizard eggs incubating on perlite.

Iguana iguana

4

VETERINARY
CARE

A veterinarian giving a green water dragon antibiotics. A reptile veterinarian is a valuable asset to the giant lizard keeper.

The time will come when you will need to bring a giant lizard to the veterinarian. The visit will usually take place when an animal is suspected of having an illness or has an obvious injury. If an animal is particularly valuable or if it is to become part of a larger collection, it may be wise to make the first visit as soon after acquisition as possible. Wild-caught animals will invariably be carriers of something with pathogenic possibilities, be it ticks, mites, internal parasites, bacteria, or viruses. A major incentive for acquiring captive-bred animals is that they are less likely to have pathogens than their wild-caught counterparts.

Finding a Reptile Veterinarian

Even before the acquisition of any new lizard, you should locate a qualified veterinarian who is familiar with herpetological medicine. Not all (or most) veterinarians are experienced in herpetocultural diseases and treatments, and reptile physiology differs considerably from that of a dog or horse. Among treatment concerns are a) the reptile's slower response time to the administration of drugs, b) calculating proper drug dosages, and c) recognizing reptile-specific diseases. Because reptile physiology is so much slower than that of mammals, a disease may manifest itself with recognizable symptoms

AGING IS GOOD FOR WINE BUT NOT FOR MEDICINES

It may be tempting to treat lizards with some old antibiotics, but there are at least two serious reasons why only the most knowledgeable herpetoculturists should attempt this route. First, you may administer a correct antibiotic in an incorrect dosage. The lizard may appear to recover, only to die for mysterious reasons a month or so later. This may be caused by overdose poisoning. A common cause of delayed death by antibiotics is renal failure, which may not manifest until several months after an inappropriate drug therapy was administered. There are no overt clinical symptoms, so death is "sudden" and seems mysterious.

A second problem that may occur from treating an animal with dated prescriptions is that drugs change in structure over time. Most simply lose efficacy; the medication becomes useless because it has done the equivalent of converting from fine wine to vinegar. Other medications, including aspirin, change into forms that can become dangerous and possibly fatal.

Self-prescribing medications for an ill lizard without the supervision of a veterinarian is further unwise. Administration of drugs at too low a dose and/or for too short a time may leave a resistant strain of bacteria in the lizard for which no treatment may exist or for which treatment is far more expensive than it would have been had the animal been treated appropriately in the first place. Humans are already facing the consequences of inappropriate and excessive antibiotic treatment in the form of drug-resistant strains of many pathogens, including tuberculosis and the infamous MRSA (methicillin-resistant *Staphylococcus aureus*). There is even a pathogen now that can survive in formalin! Veterinarians are specifically trained to anticipate such problems. I am not a vet and am not paid a percentage of the fees they charge clients I have referred to them, but I have kept reptiles for over four decades and know the value of *professional* advice in this business. Just as I don't fix my own car, rebuild my computer, or diagnose my own illnesses, I do not entrust the health of my animals entirely to my healing skills.

only in the last stages. If you wait to find a herpetologically savvy veterinarian until a specimen needs one, you may be too late.

The simplest way to find a qualified herpetologically oriented veterinarian is to ask potential vets if they are members of the Association of Reptile and Amphibian Veterinarians (ARAV), although not all reptile vets are members. You may also consult the ARAV website at www.arav.org, or ask someone at the local zoo or herpetological society for a referral. Once you think that you've located an acceptable veterinarian, make an appointment–a telephone interview is fine–to ask pertinent questions about his experience with exotic reptiles, any special training he may have had, and his membership in and participation with specialist herpetological veterinary groups. Remember that vets sell their time, so offer and be prepared to pay for a consultation.

Why You Need a Reptile Vet

With all the detailed books on reptilian medicine available today, it may be tempting to try diagnosing and treating your lizard without seeing a vet. After all, vets cost money and so do prescription drugs. But if you do decide to be your own vet, the magic word "prescription" means that you need those letters "D.V.M." after your name to be able to acquire the appropriate medications. And an ethical veterinarian will not write you a script for an animal that he has not seen and examined–even if it wasn't against the law for a veterinarian to treat an animal without a doctor-patient-client relationship. Your choice

Scar from abscess removal surgery on a green iguana. Such treatment is beyond the ability of most hobbyists and requires veterinary expertise.

will in large part be based on how much you value your animal. *If you sincerely care about your animal and it is ill or injured, take it to the veterinarian!* What you get for that money is a minimum of six years of college, including a minimum of four years veterinary training, several more years of experience in diagnosing and treating diseases, considerable knowledge in the prescribing of appropriate drugs or therapies, access to necessary diagnostic resources (such as X-rays, blood and fecal tests, etc.), plus the peace of mind that comes from dealing with a professional animal physician. Most veterinarians advise against any prophylactic drug therapies. If the animal is not sick, giving antibiotics is a waste of time, energy, and money, and it can help contribute to the increase of drug resistance problems that have become so common.

SIGNS OF ILLNESS

Signs of some diseases are relatively obvious. Any departure from a lizard's normal behavior could be a clue that something is wrong. Some symptoms are more diagnostic than others. Typical reptilian signs that disease is present include:

- loss of appetite
- loss of weight or the appearance of the bones under the skin
- lethargy
- staying hidden
- unusual behavior
- blisters, lumps, or unusual growths
- trouble righting itself if rolled over
- gasping or gaping
- wheezing
- nasal (nose) or ocular (eye) discharges
- abnormal droppings
- discoloration of limbs, tail, or even body

A lizard displaying one of these symptoms should be isolated from other lizards and housed alone in a quarantine terrarium. Persistence of these symptoms warrants a swift visit to the vet.

Incidentally, if a veterinarian prescribes drug therapy, be sure to administer the full course of treatment (which means that you should not have "old antibiotics" from treating some other animal). If you stop giving an antibiotic when symptoms seem to disappear, any remaining bacteria in the animal may cause a serious relapse and those bacteria may now be resistant to further treatment by the same drug. Result: You will have to start treatment from scratch with a new and often more expensive drug, and you may still lose the lizard because the relapse is hitting an animal already weakened from the initial illness.

What Your Vet Needs From You

The veterinarian will benefit considerably from the intimate knowledge of your lizard that only you have. There are a multitude of questions that the veterinarian may ask to help get to the cause of your lizard's illness. Has it been feeding regularly and on an appropriate diet? Does it eat all the food you offer? Are its feces loose or solid, and what color are they? Is the lizard either unusually energetic or lethargic? Does it sleep more than usual? Is it being handled more or less lately, and is it subjected to handling by school groups or other people? It is a good idea to keep a checklist of certain factors in the lizard's life that can be used for collecting baseline health information. The list should include these items:

- Daytime temperature and high/low temperature in the cage
- Nighttime temperature and high/low temperature in the cage
- Heat source(s)

- Animal's recent water intake
- Type of lighting being used and for how long per day/week
- UVB exposure, including how far source is from lizard and how often you replace it
- Terrarium cleaning materials
- Types of foods and frequency of feedings
- Date of last shed
- Type and depth of substrate
- Number of animals in same cage and when cagemate(s) were added
- Interactions between cagemates
- Number and type of hiding spots and feeding stations in enclosure

Veterinary treatment is designed to work first on relieving the symptoms of an illness. To prevent additional illnesses from infecting the reptiles in a collection or to prevent reinfection of a single animal, the probable causes for the illness must be determined, addressed, and treated directly. In most cases, the cause of an illness is

found in one of the following situations (roughly in order of likelihood):

- animal was acquired with the illness or parasite
- improper temperature regime (meaning animal is too cold or too hot)
- infection from cage mate
- unsanitary terrarium (includes use of toxic substrate, such as cedar)
- improper diet (including lack of UVB exposure)
- undetected wound (which leads to infection)
- overcrowded terrarium
- another animal in field of vision causing stress

Diseases and Other Health Issues

What follows is a list of the most common health problems seen in giant lizards, roughly in order of their likelihood of showing up in a collection. Preliminary treatments are given where appropriate, but remember that they are preliminary–a good veterinarian can best provide proper diagnosis and treatment. This is not meant to be a comprehensive list of ailments, so do not summarily dismiss symptoms that are not described here as unimportant.

Mouth Rot

This insidious, common, highly infectious, and potentially lethal disease goes by the technical name of stomatitis or ulcerative stomatitis. Early symptoms include wheezing or gurgling sounds, tiny bubbles emitted from the nostrils, and swelling of the lips. Examination of the mouth will show the teeth and gums covered in a pasty, pinkish/yellow, yellow, or cheesy substance made from decaying tissue. Too often the first symptom

Green iguana with a generally unhealthy appearance.

Green iguana with lower jaw distended from mouth rot.

the keeper notices is that the lizard will refuse food or try to eat but drop the food after biting into it. This behavior results from the pain caused by oral inflammation.

There are two main varieties of this disease, both contagious to other reptiles and both requiring prompt veterinary care. One form is treated by systemic administration (injection or oral) of an appropriate antibiotic, at the appropriate dose, accompanied by increasing the terrarium temperature and making sure that drinking water is clean and changed several times per day. The other form requires surgery as well as antibiotic treatments, and recuperation may take considerably longer than from the first type of stomatitis.

Recovering lizards must be kept in a warm, dry terrarium with clean drinking water. Do not provide water for soaking unless it is medicated or treated water. Keep recovering lizards in quarantine well away from other animals, and be sure to wash your hands thoroughly with antibacterial soap after handling sick animals or their cage accessories. The terrarium should have a very warm (95 to 115°F [35 to 46.1°C]) section and a cooler retreat area. Reptiles with bacterial infections often bask and induce a fever to fight the disease, but they still require an escape to a cool refuge when temperatures threaten their other physiological functions.

Remember that bacterial infections can easily be transmitted–or retransmitted–through infected water, so change the drinking water frequently during the course of the treatment period. Keep infected animals in separate terrariums, and do not reintroduce them to cage mates until all signs of the illness have been in remission for at least 30 days.

Temperature Stress

Most lizards like it hot–not warm but hot. Humans may find an 80°F (26.7°C) room warm and start the air conditioner, but most lizards see that temperature as cool. Lizards need heat, usually in the range that humans find uncomfortable. There are cool-adapted lizards but not among the giants.

If kept at inappropriately low temperatures, lizards will fail to metabolize properly. They will have neither the energy needed to hunt and feed nor the production of the hormones telling them to hunt or mate. A chilled animal can be active enough to eat, but if the body is not warm enough to allow normal digestion, the food may

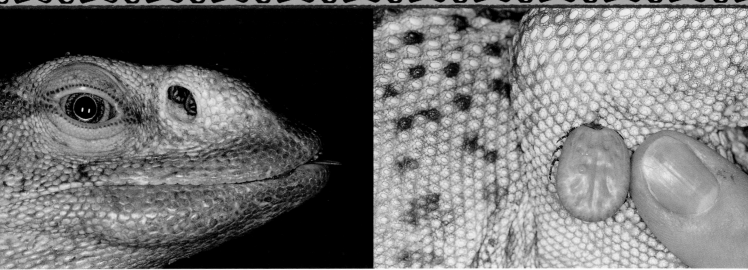

Most wild-caught lizards will have ticks, shown here in the nostril of a white-throated monitor (left) and on the underside of the thigh of a savanna monitor (right).

rot inside the animal, producing potentially fatal toxins. Also, the reptilian immune system becomes depressed at low temperatures, and the body will begin the slow process of catabolization, breaking itself down to provide the energy needed to stay alive.

Increasing the heat in a terrarium is a first step in reviving cold-stressed lizards, but a proper diet and fluid therapy regimen are also needed. Cold-stressed lizards may need to be assist fed or force-fed until they are strong enough to feed on their own. They may also require water (or electrolyte-rich fluids, such as Pediolyte) to be given to them from a dropper. In severe cases, veterinary assistance may be required to provide subcutaneous (under the skin) or even IV fluids to rehydrate the animal.

Excess heat is also dangerous and typically comes when a keeper sets up a terrarium with

the "right" temperature but no place for the resident lizards to escape from the heat. Always be sure to provide not only adequate basking areas but also adequate areas of escape from high terrarium heat for each and every animal in a terrarium. Heat-stressed lizards also require water and fluid replacement therapy, but they may also be suffering more serious internal injuries. Take such reptiles to a veterinarian for a complete examination, and have him check kidney functions.

Parasites
External Parasites

A keeper can often discover external parasites by close examination of a lizard. Mites and ticks, the former often extremely tiny, are most commonly found in a lizard's nostrils, near the eyes, in the axillae (armpits), near the cloaca, and in any skin

THE QUARANTINE TERRARIUM

The goal of a quarantine terrarium is to isolate a sick or injured animal from other animals to a) prevent illness from being spread to healthy animals, b) protect the sick or injured animal from being harmed by cage mates, c) eliminate conditions that could promote secondary complications, and/or d) provide a safe and quiet environment that promotes healing. How, then, should a quarantine terrarium be set up?

First, use the most easy-to-clean materials for the terrarium that you can. Glass terrariums can easily be washed and disinfected after each use, while wooden cages are more difficult to sanitize. Second, do not try to simulate a natural environment; use simple paper towels as substrate, and provide a hide box (especially if the animal is wild caught or not used to being around people or other animals) and a wide, low dish for water. The animal must always have access to clean drinking water, so thoroughly clean the dish at least twice daily, and keep it filled with clean water. (Discard all old water every time you refill the dish.) Always perform maintenance of the quarantine terrarium *after* doing so to your other enclosures to avoid accidentally transferring an illness from the quarantined animal to your healthy ones. Wash your hands before and after working with animals in quarantine.

Provide a thermal gradient, with one side of the terrarium always very warm (usually in excess of 100°F [37.8°C], depending on the species) and the retreat at least 10°F (5.6°C) cooler. Reptiles cannot induce bacteria-killing fever unless their environments are hot enough to make it possible.

folds. Ticks can be removed with forceps, and a topical application of an antibiotic ointment (such as Neosporin or Polysporin) may help prevent a secondary bacterial infection. Because of the nature of their biting mechanism, ticks will usually need to be removed with fine-tipped forceps. Be sure to remove the head when you remove a tick.

Mites can be suffocated by dabbing with any type of cooking oil, then removed by wiping with a paper towel an hour or two later. They may also be drowned by immersing the lizard in a tepid bath of water with a little salt (the salt hastens death in mites), then waiting until dead mites begin to float on the water. There are also some acceptable commercial products specifically made to help kill mites and ticks in terrarium specimens–be careful with these products, and follow the directions exactly. If the miticide contains the chemical ivermectin, keep it away from any turtles you may have; ivermectin is

very toxic to turtles and tortoises. Wiping with a paper towel will remove additional mites, and the process may need to be repeated two or three times to ensure that the lizard is thoroughly cleaned of parasites. Be aware that mites can and do burrow down into the spaces between scales and may not be visible.

The biggest problem with external parasites lies more in keeping them away rather than removing them from an animal. You must find and eliminate the source of the parasites. More often than not, one infected specimen was not subjected to sufficient inspection on purchase or during quarantine, or it did not spend an appropriate time in quarantine (which should minimally be 30 days and as long as 90 days). Again, veterinarians will have chemical treatments that kill local parasites and can check infected lizards for secondary signs of parasite-induced stress or infections.

Internal Parasites

Internal parasites–tapeworms, roundworms, and the like–are more difficult to detect. Large intestinal worms may be apparent in feces, but only a proper fecal analysis that microscopically checks for parasites and parasite eggs will confirm the parasites in many cases. Although a positive fecal test is always indicative of the presence of parasites, a negative result may simply mean that no eggs or parasites were present in the sample examined. While periodic fecal examinations are not usually recommended or needed, it may be wise to have annual exams performed on the specimens in a particularly valuable collection.

Destroy and dispose of ticks as soon as you find them.

Savanna monitor with retained shed. This animal likely needs a more humid terrarium to prevent recurrence.

Shedding Difficulties

Lizards shed their skins as they grow because the outer layer of dead cells (**epidermis**) is not particularly elastic. Unlike snakes that shed their skins in one piece, lizards tend to shed in patches. The process may therefore take a week or more to complete. To someone unfamiliar with this process, the loose flaps of dry skin may appear to be a skin disease.

Lizards in shed may spend more time soaking in water and will drink more water than during periods between sheds. They secrete a water and oil substance between the old and new layers of skin, which loosens the outer layer so that it separates from the body and is more easily shed. Young, well-fed (and thus fast-growing)

lizards will also shed more frequently than older specimens. Geckos often eat their own shed skins; other lizards rarely do so. Watch to be sure that the skin on the animal's toes sheds off, or the retained shed can act as a tourniquet and cause toe loss. If there is a problem with retained toe shed, a shallow dish of moss and water can provide enough additional moisture to assist in the shed. If necessary, a *gentle* massage may be used to remove toe skin.

Cage furniture should include things that are rough enough to allow the animal to rub against to aid in the shed without being abrasive enough to damage the hide. This furniture also has to be heavy and solid enough that the animal can neither knock the furniture over onto itself nor shift it enough to trap a toe or limb when it rubs.

Respiratory Disease

Reptiles resemble humans in that both may contract any of a variety of respiratory infections, including pneumonia and tuberculosis. (Mouth rot is often associated with respiratory illnesses.) The herpetological forms of these diseases are every bit as serious as their human counterparts. Proper diagnosis of which illness is present requires a veterinary examination. Aquatic and semiaquatic lizards are particularly susceptible to respiratory infections during and some time after import from overseas. Desert species are less likely to have respiratory illnesses except when caught from other animals in a collection or if kept in excessively humid or cool conditions.

Typical early symptoms of respiratory distress include loss or reduction of the appetite, listlessness, muscle looseness (the lizard goes limp when handled), and bubbling or gurgling sounds as the lizard breathes. In severe cases, bubbles may protrude from the nostrils (and is often accompanied by stomatitis) and mouth. If symptoms are detected early enough, a proper antibiotic treatment may effect a cure. Immediately isolate the sick lizard from other reptiles and handle only as necessary, preferably using disposable gloves. Respiratory diseases are usually both highly infectious (as the organism is aerosolized with each exhalation, explosively so if the animal is sneezing or coughing), and difficult to treat. The reason for the latter is that reptilian physiology is notoriously slow in revealing symptoms. By the time a keeper is aware that an animal is ill, the illness is often at a critical stage.

Keeping lizards that require high humidity, such as crocodile monitors, in dry conditions can result in numerous health issues.

After isolation, immediately provide the lizard with a thermal gradient that allows a basking site that is at least 105°F (40.6°C), as well as a dish of clean water in which the lizard may soak. At the first sign of respiratory infection, make an appointment to take the lizard to a veterinarian; recovery without a proper drug therapy is unlikely.

Gastrointestinal Blockage and Constipation

Constipation is not the same thing as blockage; however, the two problems share some causes. Constipation is difficulty passing fecal matter, which is usually seen as hard, dry stool. Blockage means that nothing is going through the gut, thus producing very little or no fecal matter.

Giant lizards may become constipated because

Snout injuries are a common problem in lizards, especially fast, nervous species like the green basilisk.

of a restricted or inappropriate diet, insufficient food, insufficient heat, insufficient water, being fed on an indigestible substrate that adheres to the food and is swallowed when the animal eats, and/or disease. In many cases, this is a condition you may safely try to correct without the immediate need to consult a veterinarian, barring any additional symptoms. Newly acquired wild-caught large lizards are especially likely to harbor an incredible number of parasites (due to horrendous caging conditions while they are stored prior to shipment), which is a primary reason why new animals must be quarantined away from your healthy older stock. Parasites are also animals and thus require water to survive. If the parasite load is large enough, it acts like a sponge and absorbs enough water to dry the fecal matter and thereby cause constipation.

In treating constipation, begin by increasing the amount of clean fresh water available to the sick lizard, and if necessary, offer the water by eyedropper. A brief soaking in warm water may help initiate a bowel movement. Or sometimes, a vigorous warm-water swimming session can be substituted for the "brisk walk" that works so well in many mammals. By adding a small quantity of vegetable or olive oil to the lizard's diet, things may move along. If any of these treatments fails to produce a substantial bowel movement within 48 hours, assume that the problem is a blockage and seek the services of a veterinarian immediately.

Some herpetoculturists claim that intestinal blockages may be caused by excessive hair or chitin collected in the gut from diets too high in rodents or insects, respectively. Giving lizards additional drinking water may treat this kind of blockage. This may facilitate movement in *minor* blockage cases, but more severe cases will not respond. This is because the chemical structure of both hair and chitin makes them waterproof, so they cannot be dissolved in water. Both substances are also indigestible by the gut enzymes present in lizards. For such cases, take the animal to a veterinarian, who can treat the condition safely and effectively.

An additional treatment can be the use of Prozyme, an over-the-counter powder made of amylase, lipase, cellulose, and protease (digestive enzymes) that can often be administered orally with a little water to act as the vehicle to get it into the animal. It will dissolve many kinds of intestinal blockages, alleviating the need for surgery.

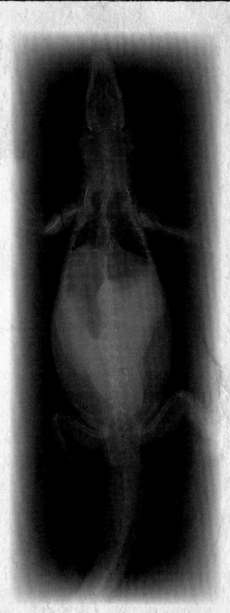

EGG RETENTION

Occasionally, a female that's carrying eggs will be unable to pass them from her body. For several possible reasons the eggs can become stuck inside the mother, a condition called egg binding, egg retention, or dystocia. Among the causes are calcium deficiency from malnutrition, obesity, temperatures that are too low in the terrarium, inadequate laying areas or substrate in which to lay, lack of privacy/cover, bacterial or parasitic infections, trauma to the mother, infertile eggs, hypercalcified egg shells in the uterus, and misshapen or abnormally large eggs.

Signs include lethargy, apathy (especially toward food and water), bloody cloacal discharge, shortness of breath, sudden weight loss, and regurgitation. Positive diagnosis should be done with ultrasound or X-ray examination.

Treating dystocia involves lubricating the cloaca with sterile gel and gentle palpating to assist the passing of the eggs; brief warm water baths; injections of oxytocin or calcium; or in the most extreme cases, surgical removal of the eggs. This is a serious condition, and veterinary intervention is necessary.

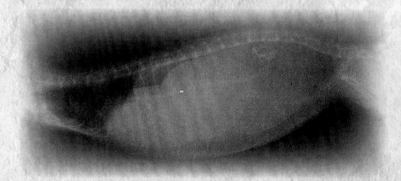

Two X-rays of a female *Varanus pilbarensis* suffering from egg binding. Note the calcified mass of eggs in her abdomen. The lizard did not survive.

Some cases of constipation caused by gravel substrate ingestion–more correctly called an impaction–can cause fatal gut damage by the simple mechanical effect of gravel on tender intestinal tissue. Consequently, you must be careful about the surface used when the animal obtains its food, remembering that many animals will take the food out of the dish and onto the substrate before consuming it.

Bites and Wounds

Most giant lizards are predators and as such have sharp claws and teeth. Even the herbivores, like iguanas, have formidable claws that allow them to climb well. Lizards housed together may bite each other when seizing the same food item, when mating, in territorial disputes, or by accident. Claws may passively open skin when one lizard walks

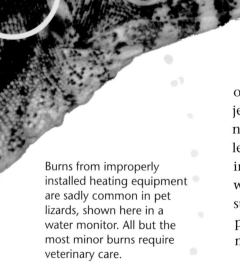

Burns from improperly installed heating equipment are sadly common in pet lizards, shown here in a water monitor. All but the most minor burns require veterinary care.

across another. Sharp objects in cages may cut the lizards, and live rodents are common causes of severe cuts and bites to reptiles, some even causing fatalities. (Lesson: Feed freshly killed or *thoroughly* thawed rodents whenever possible.)

Infections thrive in warm temperatures (recall that even small cuts are considered more serious in the tropics), so treatment, too, should be swift. Establish the cause of the cut and remove it–this may require separation of lizards into individual quarters. Wash a fresh wound with warm water, and if possible, an antiseptic.

Apply a topical antibiotic cream, such as Neosporin, Polysporin, or Nolvasan ointment, and keep the lizard warm and dry until it heals. At any sign of continued bleeding or spreading of an infection, take the lizard to a veterinarian. Many infections will require antibiotic therapy.

If you are bitten, do not jerk or pull to get away. Remember that most lizard teeth are recurved, so you'll only make the injury worse if you pull. (For fishermen, think of it as setting a hook when you jerk.) In many cases, you may need to wait for the lizard to let go. In more persistent cases, immerse the lizard in warm water. Although most can remain submerged for a considerable period, those immersed in this manner often release quickly.

99

Soaking in warm water can help resolve constipation and retained skin. This is a white-throated monitor.

Warm water generally elicits a quicker release response than does cool water. Do not try to pry the mouth open with something hard like a screwdriver unless you are willing to deal with the veterinary bill for treating a broken jaw. (Yes, that has happened on more than one occasion when the keeper was not particularly pain tolerant and/or patient.)

Bites from large lizards or from almost any sized tree crocodile monitor (*Varanus salvadorii*) may be especially serious. Tree crocodile monitor teeth are unique among lizards because they are straight and interlocking, making a bite more of a shearing wound. Such bites may remove flesh and will almost always require prompt medical treatment, possibly including stitches and antibiotic therapy.

Bites should be taken seriously, especially if given by a large lizard. The possibility of you getting an infection is not to be underestimated, so see your physician as soon as feasible. Bites from larger lizards may require stitches. If a bite or scratch draws blood, you are also advised to consult with your M.D. about starting antibiotics and/or getting a tetanus shot. Even if the bite does not draw blood, monitor the area for signs of infection (redness, swelling, excessive pain) and consult your M.D. if they occur.

Zoönoses

It is probably safe to say that most animals are capable of transmitting a disease-causing organism to humans. Humans are even capable of infecting themselves; the feared *Escherichia coli* (or *E. coli*, as it most familiarly known) is an essential bacterium that lives in our large intestines and is largely responsible for our ability to absorb B vitamins. But if introduced to the eyes or mouth, that same *E. coli* may become the source of serious, potentially fatal illness.

Zoönoses (pronounced zo o no sees, not zoo noses) are diseases that are transmitted by animals to humans, and while the incidence and variety of reptile-borne zoönoses are limited, they include some important examples. Salmonellosis has been among the most frequently cited reptile-to-human bacterial diseases and may result from colonies growing in water, among fecal material, and in decaying foods. Proper hygiene is the first line of defense against such pathogens and must include the regular and proper cleaning of terrariums and animals. Use disposable gloves when doing cage-cleaning chores, or be sure to wash your hands thoroughly with antibacterial soap and hot water after working each cage. Never let your lizard or its cage furnishings come in contact with areas used for human food preparation. If you soak your lizard in the bathtub, immediately clean the tub with bleach or another disinfectant.

Varanus varius

5

LAWS
AND
HERPETOCULTURE

There was a time when a person in the United States could go outside in practically any state and collect reptiles and amphibians. The animals could be collected for any purpose–as personal pets, for sale, to use as food, or to bring into classrooms. People who earned their livings as reptile suppliers were few and far between. If a collector in New Jersey wanted specimens of lizards from Florida, he would either have to collect them personally or make the acquaintance of a Floridian collector who wanted to sell or trade local animals. Some of the classic literature of mid-20th-century herpetology centers on the annual collecting trips by zoo curators, such as Raymond Ditmars, Carl Kauffeld, and Marlin Perkins, as they braved the swamps of Georgia or the arroyos of Arizona in search of exotic reptiles.

By the 1950s, roadside reptile "zoos" were a feature of the predominantly two-lane interstate highway system, and visitors could purchase some of the local species for incredibly low prices. Anoles sold for 25 cents, and in Arizona, young Gila monsters were sold for 2 to 5 dollars apiece! In the 1960s, it was unusual to encounter a department store that did not carry horned lizards, anoles, iguanas, and other lizards for sale at low prices.

By the late 1960s, the U.S. began enforcing a long-neglected law called the Lacey Act, which put severe restrictions on the interstate transport of live animals. The Endangered Species Act (ESA) soon followed, as did a plethora of state laws restricting the sale of many native species. There are now few places in North America where one

Many areas have banned the keeping of the truly giant lizards, such as water monitors, seen here with the author.

WILDLIFE REGULATIONS AND THEIR AREA OF AUTHORITY

REGULATION/ACT/DOCUMENT	AUTHORITY
Convention on International Trade in Endangered Species (CITES)	international treaty law; all signatory nations are expected to observe and enforce
U.S. Endangered Species Act (ESA)	protection of all species listed by the regulations, including both domestic and foreign species
Lacey Act	1. allows prosecution for the illegal taking of any species from any location 2. allows the ban of importation of any species deemed injurious
International Union for Conservation of Nature and Natural Resources (IUCN)	none; a strictly advisory body that provides information–mainly via its Red List of Threatened Species–to any agency that can be used in the establishment of regulations

may legally collect reptiles without some sort of state permit. Horned lizards and Gila monsters are nearly universally protected, and it is unlikely that any Gila monster has sold for less than several hundred dollars in the past decade.

Herpetoculturists need to be aware of the laws surrounding the collecting, selling, and keeping of reptiles. Even dead (preserved) specimens are covered by laws. These laws and regulations range from the international to local community levels. In many U.S. cities, there are ordinances–or planned ordinances–banning the keeping of exotic, large, or potentially dangerous animals. It is not illegal to keep crocodile monitor lizards in the state of California, but it is illegal in San Francisco. In that city, and others, local laws ban the private keeping of reptiles that may exceed 6 feet (1.8 m) in total length. Even a juvenile is illegal because it belongs to a species that may exceed the legal length limit.

This volume cannot possibly review all the local and ever-changing laws regarding herpetoculture. Not only are there too many states, but the laws frequently change. In Western Australia, for example, after decades of draconian bans on any private reptile keeping, it is now possible to obtain a permit and keep some species. As the keepers become more organized and numerous, the laws

I⟩◗◗◖◗◗◖◗◗◖◗◗◖◗◗◖◗◗◖◗◗◖◗◗◖◗◗◖◗◗◖◗◗◖◗◗◖◗◗◖◗◗◖

WHAT IS THE LACEY ACT?

The Lacey Act has probably caused more confusion for herpetoculturists–and anyone else interested in the keeping of animals–than all the other acts, regulations, and laws combined. So just what is the Lacey Act?

Concern about the demise of many native species, particularly passenger pigeons, prairie chickens, grouse, and bison, led Iowa congressman John Fletcher Lacey (R-Iowa, 1841-1913) to introduce laws in 1900 that would protect native American wildlife near the turn of the 20th century. Lacey wanted to give the national government the power to exterminate "unwisely" introduced foreign species and keep out such known environmental disasters as the Indian mongoose. A 1926 revised version of the act combined jurisdiction over both terrestrial wildlife and game fishes. The amended version of 1981 made it illegal to move or trade wildlife that was taken from any place in an illegal manner. A major component of the act allows legal action to be taken in support of the violation of the laws and regulations of other nations. Thus, an animal smuggled out of New Zealand could be confiscated in the United States under authority of the Lacey Act. Unlike the Endangered Species Act (ESA), which has authority only over endangered species, the Lacey Act gives the U.S. government authority over any species that was taken illegally.

will undoubtedly be altered, hopefully becoming more accommodating.

CITES

At the international level, the most encompassing regulations come from the Washington Convention, known as the Convention on International Trade in Endangered Species (CITES). The Convention was established in 1973 by 87 founding signatory nations, and although not a law, CITES has the effect of law but only at international borders. CITES was intended to regulate–not prohibit–and monitor the commercial and other traffic in endangered species. An international body periodically reviews lists of species and determines if any should be included on one of the Convention's three appendices. If an animal is listed on Appendix I, it is deemed to be endangered, and commercial and other trade is to be prohibited. Placement on Appendix II means that there is concern that if trade is not regulated, populations may decline or the species may become endangered. Listing on Appendix III means that local populations are endangered and given regional protection.

In practice, what does this mean? Suppose a zoo wishes to import a Komodo dragon (Appendix I) from Indonesia to Washington. This

is an international transfer, so an export permit is required from the Indonesian government, and the zoo needs an import permit for an endangered species as required under the ESA administered by the U. S. government. This will fulfill the CITES requirements. Now suppose the zoo in Washington is breeding Komodo dragons and wishes to sell offspring to a commercial dealer in Florida. No CITES paperwork is required now, not because the lizards are captive bred but because the transaction is all within the same country. Under the ESA, both parties must now secure interstate commerce permits to legally sell the lizards across state lines. If the sale were to take place within the same state, only local state and community laws and restrictions would apply.

If a CITES-listed animal is being sold in a store, the purchaser does not need a permit from CITES to either purchase or transport the animal within the country. If the animal is to be exported abroad, CITES documents are needed; or if it will be crossing state lines, CITES papers are needed to obtain a permit under the ESA. If you are going to purchase a CITES-listed animal, ask for a copy of the permits that accompanied the animal into the country, along with Form 3-177 (in the United States), to verify legal acquisition. In short, make sure that you can prove that the animals were legally acquired.

Other Laws

The ESA was authorized by the U.S. Congress in 1973 and aims to control interstate and international trade in endangered species.

Because the nation of Fiji bans the export of its wildlife, bringing a Fiji banded iguana (*Brachylophus fasciatus*) into the United States would violate the Lacey Act.

There are, of course, other documents that cast confusion over who may and may not collect, study, sell, or own animals. The International Union for Conservation of Nature and Natural Resources (IUCN), headquartered in Switzerland, publishes a Red Data book. The book, which is updated frequently, contains information on the status of every species of plant and animal that is deemed to be threatened with extinction or that is already endangered. The list of endangered species presented in the IUCN Red Data book, the ESA, and on CITES varies, thereby adding to potential confusion of just which creatures are actually protected by what laws in which countries.

Then there are the local municipal laws that govern what may or may not be kept by individuals. Many cities restrict ownership of

All of the *Cyclura* species are listed on CITES Appendix I. *C. nubila caymensis* is shown here.

animals that exceed a certain length or that are venomous, and many local ordinances are enacted out of apathy or whim rather than reason or need. I am aware of one town where it is illegal to own any snakes because the animal control officer at the time was afraid of them. When presented to the local town committee for a vote, no one dissented and a new law was enacted. This brings to light another important caveat for herpetoculturists: Many regulations are passed with little or no advance notice, giving the public little opportunity for rebuttal. There are also state or provincial laws and regulations that may sometimes prohibit animals not covered by more encompassing federal or international laws. As examples, Western Australia only recently relented to allow the licensed keeping of any reptiles by private individuals, and California prohibits the sale of any species native to the state even if it was captive bred or obtained out of state. (There are some extraordinary steps one may take for a rare exemption.)

Consequences

Finally, the emphasis given to arresting and prosecuting people with live animals is not warranted by either threat to society or to the animals. When I was reviewing CITES numbers for a report, I discovered that, for 1984, of 1,066,502 Nile monitors imported into the United States, only 988 were for the pet trade. That amounts to less than 1 live lizard per 1,000 skins imported for the leather trade. Similarly, in that same year, of 545,031 water monitors imported, only 1,797 were live animals, or just 30 for every 1,000 skins. This unreasonable disparity might be explained by the far greater financial influence wielded by the designers who produce fashionable leather

Most monitor lizards, including *Varanus mabitang*, are listed on CITES Appendix II; a few are on Appendix I.

is still strongly advised that anyone keeping live animals be sure that all required paperwork is at hand and that specimens were demonstrably obtained through legal channels.

Possibly because reptiles are easily cast as odd or dangerous creatures, news stories about reptile dealers and collectors are typically and easily overblown. Of six arrest and confiscation stories I have examined since 2001, all depict the reptiles as "icky," "dangerous," "potentially dangerous," or "illegal." Officials allegedly report that the animals would be worth fortunes–$50,000 is about the lowest claim and $250,000 the highest–on "the black market." While there is little doubt that a black market exists, the highest value for a shipment that I've calculated (based on prices for legally imported specimens) has been about $7,500. But all the newspaper readers and evening news watchers will ever hear is that customs officers seized illegally obtained dangerous reptiles with a street value of more than $50,000.

garments and accessories, or it may reflect the fact that one headline certainly trumps another. Consider these two samples, and decide which one makes a better newspaper headline:

"Wildlife Officials Nab Cobra and Monitor at Airport"

"Wildlife Officials Nab 1,500 Illegal Wallets."

While some herpetoculturists have become rabid in their attacks against the legal authorities (Hoser, 1993, 1996), others have taken a more moderate stance against restrictions on access to animals (Campbell and Frost, 1993). Problems among authorities and dealers and collectors have diminished considerably since 2000. However, it

This is one of many examples of why responsible herpetoculturists must observe the laws and keep their animals in ethical and safe conditions. Just one renegade hobbyist causes damage that ripples throughout the herpetological community, affecting other hobbyists, zoos, and museums.

Chlamydosaurus kingii

PART
2

THE LIZARDS

Herpetologists believed that the perentie was the largest living lizard when it was named, so it was given the scientific name *Varanus giganteus*.

The keeping of large reptiles in captivity is a considerably different proposition than keeping fishes in aquaria. Excepting the largest exhibits in some zoos, there is really no such thing as what aquarists call a "community tank," and lizards will need to be housed in small groups comprising single species. In the species accounts that follow, lizards are presented alphabetically by genus and then by trivial name.

Each species account in the chapters that follow will contain certain information elaborated in this section.

Scientific Name

Every species, living and extinct, is assigned a Latinized name according to set rules when it is first described. The name may or may not be descriptive, accurate, or even based on a real word. It is simply and solely a catalog identifier, a code name that assures anyone working with animals that they are all referring to the same species or group.

For animals, the procedures for naming are governed by the very formal International Code of Zoological Nomenclature (International Commission of Zoological Nomenclature, 1999).

EXAMPLES OF VALID SCIENTIFIC NAMES THAT ARE NOT DESCRIPTIVE, ACCURATE, OR BASED ON A REAL WORD

COMMON NAME	SCIENTIFIC NAME	COMMENTS
Spiny-tailed tree iguana	*Urocentron azureum*	The name "*azureum*," which means "blue," was incorrectly applied because the preserved specimen had turned from bright green to deep blue in preservatives.
Perentie	*Varanus giganteus*	When named it was the largest known lizard in the world, but several species have subsequently been discovered that are larger.
Spencer's monitor	*Varanus spenceri*	Named for a zoologist who may have had nothing to do with the species.
Blue-tongued skinks	Genus *Tiliqua*	The name means nothing and was coined by John Edward Gray probably because it sounded appropriate.
Solomon Island skinks	Genus *Corucia*	The name means nothing and was coined by John Edward Gray probably because it sounded appropriate.

113

GENUS NAME	LANGUAGE OF ORIGIN
Iguana	Caribb (Caribbean islands)
Varanus	Arabic (corrupted)
Scincus	Arabic
Corucia	meaningless, probably chosen simply because it sounded interesting
Tupinambis	from the extinct Amazonian tribe known as the Tupinambas
Shinisaurus	Cantonese (for a Professor Shin, a teacher at Sun Yat-Sen University in the 1920s)

An example of the classification scheme still widely used (known as the Linnean system) is provided here for the mangrove monitor:

Empire (often called Domain): Eukarya (living things made of cells that contain nuclei)
Kingdom: Animalia (multicellular organisms that must eat other living things and whose cells lack cell walls)
Phylum: Chordata (animals that have a hollow dorsal nerve tube and notochord)
Subphylum: Vertebrata (animals with a skeleton made of cartilage or bone)
Class: Reptilia (animals that reproduce with amniotic eggs, lack a larval stage, breathe with paired lungs, and have 12 pairs of cranial nerves)
Subclass: Diapsida (reptiles with two temporal openings)
Superorder: Lepidosauria (scaly diapsids with three-chambered hearts)
Order: Squamata (diapsids with paired copulatory organs and a transverse cloaca, lizards and their kin)
Suborder: Scleroglossa (squamates with scaly tongues)
Infraorder: Autarchoglossa (scleroglossans with elongated, bifid tongues)
Unnamed Clade: Anguimorpha (monitors, alligator lizards, and kin)
Superfamily: Varanoidea (monitors and their kin)
Family: Varanidae (monitor lizards)
Subfamily: Varaninae (true monitors only)
Genus: *Varanus* (monitor lizards)
Subgenus: *Euprepiosaurus* (mangrove and tree monitors)
Species: *Varanus indicus* (mangrove monitor)
Formal scientific name: *Varanus indicus* (Daudin, 1802)

Defining characteristics for each level can go much further than provided in this simplified listing. For example, the DNA structure and organization in the Eukarya are considerably different than in prokaryotes; animal cells possess structures not found in plants or fungi and vice versa; and so on.

In this classification, note that the name *indicus* is *not* the species name; in fact, the single name is known as the **trivial** name. It is only when

TYPES OF TYPES

Fundamental to describing a species is the **type specimen**. The type is the (usually) single specimen from which the original description is taken. A single designated type is the **holotype**; other specimens of the same species used in making a type description may be designated **paratypes** by the describer. Should a type be destroyed, a **neotype** may be designated. Similarly, the **type locality** is the geographic place from which the type was collected.

the genus and trivial names are used together that a species name exists. A species name's Latinized portion is always to be printed in italics or underlined. Correct representation of some other familiar scientific names are *Tyrannosaurus rex*, *Canis familiaris* (for your dog), and *Homo sapiens* (for you). Notice that I said that the names are Latinized–most genus names come from ancient Greek, and names may come from any language as long as they are converted into a Latin format. Some examples of Latinized lizard names that come from neither Greek nor Latin sources are given in an accompanying table.

A name and date also follow the Latinized part of an animal's scientific name. This is the name of the person or people who published the original description of the

species and the year in which the publication appeared. In the example given, François Daudin published the description of *Varanus indicus* in 1802. When you see a describer's name in parentheses, the parentheses indicate that the first author to describe the species assigned it to a different genus name, i.e., as *Tupinambis indicus* in 1802. If there are no parentheses, as in *Varanus acanthurus* Boulenger, 1885, then the originally published name was exactly as shown. *Varanus prasinus* (Schlegel, 1839) was originally described as *Monitor prasinus*. *Monitor* is no longer formally or properly used as a genus name, so many lizard species that were once called *Monitor* have been

Knowing the eventual size of the lizard you want to keep is essential to proper care. This baby savanna monitor will attain a length of more than 4 feet (1.2 m).

115

The captive suitability number gives the keeper an idea of how difficult keeping a given species is. The caiman lizard ranks a 2 due to its highly specialized diet and habitat.

reassigned to *Varanus*, and the original author's name must appear in parentheses.

Common Name

Common names vary considerably over time, space, and culture. Most giant lizards are creatures of the tropics, where many languages besides English are spoken. In this book, the generally used English names are given, but so are some local names for well-known creatures. In most cases, though, English common names have less stability than scientific names. Still using the earlier example, the lizard now called the mangrove monitor has also been known as the Pacific monitor, spotted monitor, and the Indian monitor at one time or another. Other species, those that range widely across different countries, may be known by many local names. The water monitor is also called biwak, biawak, kabaragoya, ora, bis-cobra, and other names (Bayless, 2004).

Etymology

Ever since I read William T. Innes's book about tropical fishes when I was a boy, I liked the idea of including translations of the Latinized names. From the comments I have received over the past decade about *Giant Lizards*, I have come to learn that I was not alone in my enjoyment of

The water monitor ranks a 3 on the captive suitability scale because, although it is hardy, it is one of the largest lizards available in the hobby.

etymology, the origins of words. Consequently, I expand that feature to retain etymology, and where appropriate, include the Greek terms using Greek letters. The Greek alphabet and pronunciation guide is provided after the glossary. Readers interested in the meanings of scientific names may also wish to consult Gotch (1986).

Range

Maps now complement the range information provided for many species and show the historic distribution of the lizard. The range indicates the area within which a species may be found. However, populations are not evenly distributed across the range. Any given species may be absent from a tall mountain even if it is in the middle of that range, or colonies might be prevalent amongst one ripe microhabitat but absent from an apparently similar habitat a few yards (meters) away.

The complete ranges for most species are incomplete. This is because many giant lizards have not been adequately collected or studied. As a consequence, some ranges will appear spotty, with discontinuous distributions. The maps may reflect reality but more likely show gaps in our knowledge.

Maximum Size

Few specimens from any species attain the maximum known size, and it is likely that larger specimens may have eluded human eyes somewhere in the wild. Still, it is good to know to what length a lizard may grow before planning to acquire it for captivity. Maximum size information

117

Green tree monitors are nervous and somewhat fragile lizards, earning them a rank of 2 for captive suitability.

is given in inches and millimeters for each species, and it represents snout-to-vent length (SVL) plus tail length (TL).

References

Here I list the most directly pertinent resources about each species so that the reader may pursue greater depth of knowledge about a subject or follow different courses of inquiry. Wherever possible, I include references to both highly technical and more general readership sources. In the first edition of *Giant Lizards*, I tried to restrict references to publications written in English, but given the number of important papers that have been published in other languages–notably German–these have been included in this second edition. I have also listed useful websites.

Captive Suitability

This is a numeric scale that indicates the suitability of each species for captivity. Factors that are considered include disposition, hardiness, and breeding potential. More specifically, each lizard species is rated on a scale of 1 to 5 as follows:

1: Extremely difficult to maintain, unsuitable for captivity except in exceptional circumstances, or critically endangered in the wild. These animals may refuse to feed, become highly susceptible to diseases, or show aggressiveness that could be injurious to the animals, handlers, or both.

2: Suitable only for veteran and successful keepers or zoos with facilities and resources needed to help assure success.

3: Moderately hardy and tend to feed after a brief settling-in period. May require a specialized diet but readily eat if that item is provided. Generally unlikely to breed given present husbandry knowledge.

4: Good animals for moderately experienced keepers; likely to breed and accept a variety of foods.

5: Beginner's-level species that are extremely easy to care for and not difficult to breed; species are not overly prone to illnesses.

For species listed on the Convention on International Trade in Endangered Species (CITES), the appendix listing will be provided. For details on CITES and other wildlife laws, see Chapter 5: Laws and Herpetoculture.

Natural History

Most of each account will briefly summarize what is known about the biology of the lizards in the wild. The intent is to provide some general information about how the lizards live in their environment and to provide the keeper with environmental data that may help improve husbandry.

Captive Care

Any special considerations needed to successfully maintain the species that are not covered in the general chapter about husbandry will be included in this section.

Lialis sp.

6

GEKKOTA

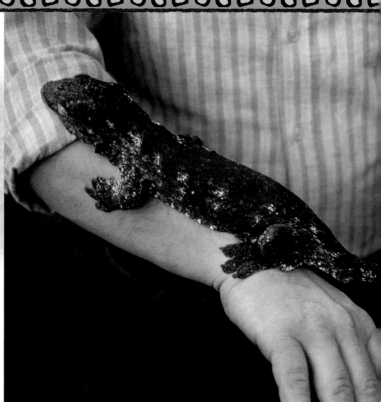

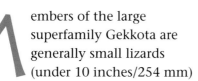
Although not large enough to be covered in this book, the giant gecko is the largest living gecko, reaching a length of 15 inches (381 mm) or more.

Members of the large superfamily Gekkota are generally small lizards (under 10 inches/254 mm) of the tropics and subtropics around the world. Included are the true geckos (Gekkonidae), Pacific geckos and flap-footed lizards (together the Diplodactylidae), and the leopard and banded geckos (Eublepharidae). Only members of the last group have moveable eyelids. The largest of living geckos are the giant gecko (*Rhacodactylus leachianus*) of New Caledonia, followed by the tokay gecko (*Gekko gecko*) and the giant cave gecko (*Cyrtodactylus louisiadensis*) of northern Australia.

Geckos have gained considerable attention through the use of gecko images to sell automobile insurance, sportswear, and fruit drinks. It seems that much of the world is coming to recognize that geckos are interesting and attractive creatures. Some, such as the Madagascan day geckos (genus *Phelsuma*) are true color gems.

Characteristics of the Gekkota include: body covered in soft, almost velvety scales; tongue broad, only slightly nicked at the tip; vocal sacs present; autotomy present; parietal bone without a pineal foramen; and jugal bone greatly reduced or absent.

Family Diplodactylidae

Members of the Diplodactylidae are distributed throughout the southwestern Pacific, from Australia and New Guinea east to New Zealand.

Lialis jicari is a poorly known lizard from New Guinea.

Lialis jicari Boulenger, 1903
New Guinea Legless Lizard

Etymology: The generic name *Lialis* is one of the meaningless terms coined by John Edward Gray; the term *jicari* probably refers to a locality in New Guinea, but its source cannot be determined. It is possible that it is one of Gray's made-up words.

Range: New Guinea.

Maximum Size: 30.7 inches (780 mm.)

References: De Rooij (1915); Murray, et al. (1991); Obst, et al. (1988).

Captive Suitability: 4

Natural History: Virtually unknown. The lizards may be found in a variety of grassland habitats from dry tall grasses to lush green areas in forest clearings (pers. obs.). The species lack moveable eyelids, having instead a clear convex spectacle that is often cleaned with the tongue. Ear openings are present. Scales are uncharacteristically (for geckos) large and stiff, similar to those in the gecko genus *Teratoscincus*.

Like the only related species, *Lialis burtonis*, there is considerable color variation in the legless lizard. The upper body may be straw colored or

Lialis jicari is sometimes available to hobbyists. It seems to need warm conditions and moderate humidity in captivity.

reddish brown, with or without longitudinal stripes. The belly is typically light in color with some darker stripes.

There is little data available for this species. Murray, et al. (1991) reported caudal luring by *Lialis burtonis*, the only other species in the genus. Caudal luring is wriggling the tip of the tail to draw the attention of prey into striking range; it may also be practiced by the very similar *Lialis jicari*.

Captive Care: Though legless lizards do not require legroom, these are active animals that do best in larger terrariums. Assume a terrarium 30 inches (76.2 cm) to each side is the minimum needed to house a single adult *Lialis*. Provide a natural substrate of potting soil and some live plants—birdseed will yield good grasses—and a thin layer of dry grass. A tall terrarium that will allow climbing by the lizards is best. Flat pieces of bark or larger logs that will allow concealment sites are also needed. The lizards seem to swim among the tall stems of grass in search of basking sites and insects and small lizards that make up their prey. Captives do well on a mixed diet of crickets, wax

worms, small worms, newborn mice, and small lizards. *Lialis* is unusual in that the lower jaw is loosely hinged, allowing the lizards to swallow prey somewhat larger than the width of the head. This is an example of parallel evolution—the same basic solution to consuming large prey seen in snakes (though to a lesser degree) that evolved quite separately in the two lineages.

Keep *Lialis* warm. Daytime temperatures should stay in the 86 to 98° F (30 to 36.7° C) range, and drop to 68° to 72° F (20 to 22.2°C) at night. Feed and lightly spray daily, but reduce feeding to three times weekly during simulated dry periods, when spraying should be eliminated. Always provide a small shallow dish of clean drinking water.

Reproduction in captivity is rare, but probably only because not many keepers are working with this lizard. One or two hard-shelled eggs are laid in logs or under loose bark on the ground, and hatch in 60 to 70 days. Young should be kept separately and fed small mealworms, bloodworms, and two-week old crickets.

NEW GUINEA

Approximate natural range of *Lialis jicari* (yellow).

Iguana iguana, albino

7

IGUANIA

The northern angle-headed dragon is rarely imported for the herp hobby; little information about its care is available.

Lizards in this group–often termed a superfamily or infraorder–share many features in common and are among the first lizard lineages to show up in the fossil record. Iguanians are all equipped with well-developed limbs and digits; there are no limbless or two-legged iguanian species, and only a single Asian agamid genus (*Sitana*) has fewer than five digits.

Family Agamidae Gray, 1827

Agamids are Old World lizards, distributed throughout Africa, Asia, Australia, and southern Europe but curiously absent from Madagascar. They are typical scaly lizards, all of which have well-developed limbs and five digits on each limb (excepting the genus *Sitana*, small lizards from southern India and Sri Lanka, which possesses only four toes on each foot), as well as tails that lack autotomy. All species are diurnal or largely

EXAMPLES OF CONVERGENCE BETWEEN THE OLD WORLD AGAMIDS AND THE IGUANIDS.

AGAMID	IGUANID
Moloch, *Moloch horridus* Australia	Horned lizards, genus *Phrynosoma* North and Central America
Asian water dragon, *Physignathus cocincinus* SE Asia	Green iguana, *Iguana iguana* Central America
Indonesian sailfin lizard, *Hydrosaurus amboinensis* Indonesia	Green basilisk, *Basiliscus plumifrons* Central and South America
Asiatic bloodsuckers/garden lizards, genus *Calotes*	Anoles, genus *Anolis* Tropical and subtropical Americas
Flying dragons, genus *Draco* SE Asia	Anoles, genus *Anolis* Tropical and subtropical Americas
Painted dragons, *Ctenophorus pictus* Australia	Collared lizards, *Crotaphytus bicinctores* North America
Netted dragons, *Ctenophorus reticulatus* Australia	Leopard lizards, *Gambelia wislezenii* North America
Mastigures, genus *Uromastyx* N. Africa and SW Asia	Spiny-tailed iguanas, genus *Ctenosaura* Central America
Mastigures, genus *Uromastyx* North Africa and SW Asia	Malagasy ring-tailed lizards, genus *Oplurus* Madagascar
Butterfly agamas, *Leiolepis belliana* Southern Asia	Desert iguanas, *Dipsosaurus dorsalis* North America
Chameleon dragon, *Chelosania brunnei* Australia	Chameleon iguana, *Chamaeleolis* Central and South America

diurnal. Agamids may also sport armor such as cephalic, vertebral, and caudal spines, and tail armature may range from simple to complex (as in *Uromastyx*) to bizarre (*Xenagama*). Agamas and chameleons are the only living lizards with acrodont teeth; among living reptiles, this condition is also in the tuatara species (order Rhynchocephalia, restricted to New Zealand) and is considered an ancestral trait. Acrodont teeth are not replaced if lost. A particular feature in the Agamidae is that the members possess two pairs (one upper, one lower) of enlarged, fang-like anterior teeth. These teeth are particularly conspicuous when the lizard gapes during a threat display.

Like the chameleons, agamids are usually excellent color-change artists, and the males of many species may assume a variety of bright breeding hues to rival numerous tropical birds.

Large agamids include several mainstays of both the zoo and private herpetocultural sectors and include water dragons (genus *Physignathus*), sailfin lizards (*Hydrosaurus*), and frilled lizards (*Chlamydosaurus*). The majority of species are insectivorous, but many are omnivorous; mastigures and some relatives are primarily herbivores. The word "agama" comes from Arabic and means "small lizard."

The giants of this family include some of the largest living lizards outside of the monitors. Sailfin dragons (*Hydrosaurus*) may exceed 4 feet (1.2 m) in total length, and with their large dorsal fins, they make awesome display animals.

Hypsilurus godeffroyi (Peters, 1867)
Northern Angle-Headed Dragon

Etymology: 'υπσι, *hypsi*, high or tall, and υρι, *uri*, tail, in reference to the tall, compressed tail. Named for J.C. Godeffroy (1813–1885), who founded the Godeffroy Museum in Hamburg, Germany.

Range: Broadly distributed from the Philippines east to the Solomon Islands; there are doubtful records from Queensland, Australia, and the Palau Islands.

Maximum Size: 43.3 inches (1,100 mm)

References: DeRooij (1915); Henkel and Schmidt (1997); Manthey and Schuster (1996).

Captive Suitability: 3

Natural History: There have been no studies of this species in nature. Related species have habits similar to those of chameleons. They are slow-moving, sit-and-wait predators that allow prey to move into proximity before lunging. Angle-headed dragons do not have long sticky tongues, thereby relying on allowing prey to approach very closely. When perching on a branch or vine, the immobile lizards are extremely difficult to spot, regardless of their considerable size. They are especially active–if that word can be used with this species–in the late afternoon and at twilight. If threatened, however, the dragons are capable of swiftly running away. They may threaten a perceived aggressor with an open mouth and hissing but are generally disinclined to bite.

Captive Care: Very little information is available for this species. Angle-headed dragons are almost exclusively arboreal, and they are slow-moving diurnal animals that feed on large insects, geckos, and small mammals. During the day, they assume

Frilled lizard in full display. This individual was photographed in Australia's Kakadu National Park.

Frilled lizard in a relaxed pose with the frill folded down.

postures such that their contours resemble the local foliage. When disturbed, they can run quickly and will bite if the opportunity presents itself. Although capable of defense, they are relatively reclusive animals that do best if housed with their own kind and with only one adult male per enclosure.

Give these lizards a tall terrarium with plenty of thin climbing branches and thicker branches for perching. There must be places where they can hide from view. Keep humidity high (70 percent or more) and provide plenty of airflow. They will do well in screened enclosures, such as those used for chameleons, as long as the mesh is strong and there is considerable room inside; otherwise, the lizards may rub their snouts against the screen and injure themselves. Provide a dish for water, and spray the terrarium to maintain the humidity. All members of this genus are oviparous.

Juvenile frilled lizards. The male (left) has a larger frill than the female (right), even at this age.

Chlamydosaurus kingii Gray, 1825
Frilled Lizard

Etymology: ξλαιδως, *chlamydos*, a frill or ruffle, and σαυρως, *sauros*, lizard. Named for lietuenant Philip Parker King, Royal Navy (1791–1856), who commanded amajor Australian charting and exploration program from 1817 to 1820.

Range: Northern coastal Australia from Western Australia to the coast along the Great Barrier Reef, and southern New Guinea

Maximum Size: 35.8 inches (910 mm)

References: Card (1995); DeRooij (1915); Henkel and Schmidt (1997); Manthey and Schuster (1996); Weis (1996)

Captive Suitability: 4

Natural History: It isn't difficult to correctly identify a frilled lizard. As herpetologist William Duellman once wrote when providing the diagnosis for a particularly conspicuous frog, "Any damn fool should be able to identify this species" (Duellman, 1978, p.65). The characteristic neck frill, usually held compressed along the lizard's flanks, may expand to a width of 10 to 14 inches (250 to 350 mm) when in display.

Despite their iconic status and unique visage, there have been very few field studies of this remarkable lizard. Frilled lizards are inhabitants of scrub forest areas, where they spend most of their time on or inside trees. Habitats may range from the predominantly dry scrub of inland Australia to the typically wet southern forests of New Guinea. Most specimens in collections outside of Australia were collected in the Indonesian portion of the island of New Guinea, where humidity

and incidental moisture levels are high. During the dry season, frilled lizards may retire to the insides of large hollow trees or mammal burrows in the ground, where humidity is high and the lizards can escape excessive heat. They resume activity with the coming of seasonal rains and the emergence of their prey, which includes insects, spiders, smaller lizards, fledgling birds, small snakes, and the occasional bird's egg.

Although resident to the tropical north of Australia, frilled lizards spend one to two months in dormancy during the southern winter. Daytime temperatures may drop to 68°F (20°C), and it may be only 63°F (17.2°C) at night. Once daytime temperatures exceed 72°F (22.2°C), the lizards emerge and begin feeding. Within days they are mating, and females will lay up to three clutches of 8 to 14 eggs at monthly intervals throughout the summer (December through April). Incubation spans 80 to 95 days, and young frilled lizards have tiny but functional frills.

Color variation appears to be geographically linked. Specimens from New Guinea are generally gray with whitish reticulations dorsally and ventrally. Australian animals from seasonally moist habitats are similar to New Guinea lizards, but those from drier forests tend to be darker, ranging from chocolate brown to black, and are marked with light reticulations. The frill of Australian animals may be marked with orange, red, and yellow spots.

Captive Care: Frilled lizards are relatively hardy animals that acclimate well to captivity and are fairly easy to breed. Essentials to the well-being of captive frilled lizards include a large and tall terrarium that allows climbing, a varied diet of insects and small rodents, small turkey sausage cubes or canned dog food, and adequate humidity. They need a large terrarium with horizontal room for running, as well as vertical objects to climb. Males should be housed alone or with females.

The frills of these lizards are delicate and often show tears and other damage. They are also excellent places for mites and other ectoparasites to take up residence, so inspect the frills regularly. Also, thoroughly inspect newly acquired frilled lizards for parasites in the mouth.

Keep frilled lizards warm (80 to 98°F [26.7 to 36.7°C]) and in moderate to low humidity (40 to 80 percent). Provide a deep substrate for females to dig their nests, and remove eggs for incubation once laid. Incubate at 83 to 85°F (28.3 to 29.4°C). This temperature range will produce a mix of males and females. Young may be safely reared together as long as sufficient live foods are offered for all. Separate them when they approach 11 inches (280 mm) total length.

The sailfin lizard (*H. amboinensis*) is the largest of the agamids and requires a very large enclosure.

Genus *Hydrosaurus* Kaup, 1827

The lizards in this genus are larger equivalents of the American basilisks, similarly sporting neck, vertebral, and caudal crests. The characteristic crest is much more developed in adult males than in females or subadults, where there may be nothing more elaborate than a series of low separated spines. Sexual dimorphism becomes apparent when lizards are 6 to 10 months of age. The digits differ from those of basilisks in that they are lobed, so each digit expands into a broad flat unit that helps act as a paddle when the lizard is submerged. The combination of their large adult size and need for considerable space for swimming and climbing make them unsuited for all but the most serious private herpetoculturist. As zoo animals, they are quite hardy. All reproduce by laying eggs.

Hydrosaurus amboinensis (Schlosser, 1788) Sailfin Lizard/Soa-Soa

Etymology: ʽυδρω, *hydro*, water, and σαυρως, *sauros*, lizard. Named for the eastern Indonesian island of Ambon, where it was first collected.
Range: Central and eastern Indonesia, including Java, Flores, Sulawesi, Ambon, and far western West Irian Jaya (New Guinea).
Maximum Size: 51.2 inches (1,300 mm)
References: Barbour (1911); DeRooij (1915); De Vosjoli (1992); Henkel and Schmidt (1997); Manthey and Schuster (1996).
Captive Suitability: 3
Natural History: This is the world's largest living agamid. There is little natural history information available. The lizards are hunted for their flesh, leather, and (in far smaller numbers) the live animal trade.

These bright marbled green and black lizards spend their time in or near water, especially along rivers and in mangroves. They bask and raise their body temperature while on stout tree limbs or logs, and they forage for food along branches and while along riverbanks. They feed on small crabs, snails, fish, large insects and spiders, fresh flowers, soft leaves, and some fruits. Soa-soas are excellent swimmers and may dive for extended periods. There are unconfirmed reports that smaller specimens can run on top of water for short distances. It is not known if they forage while submerged.

This widespread species in the East Indies can tolerate living in salty, brackish, and fresh water. Males are territorial and may engage in elaborate agonistic displays and combat against other males.

ONE SPECIES OR TWO? WHAT'S SO HARD TO DECIDE?

The two sailfins described here as *Hydrosaurus pustulosus* and *H. weberi* are very similar in appearance, but they are separated by a huge geographic distance. These lizards share nearly identical habits, habitats, adult size, and behavior. Although there have been many field observations of these large animals, there has yet to be published a taxonomic review that will settle the question of whether one species with disjunct populations or two species are involved. If they are eventually merged, the prevailing name would be *Hydrosaurus pustulosus* which has priority over *H. weberi* by 82 years. If all three taxa were to become a single species, they would become the familiar *Hydrosaurus amboinensis*.

Captive Care: These are active lizards that require extremely large terrariums. Even a single adult should be housed in a terrarium at least 6 feet (1.8 m) on each side and almost as tall. Much of their time will be spent basking on horizontal branches under heat lamps, and they will drop into the water if alarmed. They swim extremely well and may remain submerged in excess of 20 minutes.

Like most iguanians, adult sailfin lizards are territorial. Males may tolerate the presence of immature and adult female lizards but will challenge and fight other adult males. Unless extremely large facilities are available, keep sailfin lizards in small groups of one sexual pair and no more than two or three subadults. Keep lizards at 75 to 90 percent humidity with a temperature range of 80 to 90°F (26.7 to 32.2°C) during the day and 72 to 82°F (22.2 to 27.8°C) at night.

Sailfin lizards are omnivores that feed largely on leaves and flowers. Captives require a varied diet of vegetables such as collard greens, dandelion greens, chopped broccoli, fruits, and insects, supplemented with young rodents, fish, shrimps, and crabs.

Females may lay eggs any time of year. There are 5 to 12 eggs in a clutch, and a healthy female may produce as many as four clutches each year. Eggs should be incubated at 82 to 85°F (27.8 to 29.4°C) at 75 to 80 percent relative humidity. Neonates may measure 11 inches (279 mm) and require no food the first week after hatching. Once young begin to swim (at about two to three weeks), they will require finely chopped green, leafy vegetables and fruits and liberal quantities of gut-loaded young crickets. They reach sexual maturity at about two years and reach full size at about four years.

This species becomes tractable in captivity if carefully and regularly handled, but the combination of sharp claws and large size make care in handling essential.

Female *H. weberi* feeding on a nutritious salad. All *Hydrosaurus* are omnivores that feed mostly on vegetation.

Hatching *Hydrosaurus* egg. Sailfin eggs take 60 to 100 days to hatch depending on the temperature. (Langerwerf, 2006).

Hydrosaurus weberi Barbour, 1911
Weber's Sailfin Lizard

Etymology: ἔυδρω, *hydro*, water, and σαυρως, *sauros*, lizard. Named for Dutch zoologist Prof. Max Wilhelm Carl Weber (1852–1937), one of the major contributors to studies of the Indonesian fauna.

Range: The Moluccan Islands of eastern Indonesia, including Halmahera and Ternate.

Maximum Size: 35.4 inches (900 mm)

References: Barbour (1911); De Vosjoli (1992); Manthey and Schuster (1996).

Captive Suitability: 3

Natural History: Few published field observations exist, but the general ecology is similar to that of *Hydrosaurus amboinensis*.

Captive Care: Same as for *Hydrosaurus amboinensis*.

Hydrosaurus pustulosus (Eschscholtz, 1829)
Philippine Sailfin Lizard

Etymology: ἔυδρω, *hydro*, water, and σαυρως, *sauros*, lizard; and *pustula*, Latin for "blister."

Range: The Philippine Islands.

Maximum Size: 43.8 inches (1,112 mm)

References: De Vosjoli (1992); Manthey and Schuster (1996); Mertens (1934).

Captive Suitability: 3

Natural History: Few published field observations exist, but general ecology is similar to that of *Hydrosaurus amboinensis*. There has been some question among herpetologists about whether *H. pustulosus* and *H. weberi* are conspecific. If so, both populations would fall under the older name, *H. pustulosus*.

Captive Care: Same as for *Hydrosaurus amboinensis*. Based on U.S. CITES records, this is probably the most commonly imported species of sailfin lizard.

H. pustulosus exhibiting the bright blue colors of a mature male

Genus *Physignathus* Cuvier, 1829

This is a small genus of Austral-Asiatic semiaquatic lizards with a spiny vertebral crest. They are restricted to riparian habitats near fresh water, where they prey upon smaller vertebrates and large invertebrates.

Physignathus cocincinus Cuvier, 1829
Water Dragon/ Chinese Water Dragon/ Green Water Dragon

Etymology: φυς, *phys*, a bladder (such as an animal hide wine/water pouch), and γνθως, *gnathos*, teeth; *cocincinus* is the Latinized version of "Cochin China," an old name for Southeastern Asia, particularly Vietnam.

Range: Widely spread through Southeast Asia, from Burma (Myanmar) and extreme southern China east through Vietnam, Malaysia, Indonesia, and far western New Guinea.

Maximum Size: 40.7 inches (1,035 mm)

References: De Vosjoli (1992); Henkel and Schmidt (1997); Manthey and Schuster (1996); Spears (2004); Sprackland (1995b).

Captive Suitability: 4

Natural History: Not well studied; this is one of the many species better known from observations in captivity than in the wild. The adults are sexually dimorphic, with males having a short series of

Green water dragons are both semi-arboreal and semi-aquatic, spending much of their time in branches overhanging rivers.

138

pronounced femoral pores, massive cheeks, and pinkish lips during the mating season.

Captive Care: This species literally burst upon the pet trade in the late 1970s and has gone on to become one of the leading lizard species purchased as a pet (along with leopard geckos, bearded dragons, and green iguanas). Although similar in appearance to the green iguana, water dragons are easier to maintain, in part because of their broader dietary needs and smaller adult size. Water dragons are hardy, long-lived lizards that do well in a large terrarium that includes high climbing space and a pool of clean water. The lizards will generally be found basking under a heat lamp while perched on a horizontal log. Their activity is limited to brief periods of foraging and swimming. Water dragons can become quite docile with regular handling, but large specimens–particularly males–may inflict painful bites.

Give these animals a spacious terrarium with dimensions of at least 80 x 40 x 60 inches (203 x 102 x 152 cm). Do not house small animals with adults, and keep no more than one adult male per enclosure.

Their diet is broad, and healthy lizards require that variety. Provide them with some combination of the following: chopped vegetables, fresh fruits, chopped turkey sausage, fresh fish, prawns, gut-loaded large insects, and freshly thawed or live small rodents.

Preferred temperature range is 78 to 90°F (25.6 to 32.2°C) by day and 65 to 78°F (18.3 to 25.6°C) at night. Keep the humidity above 80 percent, and always have a large dish or pool of clean fresh water.

Female brown water dragon feeding on a roach.

Physignathus lesueurii (Gray, 1831)
Eastern Water Dragon

Etymology: φυς, *phys*, a bladder (such as an animal hide wine/water pouch), and γνθως, *gnathos*, teeth. Named for 19th-century French naturalist Charles Alexandre Lesueur (1778–1846), curator at the Academy of Natural Sciences in Philadelphia and later curator at the Museum at Le Havre, France.

Range: Much of eastern coastal Australia, from the central Cape York Peninsula near Coen south into Victoria.

Maximum Size: 26 inches (650 mm)

References: Cogger (2000); DeRooij (1915); De Vosjoli (1992); Henkel and Schmidt (1997); Langerwerf (1998); Manthey and Schuster (1996); Melbourne Aquarium (2003); Mertens (1934); Weigel (1988); Wilson and Knowles (1988); Wilson and Swan (2003).

KEEPING AND BREEDING *PHYSIGNATHUS LESUEURII*

By Bert Langerwerf

Australian water dragons are good candidates for breeding, especially for breeding in large outdoor terraria. The dragons can handle cold and still remain active. During frequent frosty nights, they will just hide in burrows. Additionally, the animals are not skittish and are much calmer than the comparable basilisks.

In Australia, their range is limited by three important factors:

- Winters must be cool enough to induce hibernation (lacking in the moist tropical north).
- There must be enough moisture and standing water–streams, lakes, billabongs, etc.
- Summers must be long enough to allow completion of the entire reproduction cycle.

The breeding season starts after winter hibernation. In Australia, this is September through October. In central Alabama, where I maintain my water dragons outdoors, I find the first clutches of eggs in mid-April. For 166 nests, the lowest number of eggs in a clutch was 3 eggs (three nests) and the highest 14 (one nest). The average clutch contained 7.36 eggs, and 7 (30 times) and 8 (29 times) were the most frequently found numbers per clutch. A female will lay two or three clutches per season.

At temperatures fluctuating slightly around 80°F (26.7°C), the incubation period is 68 to 74 days. Over 12 years of captive breedings, I found that the earliest baby hatched on June 17th and the latest

Male brown water dragons develop dark red coloration on the forequarters when in breeding condition.

140

on October 6th. The accumulated numbers hatched per month are: June, 147; July, 6,275; August, 9,201; September, 1,845; October, 1. With a TL of 6.1 to 6.4 inches (155 to 162 mm), the babies are quite large at hatching.

This species is subject to temperature-dependant sex determination (TDSD). When incubated at around 80°F (26.7°C), only males are produced. Females occur at both higher and lower temperatures.

Raising young Australian water dragons is easier then raising most other lizard species, including Chinese water dragons. Food includes crickets, superworms, flies, and earthworms. Neonates are given termites and fruit flies for the first few days. Adults eat larger insects, like roaches and superworms, but also earthworms, pinky mice and rats, and fish. They also accept canned cat food and baby food as supplements. They will be sexually mature in their second year.

Give water dragons a large vertically oriented terrarium. These lizards tend to defecate in water, so make sure that the water bowl is easy to clean. Keep temperatures in the 70s and low 80s°F (22 to 28°C), with mid-90s°F (34 to 36°C) under a basking light. UVB or direct sunlight is a must.

The animals are very strong and not prone to parasites. Improper husbandry causes most diseases in water dragons.

Brown water dragon nest.

141

Captive Suitability: 4

Natural History: Two subspecies have been named. The northern, *Physignathus l. lesueurii* (Gray, 1831), occurs from the southeastern edge of the Cape York Peninsula to central New South Wales. *P. l. howittii* ranges from central New South Wales into Victoria. The northern subspecies attains brighter and more distinct coloration.

Australia's water dragons are found primarily in forested areas near running water or nonstagnant lakes and billabongs. They are as likely to be basking on branches and boards over water as on riverbank clearings, and although they may allow close approach, they can run quite rapidly when alarmed. At full clip, water dragons can run bipedally, but they cannot run on water, as can basilisks. Their natural diet includes a wide variety of other animals, ranging from crayfish and large worms to frogs, small snakes, lizards, and bird eggs. They also eat a variety of soft plants, flowers, and fruit but are less herbivorous than the Asian water dragon.

Males are conspicuously marked with bright coral-pink to orange undersides, and during the breeding season, the color becomes more intense and spreads to the femoral region, cloaca, and sides of the face. The heads of males are larger and much broader behind the eyes than in females. While generally innocuous, an adult water dragon can deliver a nasty bite, driven by very strong jaw muscles.

Captive Care: Similar to that for the water dragon. See sidebar "Keeping and Breeding *Physignathus lesueurii*."

Family Iguanidae Gray, 1827

Iguanians have been subjected to more high-level taxonomic shuffling than any other lizard group. For the purposes of this book, though, the modifications are irrelevant: All the giants in the group remain in the Iguanidae. The name "iguana" comes from the Caribbean word iwana, of Spanish-Arawak origin, and refers to a large lizard. Today, that name or some variation thereof (such as "goanna" and "leguaan") is used for any large lizard, iguanid or not.

Iguanids differ from chameleons and agamids in that they have tooth placement along the inner (lingual) edge of the jawbones. This condition, the norm amongst the majority of lizard taxa, is termed pleurodont. In contrast to acrodont teeth, where a lost tooth is not replaced, pleurodont teeth are continually replaced as they are lost, excepting only in very old individuals. Also separating many iguanids from their close kin is the ability to autotomize the tail; a replacement will regrow if the original is lost. Members of this group are often adorned with vertebral crests of enlarged scales or sails.

Teeth in the subfamily Iguaninae (or the family Iguanidae, depending on the author) are the maple leaf-shaped structures mentioned earlier in Chapter 1. The triple cusps facilitate the breakup of tough plant matter, an essential part of predigestion of such difficult-to-digest foods. Lizards cannot chew–the jawbones do not accommodate sufficient side-to-side motion–so iguanids break down plant matter by manipulating it with the tongue to be cut by the teeth several times before swallowing. It is

MAXIMUM KNOWN SIZES (TOTAL LENGTHS) FOR THE LARGEST OF THE GIANT IGUANAS.

Green iguana *Iguana iguana*	6 ft (1,829 mm)
Anegada iguana, *Cyclura pinguis*	5 ft, (1,524 mm)
Antillean iguana, *Iguana delicatissima*	5 ft, (1,524 mm)
Blue rock iguana, *Cyclura lewisi*	4.9 ft, (1,520 mm)
Cayman Islands iguana, *Cyclura nubila*	4.9 ft, (1,520 mm)
Marine iguana, *Amblyrhynchus cristatus*	4.9 ft, (1,520 mm)
Mexican spiny-tailed iguana, *Ctenosaura acanthura*	4.5 ft, (1,400 mm)
Black iguana, *Ctenosaura pectinata*	4.5 ft, (1,400 mm)
Ctenosaura similis	3.9 ft, (1,200 mm)
Bahaman iguana, *Cyclura cychlura*	3.7 ft, (1,143 mm)
Rhinoceros iguana, *Cyclura cornuta*	3.6 ft, (1,100 mm)
Santa Fe land iguana , *Conolophus pallidus*	3.4 ft, (1,050 mm)
Galapagos land iguana, *Conolophus subcristatus*	3.4 ft, (1,050 mm)
Ricord's iguana, *Cyclura ricordii*	3.2 ft (1,000 mm)

precisely because the iguanid tooth structure is so unusual that Gideon Mantell quickly named his 19th-century fossil discovery of the first dinosaur tooth *Iguanodon*, meaning "iguana tooth."

The Iguanidae, in the broad sense, is an enormous assemblage of lizards, comprising some 70 genera and more than 680 species. The vast majority lay eggs in two or more clutches per year in captivity. As befits their incredible numbers, iguanids occupy the majority of habitats within their range, from mountains to deserts, from tropical and temperate forests to island and coastal beaches. Of particular interest to zoogeographers is the odd pattern of iguanid distribution. They are found widely throughout the Americas, from central Canada south to Argentina, and extend to the islands of Bermuda, the Caribbean, and the Galápagos Islands in the Pacific Ocean. Beyond that, though, they are also found in the more remote Pacific Fiji Islands (three living species) and off eastern Africa on Madagascar.

Among the large iguanas, only the basilisks are primarily insectivorous, while the remainder are primary herbivores. Most species are given to considerable latitude in color change. The changes may be related to age, sex, temperature, or mood.

Genus *Amblyrhynchus*

The only truly marine lizards on earth, marine iguanas bask on rocks in the scorching sun and then dive to forage for algae in the cold ocean. The head is blunt, with enlarged conical scales on the top and a feeble crest along the spine. Genetic analyses have shown that *Amblyrhynchus* and *Conolophus* diverged from their common ancestor some 8 million years ago (Kunstaetter, 2003), and recent discoveries that the two taxa hybridize put the recognition of two separate genera into question. In the event of amalgamation, the name "*Amblyrhynchus*" would have seniority. The genus name is from Greek, αμβλυ, *ambly*, blunt, and ρ'υνχω, *rhynco*, snout.

Amblyrhynchus cristatus Bell, 1825
Marine Iguana

Etymology: (Latin) *cristatus*, having a crest.
Range: The Galápagos Islands, Ecuador.
Maximum Size: 59 inches (1,500 mm)
References: Alberts et al. (2004); Blair (2004); Carpenter (1966); De Roy (1995); Eibl-Eibesfeldt (1962); Mertens (1934); Rassmann et al. (1997, 2004); Wikelski, M., and F. Trillmich (1997).
Captive Suitability: 1; listed on CITES Appendix I
Natural History: These are the stout-bodied "imps of darkness" described by a young Charles Darwin. They have long been the focus of study by many researchers, such that we know a considerable bit about their natural history.

Marine iguanas are the world's only living ocean-dwelling lizards. Unlike the few other species that routinely swim in the ocean and hunt along its beaches, marine iguanas obtain

Marine iguana emerging from the ocean on Santiago Island. This is the only species of lizard that forages in the sea.

the entirety of their diet from the sea floor. After basking in the tropical sunlight to raise their blood temperature, the lizards plunge into the sea. A variety of stunning physiological processes then take place; the heartbeat slows and blood is shunted away from the extremities into the brain and body. This reduces the amount of oxygen needed by the lizard, letting it safely prolong its time submerged.

Swimming is accomplished by lateral undulations of the entire body as the limbs lie along its sides. While browsing, the lizard may employ the claws to anchor it and then walk across the algae-covered substrate while it feeds. During feeding, marine iguanas are also most likely to be attacked by their primary predators, local sea lions and sharks. When finished, the iguana must return to shore and resume basking,

both to bring the body to a temperature at which digestion may take place and to recover from the immersion in dangerously cold (45°F [7.2°C]) ocean water.

In the 1830s, when humans were first interacting with iguanas, the lizards showed very little fear or concern with our large ancestors. Today, though, iguanas are considerably more wary, even though they are granted total protection throughout the Galápagos. The greatest threat to their survival on some islands is the presence of feral cats, which feed on eggs and young iguanas.

One result of the many studies on iguanas is that we have learned that each island has lizards with noticeably distinct coloration. Consequently, seven subspecies have been named. (I would opt for elevating these to species status.) Most of

Marine iguana nesting site on Española (Hood) Island.

the subspecific epithets are Latinized versions of island names. The subspecies recognized are:

1. *Amblyrhynchus cristatus cristatus* Bell, 1825: Scales on snout huge (many larger than eye) and form acute pyramids, those over the frontal region much larger than the anterior scales; Fernandina (Narborough Isl.). TL to 37.4 inches (951 mm).

2. *Amblyrhynchus cristatus albemarlensis* Eibl-Eibesfeldt, 1962: Scales on snout huge (some as large as eye), but those over frontal region only slightly larger than anterior scales; Isabella (Albemarle Isl.). TL to 49 inches (1,245 mm).

3. *Amblyrhynchus cristatus hassi* Eibl-Eibesfeldt, 1962: Scales on head huge (some much larger than eye) but only a few on frontal region may be acute; Santa Cruz (Indefatigable Isl.). TL to 59 inches (1,500 mm). Named for Israeli herpetologist George Haas (1905-1981).

4. *Amblyrhynchus cristatus mertensi* Eibl-Eibesfeldt, 1962: Snout scales large (some as large as eye), broad, and predominantly convex; San Cristobal (Chatham Isl.). TL to 27.8 inches (705 mm). Named for noted German herpetologist Robert Mertens. (See account of *Varanus mertensi.*)

5. *Amblyrhynchus cristatus nanus* Eibl-Eibesfeldt, 1962: Scales on snout about equal in size and none as large as eye, from anterior of snout to parietal region, all convex; Genovese (Tower Isl.). TL 24.8 inches (630 mm). Nanus is Latin for "small."

6. *Amblyrhynchus cristatus sielmanni* Eibl-Eibesfeldt, 1962: Snout scales large, some much larger than orbit, none acute or pyramidal; Pinta (Abingdon Isl.). TL to 26.6 inches (675 mm).

7. *Amblyrhynchus cristatus venustissimus* Eibl-Eibesfeldt, 1956: Snout scales subequal and none as large as eye, with anterior scales of snout larger than those on the parietal region, all convex; flanks characteristically coral red; Española (Hood Isl.). TL to 28.7 inches (730 mm). *Venustissimus* is a Latin superlative meaning "most attractive."

Captive Care: N/A. This is a highly specialized creature that lives in an unusual habitat, feeds only on certain sea algae, and has a very restricted distribution. For these reasons, marine iguanas have not been maintained in captivity.

MAMMALS CAN DO IT, TOO!

The automatic shunting of blood, slowing of the heartbeat, and other physiological changes that occur when marine iguanas dive in deep water are common among mammals. Physiologists call this response to immersion the mammalian dive response, and it even occurs in humans. As soon as we immerse even our feet into water, our bodies respond by rerouting blood flow and slowing the heart rate. As we go deeper into the water, more shunting occurs, especially in the limbs, and the chemical processes of many of our cells slow down. The net effect of this dive response is to keep our most essential organs warm and supplied with blood and to reduce our need for oxygen.

Genus *Basiliscus*

Basilisks are large lizards capable of an amazing feat that has secured them a place of recognition with an otherwise reptile-ignorant public: They have the ability to run bipedally across the surface of water. This ability has earned them the name Jesus Christ lizards among many local peoples. Basilisks are carnivorous iguana-like lizards that have "normal" conical teeth and very long toes with scaly phalanges that produce a snowshoe effect on water, distributing the body weight over a wide area when the lizard runs at top speed. Males possess head, vertebral, and caudal crests, making them the most adorned New World lizards.

Although male basilisks possess the largest vertebral crests of any living reptile relative to size and the crest bears remarkable similarities to those seen in extinct predinosaurian reptiles such as *Dimetrodon* and *Edaphosaurus*, there has been no study to ascertain any function of the crest in the living animals. Paleontologists have long surmised about the function of the huge crests in the predinosaurs, but no consensus hypothesis has emerged. In basilisks, it is most apparently a function of sex recognition and display, but if there are other functions, they remain unknown.

Basiliscus plumifrons Cope, 1876
Green Basilisk

Etymology: (Latin) *plum*, a feather, and *frons*, the forehead.

Range: Limited to heavily forested riparian habitats in central Nicaragua, Costa Rica, and extreme western Panama, typically at altitudes below 1,650 feet (500 m).

The crest on the back of male green basilisks (left) is one of the largest of all the lizards. Female green basilisks (right) are not nearly as adorned.

Maximum Size: 35.8 inches (910 mm)
References: Köhler (1993b); Lang (1989); Leenders (2001); Savage (2002).
Captive Suitability: 3
Natural History: This is one of the truly magnificent lizards of the New World and is the iconic image for its genus. It is the largest species of basilisk, but it also has the smallest natural range of its genus. Green basilisks show considerable sexual dimorphism, such that males have large–often double–head crests and a large vertebral crest that continues on to the tail. Females and young may have a small single head crest but lack the other adornments.

These residents of hot, humid rainforests dwell alongside streams that may be fed by water that is quite cold. The lizards spend most of their time on land or in trees, retreating to the water primarily to escape predation. They feed largely on smaller terrestrial animals, including small rodents, roaches, and frogs.

Captive Care: Care of basilisks is very similar to that described for sailfin agamas (*Hydrosaurus*) and water dragons (*Physignathus*). Basilisks are active animals that require large terrariums. Provide a space at least four times the length of the lizard and a width twice the length of the lizard. Because basilisks climb well, the terrarium should also be tall, with adequate climbing facilities. Provide at least one basking site where the temperature may reach 110 to 115°F (43 to 46.1°C); the general ambient temperature should be in the 80s°F (22 to 28°C). Because basilisks generally do not like direct light, ensure that there is adequate filtering of the light source and that they receive a UVB source.

Females lay from 2 to 17 eggs, most commonly between May and August. Incubate eggs in a 3:1 vermiculite (or your preferred incubation medium) to water mixture at 90 percent humidity. Young hatch after about 80 days and may be housed together until males begin to display their crests.

Genus *Brachylophus*

This genus contains three known living and one fossil species of enigmatic iguanas. They represent the zoological anomaly, the only iguanids between the relatively eastern Galápagos Islands and Madagascar to the west. The genus name comes from the Greek words βραχι, *brachi*, short, and λοφω, *lopho*, a crest. Two of the known living species are capable of interbreeding and producing viable hybrids.

Brachylophus bulabula Keogh, Edwards, Fisher, and Harlow, 2008
Central Fiji Iguana

Etymology: (Fijian) bula, "hello," and when repeated, is a more enthusiastic or happily surprised greeting.

Range: Central Fiji, with the largest populations on Yadua Taba, the official reserve for the crested iguana. Also native to Kadavu and Ovalau Islands.

Maximum Size: Unknown; presumably to 35.4 inches (900 mm)

References: Keogh et al. (2008).

Captive Suitability: 1. Protected by Fiji law but too newly discovered to have CITES or other status as of this printing.

Natural History: Still little known, this new species is similar to both of the other *Brachylophus*. It differs from them in that it has a green nasal area with only a few yellow scales bordering the nostrils; a distinct color pattern; and distinct genetics. *Brachylophus bulabula* is very similar to *B. vitiensis* in having a pronounced vertebral crest, males with broad lateral bands, nearly unicolor females, and distinct yellow nostrils. Juveniles are lime green with broad, dark kelly green bands. The tail is banded, with adults having white and green bands. The belly is white.

Introduced mongooses and feral cats threaten this species as much as they do its two relatives. Yadua Taba is believed to have about 10,000 individuals of the new iguanas.

Captive Care: Completely unknown but probably similar to the other species.

Approximate natural range of the genus *Brachylophus*: *B. vitiensis* (yellow), *B. fasciatus* (red), *B. bulabula* (green). *B. fasciatus* is also found on Tonga, many miles to the southeast.

Male (left) and female (right) Fiji banded iguanas. This species breeds readily in zoo collections.

Brachylophus fasciatus (Brongniart, 1800) Fiji Banded Iguana

Etymology: (Latin) *fasciatus*, banded.

Range: Fiji, with an extralimital population at Efate, Vanuatu.

Maximum Size: 35.4 inches (900 mm)

References: Alberts et al. (2004); Arnett (1979); Blair (2004); Boylan (1989); Burghardt and Rand (1982); Cogger and Sadlier (1985); Gibbons (1981); Mertens (1934); Morrison (2003); Zug (1991).

Captive Suitability: 4

Natural History: Perhaps because Fiji has moist forests instead of dry volcanic deserts, the banded iguana bears a closer resemblance to South America's green iguana than does its Galápagos cousins. Females and young are quite similar in appearance to *Iguana iguana* but lack the large subtympanic (below the ear) scale and dorsal crest.

Banded iguanas are largely arboreal and may change color to match shadow patterns on their skin. Males are more intricately colored, with grayish-blue bands on a bright green body. The nostrils and bellies of both sexes are yellow.

Mating occurs in November, and three to six eggs are laid about six weeks later. Females excavate nests in the soil at the bases of trees, deposit eggs, and then refill the nest. Hatching under captive conditions follows in 18 to 30 weeks.

As for most insular species, the biggest threats come from feral cats and habitat destruction. Introduced mongooses have reduced populations on Viti Levu and Vanua Levu.

Brachylophus vitiensis Gibbons, 1980
Fiji Crested Iguana

Etymology: (Latin) *vitiensis*, "of Fiji."

Range: Fiji. Limited to a few tiny islets of the western group: Mamanucas, Yasawas to Mali, Macuata.

Maximum Size: 35.8 inches (910 mm)

References: Alberts et al. (2004); Blair (2004); Boylan (1989); Burghardt and Rand (1982); Cogger and Sadlier (1985); Gibbons (1981, 1984); Morrison (2003); Zug (1991).

Captive Suitability: 3

Natural History: Similar to the more widespread banded iguana but with more complex and variable coloring and a pronounced set of vertebral spines. The body stripes are white and narrow on a green body that can quickly turn charcoal black when the lizard is annoyed. The belly is mottled creamy white and pale green. The nostril is yellow and the dewlap is larger than that of the banded iguana. There is no significant sexual dimorphism in the crested iguana, but males do have larger and more pronounced femoral pores.

The discovery of this large and dramatic lizard began in 1980, when Professor John Gibbons of the University of the South Pacific (USP) in Fiji was watching a special screening of the movie *The Blue Lagoon* starring a teenaged Brooke Shields. Part of the filming was done on a remote island in Fiji. The footage Gibbons got to watch included a few fleeting shots of an unusual and unknown iguana. Gibbons quickly found out which island had been filmed and visited it himself. The result was the discovery of this extraordinary species,

Captive Care: Males are highly territorial and should only be housed with females. The diet of this species is limited, consisting of bananas, hibiscus leaves and stamens, and pawpaw fruits. They rarely drink from a dish but take water droplets from leaves.

There has been considerable success in breeding banded iguanas in captivity. Eggs are kept in vermiculite and water in a 3:2 ratio by volume and will incubate in five to five and a half months if kept at 75 to 81.2°F (24 to 27.3°C). Young are aggressive toward each other and should be separated until sexes can be determined, usually after four to six months of age.

described in the *Journal of Herpetology*. Prof. Gibbons went on to study the biology of this critically endangered lizard and saw to the establishment of a preserve for its protection. Sadly, Gibbons and his family drowned in a boating accident in 1987.

From Gibbons's study, we know that the crested iguana mates in November and lays eggs in April. They hatch some 35 weeks later, in December, representing perhaps the longest incubation time for an iguanid lizard.

Captive Care: Similar to that of the banded iguana. It seems that the two species hybridize readily in captivity, and many zoo specimens seen today look like hybrid animals.

Male Fiji crested iguana in its natural habitat. This species was unknown to science until 1980.

152

C. *subcristatus* takes its trivial name from the short scaly crest on its nape.

Although *C. subcristatus* is primarily herbivorous, they will feed on animals opportunistically. This one is scavenging off a dead sea lion.

Genus *Conolophus* Fitzinger, 1843

Two species of stout, aggressive, cactus-eating iguanas live on the Galápagos Islands. They are very similar in appearance to the marine iguana but differ in that they are more robust, with shorter and rounded tails. The genus name comes from the Greek words κονω, *kono*, a cone, plus λοφωσ, *lophos*, a crest; the vertebral crest of these lizards comprises a series of numerous small individual cone-shaped scales. Both species are quite similar and may represent a single taxon. At present, *Conolophus pallidus* is considered to have larger, thinner, and more distinct vertebral spines, as well as lighter and more uniform coloration than *C. subcristatus*.

Conolophus subcristatus (Gray, 1831)
Galápagos Land Iguana

Etymology: (Latin) *subcristatus* refers to a short crest.
Range: Fernandina, Isabella, Plaza, and Santa Cruz Islands.
Maximum Size: 41.3 inches (1,050mm)
References: Alberts et al. (2004); Blair (2004); Burghardt and Rand (1982); Mertens (1934).
Captive Suitability: 1
Natural History: Identical to *Conolophus pallidus*.
Captive Care: N/A. These animals are only maintained in captivity at the research station in the Galápagos Islands.

153

The two species of Galápagos land iguanas feed heavily on the native cacti.

C. pallidus is only found on one of the major islands of the Galápagos.

Conolophus pallidus Heller, 1903
Galápagos Land Iguana

Etymology: (Latin) *pallidus*, pale.

Range: Santa Fe Island; became extinct on Santiago sometime after 1840.

Maximum Size: 41.3 inches (1,050mm)

References: Alberts et al. (2004); Blair (2004); Burghardt and Rand (1982).

Captive Suitability: 1

Natural History: These are large, primarily herbivorous lizards that feed on *Opuntia* cactus and a variety of other local flora. On occasion, they are opportunistic enough to consume insects, small vertebrates that stumble into an iguana's burrow, and carrion. The lizards consume small cactus spines but scrape larger spines off food with the front legs.

Females lay 1 to 20 eggs in specially excavated nests, and young hatch in 85 to 110 days. During the first year or so, young iguanas are largely insectivorous, but they also take soft vegetation such as flowers and berries. Lizards attain their adult size in 3 to 5 years and may live for 50 or 60 years. A large male may weigh 32.5 pounds (14.7 kg).

Major threats to land iguanas are cats, brought with settlers and ships' crews, and until recently, hunting by humans. It was the now-extinct Santiago population that Charles Darwin observed during his famous visit to the Galápagos.

Captive Care: N/A. These animals are only maintained in captivity at the research station in the Galápagos Islands.

ONE GENUS OR TWO?

It should not come as much of a surprise to learn that the two species of Galápagos land iguanas could mate, but when it was discovered that hybrids exist in which the male marine iguanas successfully mate with female land iguanas (Kunstaetter, 2003), it sent new waves of Darwinian enthusiasm into the zoological world. One widely accepted definition of species is members of a group of organisms that can mate and produce viable offspring. It is not yet known if the iguana hybrids are sterile or viable, but the mere fact of healthy hybrids is a strong argument to unite all Galápagos iguanas into the single genus *Amblyrhynchus*. If you compare the skulls of the two "genera," you will note that they are exceptionally similar.

So far the two species of Galápagos land iguanas have not been known to mate.

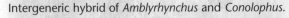

Intergeneric hybrid of *Amblyrhynchus* and *Conolophus*.

Genus *Ctenosaura* Wiegmann, 1828

The spiny-tailed iguanas of Mexico and Central America are probably closely related to both the iguanid genera on the Galápagos and the Caribbean genus *Cyclura*. In general, they are distinguished from the other large iguanas in possession of cylindrical, spiny tails and somewhat elongated and depressed heads. They are adapted for dry habitats with shrubby and forest vegetation, and although primarily insectivorous, will also take flowers, fruits, cacti, and soft leaves in their diets. Males have enlarged crests that are taller than those seen in females; some females lack crests completely. Life spans for the largest species of ctenosaurs may exceed 30 years.

The taxonomic status of ctenosaurs has been in flux for much of the past ten years. The former genus *Enyaliosaurus* has been synonymized with *Ctenosaura*, providing the genus with a number of smaller and very brightly colored species. Köhler et al. (2000) have divided *Ctenosaura* into three subgenera:

1. subgenus *Enyaliosaurus*, comprising small, short-tailed species
2. subgenus *Loganiosaurus*, containing the larger species *Ctenosaura bakeri*, *C. melanosterna*, *C. oedirhina*, and *C. palearis*
3. subgenus *Ctenosaura*, containing the remaining large species

Many subspecies, especially those allied with *Ctenosaura hemilopha*, have been raised to species status, while a minority of researchers consider them minor variants of a single widespread taxon. The genus name is from the Greek words κτ νο, *kteno*, a beast, plus ϛαυρωϛ, *sauros*, a lizard.

Mexican spiny-tailed iguana in Veracruz, Mexico. This is probably a young or female individual because it lacks a developed crest.

Subgenus *Ctenosaura*

This subgenus contains iguanas with a long flat snout, two rows of smaller scales between the keeled tail whorls, and more than 66 dorsal spines in the crest.

Ctenosaura acanthura (Shaw, 1802)
Mexican Spiny-Tailed Iguana/ Northeastern Spiny-Tailed Iguana

Etymology: (Latin) *acantho*, spiny.
Range: Eastern Mexico along the central Gulf coast.
Maximum Size: 55 inches (1,400 mm)
References: Blair (2004); Grzimek (1984); Köhler (1993a, 2002); www.westcoastiguana.com/oedirhina.htm.

Captive Suitability: 4
Natural History: Mexican spiny-tailed iguanas prefer arid, rocky habitats with plenty of perching sites that allow them to beware of approaching predators. Although awkward in appearance, they can move quickly and will bolt up a tree or under boulders at any sign of possible danger.

This species has a conspicuous vertebral crest, but the largest scales are no longer than the length of the eye. The body is slate gray without notable markings. The caudal keels are large, with two rows of smaller scales between each keeled whorl. Hatchlings are bright green but begin to change color as they approach sexual maturity.
Captive Care: Same as for the western black iguana, *Ctenosaura hemilopha*.

157

C. conspicuosa resting on a branch at night.

Ctenosaura conspicuosa Dickerson, 1919

Etymology: (Latin) *conspicuum*, a sight or something noticeable.

Range: Cholludo and San Esteban Islands in the Gulf of California, Mexico.

Maximum Size: 38.4 inches (975 mm)

References: Grismer (2002); Köhler (1993a, 2002).

Captive Suitability: 4

Natural History: Not well known. This insular species lives in the Gulf of California (Sea of Cortez). It is a slate gray lizard with a very low vertebral crest. Adults have two or three prominent but short black bars across the shoulders. Juveniles are gray with a series of thin light bands. There are four to six postmental scales.

Captive Care: Most likely same as for the western black iguana, *Ctenosaura hemilopha*.

Juvenile (left) and adult (right) western black iguanas. As in several other ctenosaurs, the young start out green and change color when they reach maturity.

Ctenosaura hemilopha (Cope, 1863)
Western Black Iguana/Cape Spiny-Tailed Iguana

Etymology: (Latin) *hemi*, half, and *lopha*, a crest.
Range: Eastern and southern Baja California and the western coastal mainland of Mexico.
Maximum Size: 38.4 inches (975 mm)
References: Blair (2004); Grismer (2002); Köhler (1993a, 2002); Köhler et al. (2000).
Captive Suitability: 4
Natural History: This large iguana is recognized by the two or three broad black bands across the shoulders, the posterior band nearly encircling the body. A low vertebral row of scales and light bands that encircle the tail are also characteristic. Juveniles are bright green. There are only four postmental scales. The body is slightly depressed, and the tail is ringed with strongly keeled scales.

These lizards inhabit arid, rocky areas and may often be observed perching atop large rocks. Western black iguanas are often observed in sexual pairs that live in a well-defined territory. Several females and young may also be present.
Captive Care: Captives require roomy enclosures, and males–which are extremely territorial–should be housed alone or only with females. Given their adult size, territoriality, and relative activity, these animals should be housed in terrariums no less than 32 square feet (3 square m) in floor space and 6.5 feet (2 m) tall. Broad-spectrum UV light is essential. Temperatures should be hot (88 to 120°F [31.1 to 48.9°C]), but humidity is less critical and may range from 35 to 100 percent.

Mating generally occurs in the early spring (March to April), and egg laying takes place a month or so later.

C. macrolopha was formerly considered a subspecies of *C. hemilopha*. This species may range into extreme southern Arizona.

Ctenosaura macrolopha Smith, 1972
Large Crested Iguana/Mainland Spiny-tailed Iguana

Etymology: (Latin) *macro*, large, and *lopha*, a crest.
Range: The western coast of northern Mexico along the Gulf of California and inland.
Maximum Size: 37.4 inches (950 mm)
References: Köhler (1993a, 2002).
Captive Suitability: 3
Natural History: Not well known but presumably similar to that of the western black iguana; it was once considered a subspecies of that species.
Captive Care: Same as for the western black iguana.

Ctenosaura nolascensis Smith, 1972

Etymology: From Latin for the name of the island from which the species comes.
Range: San Pedro Nolasco Island, Baja California, Mexico.
Maximum Size: 38.4 inches (975 mm)
References: Grismer (2002); Köhler (1993a, 2002); Köhler et al. (2000).
Captive Suitability: 4
Natural History: Differs from *Ctenosaura hemilopha* in having five or six postmental scales and reaching a smaller adult size. The iguanas live on a small and very dry, rocky island, where they climb tall cacti to feed upon their fruits. The lizards mate in spring, with hatching taking place in October.
Captive Care: Same as for the western black iguana.

Despite having the common name black iguana, *C. pectinata* usually has patches of white or other pale colors.

SEXING SPINY-TAILS
By Gunther Köhler, A.J. Gutman, and John Binns

It is difficult to determine the sex of immature *Ctenosaura* species. In fully grown males of most species, the dorsal crest is substantially more developed than in females. Exceptions are *C. alfredschmidti*, *C. clarki*, *C. defensor*, and *C. flavidorsalis*, in which neither males nor females have particularly well-developed dorsal crests. Adult males also usually have clearly visible hemipenial bulges under the base of the tail. The femoral pores are always larger in males than in females. In adult male *C. similis*, the femoral pores can attain diameters of 2.5 mm, whereas they are rarely more than 1 mm in diameter in females.

Ctenosaura pectinata (Wiegmann, 1834)
Black Iguana/Mexican Spiny-Tailed Iguana
Etymology: (Latin) *pectin*, a comb or crest.
Range: Coastal mainland Mexico (not Baja) south to Panama.
Maximum Size: 49 inches (1,245 mm), the largest member of the genus
References: Blair (2004); Köhler (1993a); Köhler et al. (2000).
Captive Suitability: 4
Natural History: This species is a resident of arid forest areas, where it will be seen on rocks or the ground as often as in trees. It is also an excellent burrower. These lizards prefer a temperature range of 85 to 95°F (29.4 to 35°C). Like other ctenosaurs, the black iguana is omnivorous, the diet shifting seasonally. At times insects and small vertebrates may constitute the bulk of prey, while at others the diet is largely made up of fruits, leaves, and flowers.

Mating occurs in January through March, with egg laying following some 9 to 12 weeks later. Incubation takes 12 to 15 weeks. Hatchlings are bright green with black mottling, but the green fades by the end of the first year. Adults are black with white dorsal markings; the head is always completely black.
Captive Care: Same as for the western black iguana.

Adult (left) and juvenile (right) *C. similis*. This lizard holds the record for being the fastest lizard on earth.

Ctenosaura similis (Gray, 1831)
Black Spiny-Tailed Iguana

Etymology: (Latin) *similis*, similar to.

Range: Coastal mainland Mexico (not Baja) and the Yucatan Peninsula south to Panama. This species has the largest natural range for the genus.

Maximum Size: 47.2 inches (1,200 mm)

References: Blair (2004); Köhler (1993a); Köhler et al. (2000); Savage (2002).

Captive Suitability: 3

Natural History: This species is the second largest of the ctenosaurs, and males have the longest vertebral spines in the genus. Color and pattern are extremely variable. Hatchlings and young iguanas are bright leaf green with black dorsal bands. As the lizards mature, the green markings become black, often with numerous tiny light scales interspersed. As adults, males are almost uniformly black, although females may have intricate banded patterns of black, gray, and pale green. Caudal bands are distinct in young and females but indistinct in adult males. Variations in pattern, color, and especially juvenile coloration are geographically influenced.

The caudal spines of this species, although distinct, are considerably smaller than in other ctenosaurs.

Some 12 to 88 eggs (Savage, 2002) may be laid in the spring between March and April. Eggs measure 0.6 to 0.7 inches (15 to 18 mm) in diameter. They hatch between June and July. Köhler (2002) notes that when hatchlings emerge, they measure 1.9 to 2.3 inches (48 to 59 mm) SVL and weigh less than one-fifth of 1 ounce (4 g). By the end of the first year, they measure 5.7 to 7.3 inches (145 to 185 mm) SVL and weigh up to 7 ounces (200 g).

Captive Care: Same as for the western black iguana.

Subgenus *Loganiosaurus*

This subgenus contains iguanas with a normal, slightly truncated snout with a blunt tip, one row of smaller scales between the keeled tail whorls, and fewer than 48 dorsal spines in the crest. They are restricted to Guatemala and Honduras and their Caribbean islands.

Ctenosaura bakeri Stejneger, 1901
Utila Iguana/Swamper

Etymology: Named for the director of the U. S. National Zoo, Frank Baker, where the specimen used by Stejneger for the type description had been kept as a display animal.
Range: Utila Island, east of Honduras.
Maximum Size: 31.4 inches (800 mm)
References: Köhler (1993a); Köhler et al. (2000); www.westcoastiguana.com/oedirhina.htm.
Captive Suitability: 2
Natural History: A pretty species that ranges in color from dusky tan to yellow to blue. It is also more arboreal than other spiny-tailed iguanas, and the diet contains a higher percentage of invertebrate prey. A mangrove resident of tiny (16 square miles [41 km²]) Utila Island, its habitat is threatened by tourist site developers. They feed upon local vegetation and small crabs and are thus extremely salt tolerant. They are also found in much wetter habitats–mangrove forests–than other members of the genus. The snout of this species is more truncated than in other ctenosaurs.
  This species is endangered.
Captive Care: Unknown.

C. melanosterna has a small range in northern Honduras and some offshore islands and is considered critically endangered by the International Union for Conservation of Nature (IUCN).

Ctenosaura melanosterna Buckley and Axtell, 1997
Rio Aguan Valley Iguana

Etymology: (Latin) *sterna*, breastbone, and *melano*, black.
Range: Northern coastal Honduras and offshore islands.
Maximum Size: 38.4 inches (975 mm)
References: Buckley and Axtell (1990); Köhler (1993a, 2002); Köhler et al. (2000).
Captive Suitability: 4
Natural History: The Rio Aguan Valley iguana occupies one of the smallest ranges for the genus *Ctenosaura*. It is a conspicuous animal, with a large gray dewlap that is more similar to what is seen in green iguanas than in other ctenosaurs. The body is beautifully marked with brown, tan, and black,

KEEPING *CTENOSAURA* IGUANAS

By Gunther Köhler, A.J. Gutman, and John Binns

Healthy spiny-tailed iguanas typically exhibit lively and inquisitive behaviors. During the active phase (daytime), the animals eat, threaten, court, or patrol their territory with alternating periods of basking or sleeping. Sick animals, on the other hand, will have sunken eyes and protruding pelvic bones due to loss of weight, and they will lack muscle on the legs and tail. They tend to lie apathetically at the bottom of the enclosure and do not react to their surroundings. Any movements tend to be halting and insecure, and the lower abdomen often rests on the ground.

HOUSING

The size of the enclosure will determine the degree of flexibility in design and setup. Planning must include provisions for animal barrier isolation and for developing lighting and temperature zoning for thermoregulation. To adequately provide for a complete behavioral repertoire, a ctenosaur enclosure must be large and sturdy. For an adult pair of any of the medium-sized or large species, a habitat should be at least 6.5 x 5 x 4.5 feet (2 x 1.5 x 1.4 m).

Hatchling spiny-tailed iguanas are best housed in groups of three or four in at least a medium-sized terrarium about 24 x 16 x 24 inches (61 x 40.6 x 61 cm) in size. Certain juveniles in captivity, like their counterparts in the wild, can be distinct loners and may be incompatible with other individuals. A well-structured terrarium with multiple basking spots and hiding places is required for raising juveniles together. Sometimes, however, despite all these measures, combatants must be separated.

The territorial nature of spiny-tailed iguanas must be considered when deciding the number of animals to place in a single enclosure. Sex is not easily determined in very young ctenosaurs, and although a male and a female or a pair of young females is likely to be compatible, two males will definitely fight. The size of the enclosure (generally bigger is better) may be the deciding factor in providing sufficient territory for more than one animal. Dominance develops at a very young age and can range from establishing a natural pecking order to violent biting and life-threatening aggression. A second enclosure must be available should the dominant animal create an unhealthy, irresolvable situation with its mate or other female animals in the enclosure.

GENERAL SETUP

Because spiny-tailed iguanas are territorial, the habitat should be structured to permit animals to avoid one another, particularly if they vary in size. Visual barriers and hiding places can be created using rocks, tree roots, PVC tubing, cork bark tubes, or whole pieces of cork bark attached to walls. All structures and components must be sufficiently secured and stable to prevent injury to the iguanas.

Isolation barriers may necessitate the provision of individual basking areas, and this should be considered when developing the enclosure design. Basking locations should be designed that allow declining temperature zones for proper thermoregulation. This entails creating a surface that allows the animal to adjust its position relative to the central "hot spot" (high temperature area) to maintain the correct body temperature. In the wild, animals can maintain body temperature within a few degrees by repositioning themselves between bright sun and shade or retreating into cooler burrows. Providing temperature zones is a mandatory habitat design element to ensure good health. Because iguanas require heat to effectively digest food, inadequate thermal design of the enclosure will limit the benefits of providing a healthy nutritional diet, even with the presence of sufficient ultraviolet (UV or UVA/B) light.

A food bowl can simply be placed on the bottom of the enclosure. The use of commercially available garden cement tiles or walkway liners that keep the bowls from being upset will aid in housekeeping. Some animals, however, will not readily descend from an elevated perch and are much more likely to eat if their food is placed higher. Driftwood structures can be used to construct a secondary platform higher in the enclosure. Although adult spiny-tailed iguanas normally meet all their fluid

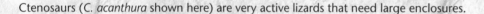

Ctenosaurs (C. *acanthura* shown here) are very active lizards that need large enclosures.

requirements from the food they eat, a water bowl should always be provided–and cleaned daily. In cases where territorial disputes occur, assuming the disputes do not result in injury, separate food bowls and water dishes should be used to minimize conflict.

SUBSTRATE

A mixture of sanitized soil, sand, and cypress bark mulch composes an appropriate substrate for the naturally appearing environment. The use of unprocessed soil, sand, and bark mulch is not recommended due to the potential of introducing insects, bacteria, or other undesirable elements.

HEAT AND LIGHT REQUIREMENTS

Spiny-tailed iguanas will be fully active and can display their intense coloration only with proper illumination. The daily photoperiod varies seasonally and according to the geographic origin of the species. Regulating a consistent photoperiod as well as appropriate daily temperature fluctuations in the enclosure is recommended. To simulate the 24-hour cycle, the method of controlling light and heat should be considered prior to setting up the enclosure. Commercially available timers are useful for regulating the photoperiod.

In nature, the ctenosaurs spend much of their time basking. In captivity, they require access to high temperatures and UV lighting.

Although many lighting products are readily available, *Ctenosaura* (and other iguanas) require higher levels of UVA/B than most other reptiles. The products selected should include lamps that produce sufficient quantities of light in the UV range. Regular ultraviolet (UV) light is critical for proper calcium metabolism and breeding.

As a final word on illumination, no light supplement for captive animals is better than natural sunlight. When possible, regular periods of exposure should be employed. In designing enclosures, any access to natural sunlight (window, porch, skylight, etc.) should be optimized. To utilize the sun's UV light, glass and plastic panels must be replaced with UV-transmittable substitutes.

Ambient temperatures in an enclosure should range from 82 to 91°F (27.8 to 32.8°C) during the day and be reduced to 64 to 76°F (17.8 to 24.4°C) at night.

FOOD AND WATER

Spiny-tailed iguanas are omnivorous. Juveniles, however, prefer animal-based foods. Between 40 and 80 percent of the food consumed by young *C. similis* consists of insects. In contrast, adult spiny-tailed iguanas are predominantly vegetarian. Vegetables, such as sweet potatoes, squash, and green beans, as well as leafy greens, such as dandelions, collard greens, mustard greens, endive, and chicory, are readily accepted. Various seeds and sprouts (linseeds, sunflower seeds, soybeans), flowers (dandelions and hibiscus), and fruits (nectarines, peaches, pears, apples, melons, berries, plums) are good supplements. The colors red and yellow are particularly attractive to spiny-tailed iguanas (as they are for many other reptiles), so hibiscus flowers, grated carrots, tomatoes, strawberries, dandelion flowers, and other red or yellow foods are usually consumed greedily and often may be used to convince reluctant eaters to feed.

Mineral supplements should be added to food daily. All insects should be dusted with mineral powder before they are offered. In addition, a regular vitamin supplement must be provided. Many vitamin supplements are available commercially, but caution is advised. Overdosing or excessive use of these supplements can result in a number of nutritional disorders.

Hatchlings have a much higher fluid requirement than adult iguanas and should be provided with sufficient drinking water. Water bowls should be cleaned and filled daily and the terrarium misted regularly. A heating mat may be used to warm the water bowl from below to 77 to 86°F (25 to 30°C). Adults may obtain all their water needs from their food, but it is best to include a water bowl.

Two views of *C. palearis*. The animal on the right has healed skin lesions (white areas), possibly from being kept too humid in captivity.

with a broad black band that covers the shoulders and upper arms. The dark bands are bordered by tiny white spots that also form bands. The blunt snout is lighter than the body and ranges in color from pale yellow to tan. The tail has five to six broad black bands.

Captive Care: Same as for the rest of the genus.

HELP SAVE THE UTILA IGUANA

Information on the efforts to preserve this iguana and its habitat, along with the contact to provide financial support for that work, may be reached at the Utila Iguana Recovery Program at www.utila-iguana.de.

Ctenosaura palearis Stejneger, 1899

Etymology: (Latin) *palearia*, dewlap, referring to the throat fan of lizards.

Range: Restricted to a small region of eastern central Guatemala.

Maximum Size: 38.4 inches (975 mm)

References: Buckley and Axtell (1990); Köhler (1993a, 2002); Köhler et al. (2000).

Captive Suitability: 4

Natural History: A reddish-brown lizard with thin triangular black body bands. The head is very blunt, and there is a large gray-mottled dewlap. There are seven to nine conspicuous broad black caudal bands, the last coloring the posterior third of the tail.

Captive Care: Same as for the rest of the genus.

Genus *Cyclura* Harlan, 1824

To this genus belong the nine large species of iguanas of the Caribbean islands where, in relative isolation from mammalian predators, they have been able to grow to large and bulky dimensions. These animals are collectively known as rhinoceros iguanas because of the conical structures seen on the snout in many specimens.

The species in this genus tend to occupy very small ranges, and populations have suffered from the introduction of non-native mammals–notably cats and mongooses–to their islands by European colonists. As a result, the genus is listed on CITES, meaning a permit is required to collect them and may be required to purchase or keep specimens. Several species are being bred in considerable numbers by zoos and herpetoculturists, and a few species are quite popular in the live animal trade. Only two species do not qualify as giants but are included in the key for completeness.

Rhinoceros iguanas are predominantly herbivorous, feeding on a variety of vegetables and fruits. Although they will consume meat, and at least when young, insects, these potential food items should be offered only sparingly, if at all. Some keepers recommend mineral supplementation.

These lizards require well-lit and roomy terrariums, preferably with considerable exposure to natural sunlight. Males are highly territorial and should not be housed with other males. Minimum terrarium size should be about 45 square feet (4.2 square m) in floor space and 6.5 feet (2 m) tall. Females typically grow larger than males and have narrower heads and thinner postcloacal tail regions. Mature males have well-developed femoral pores. You can sex these lizards with a snake sexing probe. The probe will insert about three times further in males than in females. Mating occurs in May through June, with egg deposition in late June through August. The large eggs–among the largest for living lizards, at 2.75 to 4.7 inches (70 to 120 mm) long–are laid in deep holes excavated by the females and rigorously guarded. Incubation time ranges from 50 to 70 days.

The nine species listed here are generally accepted as valid, but many subspecies are either added to the list or elevated to species level. Although there has been a good deal of study on reproductive biology and work on breeding the rarer taxa in captivity, the taxonomy of the group is far from resolved and has received surprisingly little attention. No doubt the species list will continue to change over the coming years. The genus name comes from the Greek words κυκλω, *cyclo*, ringed, and υρω, *uro*, tail.

Approximate natural ranges of *Cyclura nubila* (red), *C. cornuta* (yellow), *C. lewisii* (green), and *C. collei* (blue).

The Jamaican iguana was believed to be extinct but was rediscovered in 1990. Conservation efforts for this species have been fairly successful.

Cyclura collei Gray, 1845
Jamaican Iguana

Etymology: Named for someone associated with presenting John Gray with the specimen. In Gray's words "Colley's *Cyclura*. Adult, stuffed, presented by the Admiralty, from Haslar Hospital."

Range: Restricted to dry rocky forests of extreme south central Jamaica.

Maximum Size: 35.4 inches (900 mm)

References: Hudson (2007); Hudson et al. (1994); Noegel (1989); Schwartz and Henderson (1991); Vogel et al. (1996); www.cyclura.com.

Captive Suitability: 2

Natural History: This species, once a common animal on Jamaica, was nearing extinction because of overhunting by humans and introduced predators. By 1940, only 22 specimens were known to exist, and all were collected to attempt captive breeding. Given the sorry state of herpetoculture in the 1940s, all the animals died by 1946. In 1990, a local pig hunter and his dog secured a specimen, and subsequently conservation biologists and Kingston's Hope Zoo have had a second–and successful–chance to try captive breeding. By 1999, there were more than 100 known specimens of the "extinct" iguana, and many captive-bred animals have been released back into the wild. The major remaining threat comes from the many non-native predatory mammals now resident in southern Jamaica, including cats, mongooses, and feral dogs.

The only known populations exist in the Hellshire Hills, a region of sharp limestone rocks and dry forests. Females use communal nests and lay up to 17 eggs per clutch in June. Young hatch in 85 to 87 days.

Captive Care: The few zoos working with this species are breeding lizards and reintroducing subadults back into the wild. All simulate natural environmental conditions as closely as possible.

KEY TO THE SPECIES OF *CYCLURA*

1a. Snout of males with conical rhinoceros horns	*Cyclura cornuta*
1b. Snout of males without conical rhinoceros horns	2
2a. Nuchal scales longer by 1.4 to 1.7 times than vertebral spines	*Cyclura carinata**
2b. Nuchal scales no longer than 1.2 times vertebral spines	3
3a. Vertebral crest very low and indistinct	4
3b. Vertebral crest distinct, made of thin, comb-like scales	5
4a. Enlarged posterior scales along lower jaw subequal	*Cyclura pinguis*
4b. Three most posterior scales along lower jaw larger than others	*Cyclura rileyi**
5a. Caudal scales in whorls, all keeled, but each whorl subequal	*Cyclura collei*
5b. Caudal scales in whorls, some made of distinctly larger rings of keeled scales	6
6a. Head and snout somewhat depressed and elongate	7
6b. Head high, snout blunt	8
7a. Enlarged caudal whorls very spiny; body, especially anterior third, pale blue	*Cyclura lewisi*
7b. Enlarged caudal whorls less developed than in *Cyclura lewisi*; body gray or olive green, but not blue	*Cyclura nubila*
8a. Greatly enlarged and rounded scales on snout; enlarged whorls of caudals only slightly larger than others	*Cyclura cychlura*
8b. Scales on front of snout not greatly larger than others; enlarged whorls of keeled caudals much larger than others	*Cyclura ricordi*

* This species is not a giant but is included here for completeness.

171

Rhinoceros iguana displaying the conical scales on the snout for which this species is named. This is a female with well-developed "horns."

Cyclura cornuta Bonnaterre, 1789
Rhinoceros Iguana

Etymology: (Latin) *cornu*, horn, in reference to the snout horn.

Range: Hispaniola and Mona Island.

Maximum Size: 43.3 inches (1,100 mm)

References: Blair (1994, 2004); Boylan (1985); Schwartz and Henderson (1991); Wiewandt (1977, 1979); www.cyclura.com.

Captive Suitability: 3

Natural History: These large iguanas are among the least endangered of their genus, with well more than 10,000 individuals known to exist in the wild. They are resident of xeric habitats where plant life is dry-adapted and temperatures generally hover near 77°F (25°C). Iguanas feed primarily on fruits, flowers, and soft leaves, but they also reportedly consume a fair number of caterpillars and pupae. Habitat destruction, especially in Haiti, is the major threat to their survival. Their great bulk, horned snout,

MONA ISLAND IGUANA

One subspecies of the rhinoceros iguana, *C. cornuta stejnegeri* Barbour and Noble, 1916, the Mona iguana, has been elevated to species status by some workers based on differences in the reproductive biologies of the lizards, but this designation is not universally accepted. The Mona iguana was named to honor Leonhard Stejneger (pronounced "sty-nuh-ger")(1851-1943), the Norwegian-born herpetologist who worked at the Smithsonian Institution from 1881 until 1943.

Pair of wild rhinoceros iguanas engaged in courtship. The female is in the foreground.

and aggressive displays have made them favorites at zoos and as stand-in dinosaurs in old movies.

This is the species most familiar as the rhinoceros iguana, owing to the two or three conical horns on the upper snout. Males are particularly territorial and will display at and eventually charge interlopers. Actual bouts of aggression involve two males engaged in pushing matches. Although the jaws typically remain open, biting or serious injury are extremely rare.

The bout ends when one lizard withdraws.

Reproductive behavior is similar to that described for *Cyclura cychlura*. Females lay eggs in yard-long (meter-long) nests, but as competition for good burrows is keen, the lizards often fight over the sites.

Captive Care: Same as for *Cyclura cychlura*.

Adult *C. cychlura inornata* (left) and a juvenile *C. cychlura figginsi* (right). *C. cychlura figginsi* is unusual for the genus in that it is not territorial.

Cyclura cychlura (Cuvier, 1829)
Andros Island Iguana/Exuma Island Iguana

Etymology: The trivial name is simply an alternative spelling of the genus name and also means "ringed tail."

Range: Caribbean islands to the north of Cuba. (See "Natural History," this section.)

Maximum Size: 45 inches (1,143 mm)

References: Blair (2004); Iverson et al. (2004); Schwartz and Henderson (1991); www.cyclura.com.

Captive Suitability: 3

Natural History: These are large, bulky lizards, once used as prehistoric beasts in 1950s science fiction films. Three subspecies have been described:

Cyclura c. cychlura Cuvier, 1829 (Andros and Bahamas Islands); *C. c. figginsi* Barbour, 1923 (Exuma Island); and *C. c. inornata* Schwartz and Thomas, 1975 (Bahamas). All are distinguished by distinct whorls of enlarged spiny scales around the tail, giving the species its trivial name.

Members of this species may sport beautiful coloring and patterns. *C. c. figginsi* can be a slate gray with bluish dorsal spines and brilliant orange markings on the snout, shoulders, and chest.

Captive Care: Cages must be large and sturdy. Because males are aggressively territorial, there should be no more than one male per enclosure, regardless of enclosure size. *Cyclura* breeding expert David Blair recommends a space no smaller

than 400 square inches (26 square m) per adult lizard, including basking sites. Though these are largely terrestrial lizards, they can and will climb, so terrariums should be at least 6.6 feet (2 m) in height. All fixtures must be sturdy enough for these strong lizards.

There is only a two-hour change in seasonal photoperiod in much of the Caribbean, so the photoperiod can remain close to 12 hours of light and 12 hours of dark all year. Temperatures vary considerably, though, from nighttime lows of 55 to 63°F (12.8 to 17.2°C) to daytime highs of 95 to 100°F (35 to 37.8°C). Include a basking site that reaches 100 to 110°F (37.8 to 43.3°C), but make sure the lizards can retreat to cooler areas within the enclosure. Daily exposure to natural sunlight or full-spectrum lighting including UVB is essential to their good health.

Feed rock iguanas a primarily vegetable diet that includes leafy greens, such as collard and mustard greens, plus beans, carrots, squash, yams,

zucchini, grated turnips, and corn. Supplement with a variety of chopped fruits to which a calcium/phosphorus supplement is added weekly. Feed lizards under 5 inches (127 mm) SVL thrice weekly, and adults three or four times per week.

This species tends to mate in May and June, and eggs are laid some four to six weeks later. Females reduce or cease eating around the time they engage in digging holes for the eventual nesting site. Captive breeding seems to be most successful when the iguanas have soil deeper than 12 inches (30.5 cm) in which to nest. After laying her eggs, the female will guard the nest area for several weeks—be very careful removing them for incubation. Incubate eggs in a substrate such as Perlite deep enough to cover the eggs. Prior to adding the eggs, mix one part substrate to 1.25 to 1.5 parts water. Do not cover eggs completely, leaving about half of each egg exposed. Incubate at 86° F (30°C).

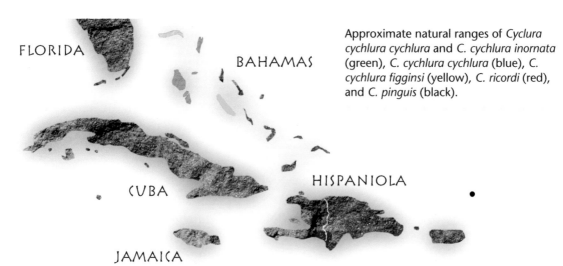

Approximate natural ranges of *Cyclura cychlura cychlura* and *C. cychlura inornata* (green), *C. cychlura cychlura* (blue), *C. cychlura figginsi* (yellow), *C. ricordi* (red), and *C. pinguis* (black).

FLORIDA

BAHAMAS

CUBA

HISPANIOLA

JAMAICA

The Grand Cayman blue iguana is critically endangered and may no longer exist outside of protected areas.

Cyclura lewisi Grant, 1940
Grand Cayman Blue Iguana/Blue Rock Iguana

Etymology: Named in honor of Charles Bernard Lewis, an American herpetologist who specialized in the study of Jamaican frogs and lizards. Chapman Grant, who founded the Herpetologists' League in 1936, named the species.

Range: Grand Cayman islands.

Maximum Size: 59.8 inches (1,520 mm)

References: Dorge (1996); Schwartz and Henderson (1991); www.cyclura.com.

Captive Suitability: 3

Natural History: Researchers call this critically endangered lizard the most endangered iguana on earth. Recent surveys put wild populations at 15 to 30 individuals, although captive propagation efforts have been successful in keeping total numbers much higher. Causes of extermination include habitat destruction and predation by feral animals, notably introduced rats and cats.

The success in breeding these animals is no doubt partly related to their beautiful blue coloring, making them highly desirable species with which to work. They are also considerably slimmer in aspect than other *Cyclura*, arguably making them the most striking of the rhinoceros iguanas.

These are huge lizards, growing to some 5 feet (1.5 m) in length and weighing in excess of 18 pounds (8.2 kg) as adults. The head is notably more elongated and depressed in shape than all other species of *Cyclura* except *C. nubila*. Blue iguanas are residents of dry scrub, where they are primarily terrestrial. Young iguanas, and to a lesser extent adults, may climb when in search of foods, including fruits, soft leaves, and flowers. Mating takes place in April through May, and females lay clutches of 2 to 20 eggs some 30 days later.

Captive Care: Same as for *Cyclura cychulra*.

Cyclura nubila Gray, 1831
Cayman Islands Iguana/Cuban Iguana

Etymology: (Latin) *nubilis*, cloudy or gloomy.

Range: Cuba and the Cayman islands.

Maximum Size: 59.8 inches (1,520 mm).

References: Blair (2004); Lemm and Alberts (1997); Schwartz and Henderson (1991); www.cyclura.com.

Captive Suitability: 4

Natural History: Three subspecies have been described: *Cyclura n. nubila* Gray, 1831 (the Cuban iguana, Cuba), *C. n. caymanensis* Barbour and Noble, 1916 (Little Cayman iguana, Little Cayman and Cayman Brac Islands; about 1,000 left in the wild), and *C. n. lewisi* Grant, 1940 (blue iguana, fewer than 100 left in the wild). The last is now generally regarded as having status as a full species. (See account of *C. lewisi* above.)

Cuban iguanas are found over a broad geographic area, and not surprisingly, they have access to and feed upon a greater variety of vegetation than other rhinoceros iguanas. They similarly occupy a variety of habitats, including mangrove forests, moist forests, and most commonly, xeric scrub forests with limestone outcrops and sandy soil.

Captive Care: Same as for *Cyclura cychlura*.

Female Cuban iguanas guard their nests for weeks. Some other rock iguanas do this as well.

177

Like the other *Cyclura*, *C. pinguis* serves as an important seed disperser on its native islands.

Cyclura pinguis Barbour, 1917
Anegada Island Iguana

Etymology: (Latin) *pingu*, stout.

Range: Anegada Island, British Virgin Islands. Regionally extinct on Puerto Rico; populations were established on the islands of Guana and Necker.

Maximum Size: 60 inches (1,524 mm)

References: Blair (2004); Schwartz and Henderson (1991); www.cyclura.com.

Captive Suitability: 3

Natural History: Similar to that of other rhinoceros iguanas, these lizards live in dry scrub habitats. It is estimated that only about 200 individuals are left in the wild. Decimation has followed the use of the islands for domestic animals (burros, cattle, goats, and sheep) and the presence of feral cats and dogs. Cats are the most serious predators, and government funding is being used to eradicate the feral felines from iguana habitats.

While adults feed largely on plant matter, hatchlings and young consume insects and may take carrion as regular food items. More than half the diet comprises fruits, including nance fruit (*Byrsonima*), sea grapes (*Coccoloba*), leaves and fruits of mangrove trees of the genus *Elaeodendron*, and myrtles (*Eugenia*).

Captive Care: Same as for *Cyclura cychulra*.

C. *ricordi* is the only rock iguana that overlaps in range with C. *cornuta*.

Cyclura ricordi Duméril and Bibron, 1837
Ricord's Iguana/Banded Rock Iguana

Etymology: Unknown.

Range: Hispaniola, in southwestern Dominican Republic.

Maximum Size: 39 inches (1,000 mm)

References: Blair (2004); Schwartz and Henderson (1991); www.cyclura.com.

Captive Suitability: 3

Natural History: Ricord's iguanas are now limited to six tiny sites in the southwestern portion of the southwestern Dominican Republic's most arid scrubland. Their range includes considerable variation, with two pronounced wet and dry seasons. They prefer loose sandy soils in which they can excavate long, deep burrows.

Females lay up to 18 eggs per clutch in burrows that they excavate, and young emerge in 95 to 100 days. Hatching generally coincides with the October rains.

The decline of populations is the result of extensive conversion of suitable habitat into agricultural land, coupled with predation by introduced mammals such as rats and cats. Contemporary surveys have documented about 1,500 remaining wild Ricord's iguanas.

Captive Care: Unknown. Captive management plans are in their infancy.

Genus *Iguana* Laurenti, 1768

The two members of the genus include one of the most familiar of all lizards. Green iguanas are perhaps the most widely sought lizards in the world, with their skin used for leather goods, the flesh and eggs eaten in many Latin American countries, and vast numbers harvested for export to the pet trades in North America, Europe, and Asia. So popular are green iguanas in the pet trade that they are the only lizard species listed by CITES documents as being traded in far greater numbers as live animals than as leather goods. In contrast, monitors and teiids are in far greater trade demand for their leather than as live pet or show specimens.

It is true that some iguanas, notably young lizards, will consume insects or the occasional small mammal as food, but the species are almost entirely herbivorous. Natural foods include leaves and fruits, particularly small berries.

Iguana delicatissima Laurenti, 1768
Lesser Antilles Iguana

Etymology: See family account; *delicatissima*, Latin superlative for "most delicate."
Range: The islands of the Lesser Antilles, southeastern Caribbean, including (north to south) Anguilla, St. Maarten, St. Barthelemey, St. Eustatius, Guadeloupe, Dominica, and Martinique.
Maximum Size: 60 inches (1,522 mm)

The Lesser Antilles iguana is declining in numbers due to a number of factors, including hybridization and competition from feral green iguanas.

References: Blair (2004); Schwartz and Henderson (1991).
Captive Suitability: 3
Natural History: Very poorly known but reportedly similar to that for *Iguana iguana*. They differ from the far more wide-ranging green iguanas in that they lack the large scale beneath the ear, are more gracile in build, and have a shorter set of dorsal spines. They are known to be very adaptable to the conditions on the small islands they inhabit, living in forests, cactus and rock flatlands, and dry grasslands. They feed on a variety of plant

Feral male green iguana eating leaves on the edge of a Florida lawn. This species has become established in many areas outside its natural range.

materials, notably the fruits of the prickly pear cactus (*Opuntia*), other soft plants, large insects, and small vertebrates. Mating occurs in spring, and eggs are laid in August through October. According to Day, Breuil, and Reichling (www. iucn-isg.org/actionplan/ch2/lesserantillean.php), "There are localized [population] decreases as a result of habitat loss and hunting, but at present these pressures affect a small percentage of the range within each island. In all other cases, populations are believed to be decreasing due to a combination of habitat loss and fragmentation, introduced predators, browsing competitors, or hybridization with common iguanas."

Captive Care: Same as for *Iguana iguana* but requires less moisture and lower humidity levels.

Iguana iguana Linnaeus, 1758
Green Iguana

Etymology: See family account.

Range: Broadly distributed from forested areas of Sinaloa in northern Mexico south into Uruguay and Paraguay, primarily in lowland (to 3,300 feet [1,000 m]) forests. The species has also been transported by human activity and has established colonies in Florida, Bali, Hawaii, and probably other tropical localities.

Maximum Size: 72 inches (1,829 mm).

References: Alberts et al. (2004); Avila-Peres (1995);

Bernard (1996); Blair (2004); Burghardt and Rand (1982); De Vosjoli (1998); Gasc (1980); Hudson et al. (1994); Kiat (2007); Mazorlig (2004); Obst et al. (1988); Savage (2002); Zimmermann (1983).

Captive Suitability: 3

Natural History: Green iguanas have a huge geographical range and occur in almost any habitats that have trees and at least some degree of water. Consequently, there is considerable variation in scalation and coloration. Adults may vary from bright lime green with gunmetal blue crossbands to animals that are predominantly orange with gray and tan markings. Although numerous field studies have focused on ecology, behavior, and reproduction of iguanas, systematic studies are largely nonexistent. It is possible, if not probable, that "the" green iguana is a mosaic of several similar species.

Adult iguanas are predominantly arboreal, spending time in trees where they can forage for soft leaves and flowers that form much of their diet. Females come to the ground to excavate a deep nest into which eggs are laid, then return to the trees. Juveniles are also arboreal but differ from adults in that they sometimes include insects in their diets. At any age, these lizards can run well and climb and swim with considerable agility. Although often disinclined to bite, some iguanas–possibly representing distinct populations–are aggressive and may rush and bite a keeper. Males are normally very territorial and do not do well if housed within sight of other males. Aggressive displays include head bobbing and violent tail lashing.

Iguanas are amazingly **vagile** (able to move and colonize with ease) creatures, showing up on the

Male green iguanas engaged in territorial combat. Never house male iguanas together in one enclosure.

mainland and many offshore islands. Their size makes them a much sought food item by many local peoples, and they are, in some places, the alternative to chicken. Both eggs and meat from the adults are eaten. Iguanas are also heavily hunted for their skins, which make a fair leather product; for making stuffed tourist souvenirs; and for the live animal trade. In some places, iguanas are commercially harvested, while in others only wild animals are taken.

Mating takes place at varying times, but egg laying follows some 35 to 45 days later. Females excavate deep nests in moist soil, then pack soil firmly over the eggs once they are laid. There may

Female green iguana laying eggs in a nesting box made from a kitchen garbage can.

be from 10 to 63 eggs per clutch, and hatching occurs in 70 to 80 days.

Captive Care: There has probably been more written about the care of iguanas than for any ten other lizards combined. This wealth of information spans the gamut, from abysmally inaccurate to extremely useful. Much (but most certainly not all) of the varying opinions and different husbandry methods reflect the rather catholic tastes of iguanas, in that they are capable of adapting to a variety of habitats, temperature ranges, and diets. I have known adult iguanas kept on an "Italian" diet of cooked plain pasta, chopped zucchini, and vegetable pizza and others fed a combination of assorted leafy greens, cooked carrots, and canned dog food, to apparently no ill effect. Others were thriving when offered nothing more than iceberg and romaine lettuce salads. While I doubt that any of those regimens was especially proper, I also cannot discount the fact that many iguanas are successfully maintained in unorthodox ways. Possibly this very reality contributes to their continued popularity: They may be as adaptable as their keepers are eccentric.

A more acceptable diet should include mostly a mixture of leafy green vegetables along with some fruits and other vegetables. Provide some combination of sweet potatoes, kernel corn, chopped beets, kale, collard greens, zucchini, pumpkin and other winter squash, dandelions, green beans, melons, and berries. The use of a dietary mineral supplement is often recommended. Iguanas should always have a large dish of clean drinking water available, and a container that is large enough to allow the lizard to immerse itself completely is advised.

These large lizards are diurnal and require both heat and intense full-spectrum light, as well as sufficient shaded cover. Daytime temperatures should range from 75 to 100°F (23.9 to 37.8°C) and lower at night to 68 to 84°F (20 to 28.9°C). Daily exposure to UVA and UVB is critical to successful iguana keeping.

Iguanas, although universally available in the pet trade, are not lizards for the novice. Young iguanas–those under 5.5 inches (1,829 mm) SVL–are notoriously difficult to raise unless in the care of an experienced keeper.

Tupinambis merianae

8

SCINCOMORPHA

To this superfamily belong the majority of known lizard species, including several hundred skinks, the teiids, Africa's plated and armadillo lizards, and some smaller and specialized groups. These lizards generally have strong scales that contain bony reinforcements called **osteoderms**. Many species have highly polished, shiny scales, but others have strongly keeled scales and spines. Most scincomorphs have a conspicuous parietal eye, although many species are not primarily diurnal. Morphology of scincomorphs runs the lizard gamut, ranging from species with large and well-developed legs and digits to completely limbless burrowers. Most have autotomous tails. Many species produce live young in lieu of laying eggs.

Family Teiidae Gray, 1827

Teiids (pronounced "tee-ids") are strictly American lizards that extend from the central United States into southern South America. They range in size from small racerunners (*Aspidoscelis* and *Cnemidophorus*) to caiman lizards and tegus (*Dracaena* and *Tupinambis*). Limbs and digits are well developed, and autotomy is present. Ventral scales are arranged in symmetrical columns and rows and are generally much larger than dorsal and lateral scales. Reproduction is by egg. Giants of the family resemble the Old World monitors, complete

The black tegu (*Tupinambis teguixin*) is the largest lizard in the superfamily Scincomorpha. It can reach a length of 56 inches (1,425 mm).

with strong bodies, long forked tongues, and predatory habits. Despite superficial similarities, though, teiids are not closely related to monitors. Their closest relatives are the Old World lacertids (Lacertidae), from which teiids may be distinguished in that they have an upper temporal arch and solid bony tooth bases. There are four genera of giant teiids.

Genus *Callopistes* Gravenhorst, 1838

There are only two species in this genus of streamlined, active, predatory teiids. Only one, the false monitor, is a giant, but it is one of the largest American lizards found in arid habitats. The genus name is from the Greek word καλωπιστικ–ς, *kallopistikos*, meaning "ornamental."

Callopistes flavipunctatus (Duméril and Bibron, 1839)
False Monitor/Monitor Tegu
Etymology: (Latin) *flavus*, yellow, plus *punctatus*, spotted.

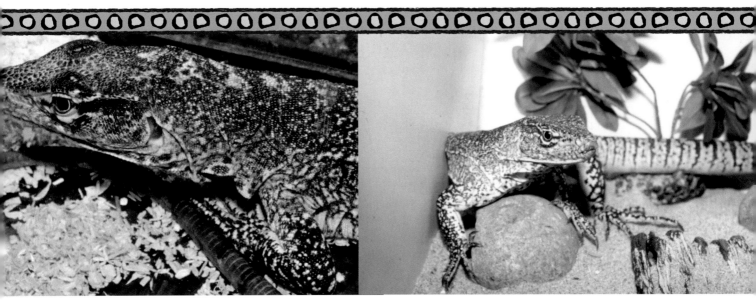

False monitors are very poorly known animals that occasionally drift into the herp hobby. They often fare poorly in captivity, and there are no known captive breedings.

Range: Dry habitats in Ecuador and Peru.

Maximum Size: 39.6 inches (1,006 mm)

References: There is very little published information available for this species, except the type description and a few papers describing teiid lizard sperm structure and evolution.

Captive Suitability: 3

Natural History: Poorly known. This species lives in arid, rocky areas where it is a formidable predator that preys upon smaller animals. Habitat includes arid semi-desert and scrubland and dry, rocky valleys. The species was once assigned to the genus *Teiovaranus*, meaning "monitor tegu," in reference to the marked similarities between this lizard and many monitors. It was later transferred to *Callopistes*.

Captive Care: Little information is available, but captives can be cared for in the manner prescribed for the tegus. These lizards tend to be somewhat aggressive and will typically (but not always) attempt to bite a handler. They may first engage in a display of inflating the body and hissing loudly, but sometimes they merely lunge at a perceived aggressor.

These large lizards require very warm daytime temperatures in excess of 90°F (32.2°C). Humidity should be 40 to 50 percent. Water may be taken from a dish but is generally obtained from dew droplets and from foods. False monitors of all sizes will take live foods, from crickets and roaches to mice and small lizards to small rats. They will also take moistened solid dog food, monkey chow, and lean raw beef strips. These lizards are excellent burrowers, and if given a large enough enclosure, should have adequate substrate to allow extensive digging. House males separately.

Crocodilurus amazonicus is a primarily aquatic species that feeds heavily on frogs.

Genus *Crocodilurus* Spix, 1825

There is but a single species in this genus. Live specimens are rarely imported, although the skin is collected for use in the leather goods trade. The genus name comes from the Greek κροκ δειλος, *crocodilos*, crocodile, plus ουρα, *ura*, meaning "tail."

Crocodilurus amazonicus Spix, 1825
Crocodile-Tailed Tegu/Jacarerana

Etymology: Latinized term for "of the Amazon."
Range: Amazonia, including Brazil, Guiana, Peru, Venezuela, and far eastern Columbia.
Maximum Size: 26 inches (654 mm), possibly longer
References: Avila-Peres (1995); Martins (2006); Massary and Hoogmoed (2001).
Captive Suitability: 2

Natural History: Very poorly known. The species is largely aquatic, living along riverbanks. Its ecology and behavior are presumably similar to that of *Dracaena*. They have been observed in swamps and along forest streams and narrow rivers, almost always in or within a few yards (meters) of water. Although they are expert swimmers, they are wary of deep water and stay close to the shoreline. During the wet season, when the forest floods, they forage almost exclusively in the water. They feed primarily on frogs but presumably consume any prey items–large insects, small fishes, frogs, and small mammals–that they can find and overpower. Other species include prawns, small crabs, large insects, and spiders.

When handled, crocodile-tailed tegus emit a croaking sound. Some researchers believe the sounds might accompany mating or establishing territories.

Previously known as *Crocodilurus lacertinus* Daudin, 1802 (Massary and Hoogmoed, 2001).
Captive Care: This species is almost never encountered in captivity outside of South America. The few observations and photos available have come from a handful of zoo specimens. It is possible that the species reaches 36 inches (91.4 cm) in total length, but such reports have not been confirmed.

Genus *Dracaena* Daudin, 1802

This is a genus of two large and largely aquatic species. The caiman lizard has shown up in the live animal trade from time to time but so infrequently that it generally commands a hefty price. Caiman lizards have enlarged dorsal scales and a pair of rows of crocodile-like scales that run from the nape and along the length of the tail– hence the name. (Caimans are South American alligators.) Like many South American giant lizards, these species are collected primarily–and in tremendous numbers–for their leather. The genus name is a diminutive form of the Latin *Draco* and refers to a small dragon.

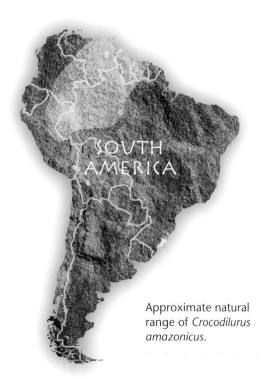

Approximate natural range of *Crocodilurus amazonicus*.

Dracaena guianensis Daudin, 1802
Caiman Lizard

Etymology: (Latin) meaning "from Guiana."
Range: Riparian habitats along the Amazonian drainage, from Columbia east to coastal Brazil.
Maximum Size: 49.9 inches (1,268 mm), possibly larger
References: Avila-Peres (1995); Dalrymple (1979); Duellman (2005); Goulding (1989); Häberle (1974); Norman (1994); Rehak (1999); Vance (1980); Vanzolini and Valencia (1965).
Captive Suitability: 2
Natural History: Almost nothing is known about this brightly marked species in the wild. It is found along riverbanks, where it may lie basking

189

Caiman lizards spend much of their time basking on limbs overhanging bodies of water. They enter the water to forage and to escape danger.

on branches over the water. At the first sign of danger, the lizard drops into the water and may remain submerged for several minutes. They are also common in areas of dense aquatic vegetation, a preferred habitat of anacondas. Although noted for their ability to crush and eat snails, caiman lizards also feed on small animals (invertebrate and vertebrate) and eggs that they find while foraging in trees (Goulding, 1989). Natural foods include shrimps, crabs, clams, tadpoles, spiders, frogs, small lizards and snakes, and small mammals.

Captive Care: This species needs a particularly large terrarium because it is a tree climber that dives into the water. When not foraging on land or basking on a branch, it will be in the water, often lying submerged for several minutes. Provide an intense heat source above one basking site, and allow the daytime basking temperature to reach 105 to 115°F (40.6 to 46.1°C). Areas not under basking lamps should have filtered light; use plants and natural cover to provide the right effect. There must be a large pool in which lizards can bask and swim.

Caiman lizards, like tegus, may become docile in captivity if handled regularly and properly. However, the incredible strength of their jaws makes the possible bite potentially dangerous, so handle them with extreme care.

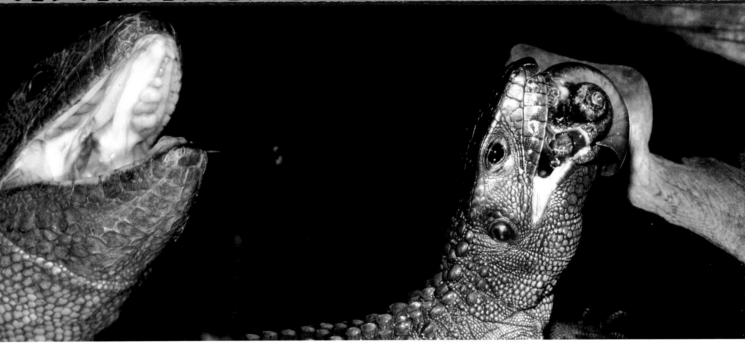

As they grow, caiman lizards develop rounded teeth (left) suitable for crushing the shells of mollusks and crustaceans, their major foods.

Caiman lizards are relatively rare in captivity, having appeared on dealers' lists only since about 1994. Captive breeding has been reported in a few zoos and large collections, but availability of captive-bred lizards is still the exception. Recently imported individuals are routinely dehydrated, stressed, parasitized, and injured. I suggest that all wild-caught specimens be taken to the veterinarian promptly and then kept in strict quarantine for at least two months.

Although they eat a greater variety of foods than just shellfish, it is probable that a diet heavy in shellfish is beneficial and perhaps necessary for proper tooth development and general health.

Approximate natural range of *Dracaena guianensis* (yellow) and *D.paraguayensis* (red).

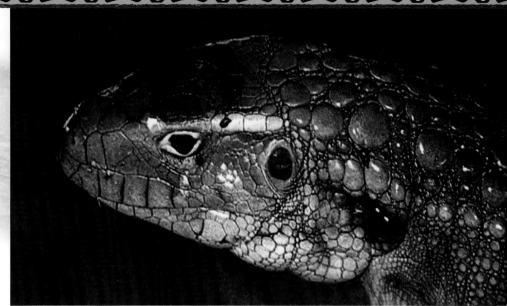

Very little is known about the southern caiman lizard. It inhabits drier habitats than the more commonly seen northern species of caiman lizard.

Dracaena paraguayensis Amaral, 1950
Southern Caiman Lizard

Etymology: (Latin) meaning "from Paraguay."

Range: The lower Amazonian drainage, including extreme southern Brazil and Paraguay.

Maximum Size: Unknown but presumably near 36.9 inches (936 mm)

References: Dalrymple (1979); Norman (1994); Vanzolini and Valencia (1965).

Captive Suitability: 2

Natural History: Very poorly known. This species more closely resembles *Crocodilurus amazonicus* than the other species of *Dracaena* in coloring. The head and body are uniformly pale golden brown, sometimes with a few scattered dark brown dorsal and lateral markings. The head scales are comparatively larger than those of *D. guianensis*. Although largely aquatic, *D. paraguayensis* is also found in drier habitats than *D. guianensis*.

It is unfortunate that this species, which is probably widely harvested by leather traders for its skin, is so poorly known as a living animal. In Portuguese, this lizard is known as "víbora," which means "viper."

Captive Care: Unknown, presumably same as for *Dracaena guianensis*.

KEY TO THE SPECIES OF TEGUS, GENUS *TUPINAMBIS*

1a	No row of small scales separates the mental scale from infralabials; a single loreal scale is present.	2
1b	A row of small scales separates the mental scale from the infralabials; two loreal scales are present	4
2a	More than 20 femoral pores present	*Tupinambis longilineus*
2b	18 or fewer femoral pores present	3
3a	One to three light stripes along the back and sides	*Tupinambis quadrilineatus*
3b	No stripes on the sides of the dorsum	*Tupinambis teguixin*
4a	Neck scales subequal in size to dorsals; 123 or more dorsal scale rows	*Tupinambis merianae*
4b	Neck scales much larger than dorsals; 103 or fewer dorsal scale rows	*Tupinambis rufescens*

Genus *Tupinambis* Daudin, 1803

To this genus belong the five species of true tegus, monitor-like lizards endemic to South America. They are readily distinguished from the true Old World monitors in that the tegus possess enlarged upper head and labial scales, shiny scales, femoral pores, and ventral scales that are larger than dorsal and lateral scales and arranged in rows. Like monitors, tegus have elongated snouts, powerful limbs, and long, protrusible bifid tongues. Tegu tongues are considerably broader than those of monitor lizards. They are diurnal and active foraging predators. Tegus are oviparous.

In South America, tegus are seen as pests because of their habit of entering farms and eating chickens and eggs. They are widely sought for the leather trade, which is a leading factor in the reduction of their numbers in the wild. Fortunately, professional breeders have repeatedly succeeded in getting some tegu species to reproduce in captivity.

Argentine tegu eating a melon. This species consumes a significant quantity of fruit; feeding them fruit can stimulate breeding (Langerwerf, pers. comm.)

Tupinambis longilineus Avila-Peres, 1995
Striped Tegu

Etymology: (Latin) *longi*, long, and *linea*, lined.

Range: The southwestern Brazilian states of Rondonia and Amazonas.

Maximum Size: 48.4 inches (1,230 mm)

References: Avila-Peres (1995); Fitzgerald et al. (1999); Kohler and Langerwerf (2000).

Captive Suitability: 4

Natural History: Poorly known. The striped tegu is most similar to the black tegu (*T. teguixin*), from which it differs in that it has a rectangular (versus oval) body in cross section, long, thin limbs, and lateral stripes instead of bands on the dorsum.

Captive Care: Presumably same as for *T. teguixin*.

Approximate natural range of *Tupinambis longilineus*.

Pair of Argentine tegus mating. Breeding activity begins about a month after the lizards emerge from hibernation.

Tupinambis merianae (Duméril and Bibron, 1839)
Black Tegu/Argentine Tegu/Giant Tegu

Etymology: Named for Maria Sibylla Merian (1647-1717), extraordinary natural history artist noted for some of the earliest realistic representations of animals and plants in print. There is an excellent biography of Merian by Sharon Valiant in the December 1992 *Natural History*.

Range: Southern Amazonian Brazil south to northern Argentina, Bolivia, Uruguay, and Paraguay.

Maximum Size: 51.2 inches (1,300 mm)

References: Avila-Peres (1995); Canepuccia (2000); Fitzgerald et al. (1999); Kohler and Langerwerf (2000); Langerwerf at www.agamainternational.com.

Captive Suitability: 4

Natural History: This species was long also known as *Tupinambis nigropunctatus* (which means "black spotted"). Although similar to the Columbian

tegu, the Argentine species can readily be distinguished with its two (versus one) loreal scales, small bead-like (versus smooth, skink-like) scales, and a distinct pale dorsolateral line from the nape to the tail on each side of the body. A resident of grasslands, particularly near permanent fresh water sources such as rivers and lakes, this species runs, digs, swims, and burrows well but is disinclined to climb.

Argentine tegus have a considerable southern distribution and are among the most cold tolerant of the giant lizards. Tegus hibernate from late March or April until August, after which they engage in heavy feeding for several weeks. As they gain mass, young males develop the enlarged mandibular region that distinguishes them from adult females. Mating occurs from September through January, and eggs are deposited in deep burrows excavated by females. The burrows may be partially filled with moist leaves and grasses,

Argentine tegu eggs in nest the mother made in an outdoor enclosure (left). Most breeders incubate the eggs in incubators, and they hatch in 45 to 75 days (right). The head and forequarters of the hatchlings are bright green, but this coloration fades in a few months.

presumably to maintain humidity levels. The 20 to 25 eggs hatch after 45 to 75 days.

When alarmed, tegus may raise the body on stiffened limbs, open the mouth, and issue a series of short loud hisses. If a potential predator comes too close, the tegu may use its stout tail as a lash and with considerable effect. If all else fails, a tegu may lunge and bite an attacker, and the strong jaws make any such bite potentially very painful.

Captive Care: Keep this large and active species in a large terrarium that's at least four times the length of the lizard and one and a half times as wide. They are very active animals that will damage all but the most solid of terrarium accessories, such as rocks, logs, and plastic or concrete water containers. Because of their digging activity, provide either enough substrate to allow a burrow to be constructed or no substrate except a thin layer of rodent chow, paper, or similar easy-to-clean material.

Keep daytime summer temperatures at 86 to 95°F (30 to 35°C), and allow a nighttime drop of 10 to 15°F (5.6 to 8.3°C). Lizards may be hibernated for two to four months if desired. After hibernation, tegus will need consistent high temperatures and large quantities of live or freshly killed animal foods. Provide a varied diet of insects, small rodents, canned cat or dog food, vegetables, and fruits after about three weeks of posthibernation diet.

Tegus are not aquatic but will retreat to a pool of water to drink and cool the body. They are also likely to pass wastes into pools, so the water source must be cleaned regularly.

Tupinambis quadrilineatus Manzani and Abe, 1997
Four-Lined Tegu

Etymology: (Latin) *quadri*, four, and *linea*, lined.
Range: West central Brazil.
Maximum Size: 30.2 inches (768 mm)
References: Avila-Peres (1995); Colli et al. (1998);
Fitzgerald et al. (1999); Kohler and Langerwerf
(2000); Manzani and Abe (1997).
Captive Suitability: 4
Natural History: This species was described by Brazilian
researchers in 1997 and again, in error, in 1998,
as *Tupinambis cerradensis*. Because of the rules of
nomenclatural priority, the earlier name is correct.
Captive Care: Presumably same as for the black tegu
(*T. teguixin*). This species does not qualify as a
giant lizard, but because it is often confused with
other tegu species, it is included for identification
purposes.

Adult male red tegu. The males are often redder than the females.

Approximate natural range of *T. quadrilineatus* (red) and *T. merianae* (yellow).

Tupinambis rufescens (Günther, 1871)
Red Tegu/ Golden Tegu

Etymology: (Latin) *rufescens*, red.
Range: Northern Argentina, Paraguay, and the
southern half of Brazil.
Maximum Size: 48.4 inches (1,230 mm)
References: Balsai (1997); Fitzgerald et al. (1999);
Hurt (1995); Kohler and Langerwerf (2000);
Norman (1994); Obst et al. (1988).
Captive Suitability: 4
Natural History: This is a truly wonderful species
of large lizard, for it comes in two extremely
distinct color varieties. One is predominantly
a golden tan marbled on a black background
(formerly named *Tupinambis duseni*), while the
other replaces red for the gold. These are large

197

There are two color varieties of the red tegu. On the left is a young red tegu of the common red form, and on the right is a hatchling of the more rarely seen golden form.

and bold lizards that have been reported stealing into chicken houses to feed on the fowl and their eggs. They are hunted for their meat and skin, which makes a highly sought source of leather for women's fashions.

Red and gold tegus are among the most spectacular large lizards. Although their coloration in captive settings seems intense, they actually blend in quite well with the rock and soil types in the arid habitats in which they are found. Red tegus are found in semi-desert areas with rocky arroyos, fallen trees, or other plentiful cover. Living farther south than any other *Tupinambis*, red tegus are able to tolerate much lower temperatures than their relatives. However, when daytime temperatures dip below 70°F (21.1°C), the lizards may retreat to a deep burrow or cave in rocks to prepare for hibernation. During the summer months, though, they prefer very warm temperatures.

This species, if healthy, is stockier than other tegus. Males have very broad heads and large jowls.

Captive Care: Care is similar to that required by black tegus (*T. teguixin*), with some modifications. Red tegus need lower humidity, higher daytime temperatures (provide a high-intensity basking site in a small portion of the terrarium that may reach 120°F [48.9°C]), and more airflow. Don't let red tegus stifle in completely solid-walled vivariums.

Provide a diet of large insects, cooked eggs, and appropriately sized rodents. Supplement with fruits such as apples, cantaloupe, and grapes. Feed adults three to four times weekly, and feed young lizards daily.

Black tegu photographed on Trinidad. This species ranges over most of northern South America.

Tupinambis teguixin (Linnaeus, 1758)
Black Tegu/Gold Tegu/Black and White Tegu/Jacuaru

Etymology: From an Amazonian tribal word for "large lizard."

Range: The northern half of South America south to Sao Paulo, Brazil.

Maximum Size: 56 inches (1,425 mm)

References: Avila-Peres (1995); Balsai (1997); Fitzgerald et al. (1999); Kohler and Langerwerf (2000); Langerwerf (1995); Langerwerf and Paris (1998); Norman (1994); Sprackland (1992).

Captive Suitability: 4

Natural History: Also known as the Colombian tegu and the Venezuelan tegu, this species is widely hunted throughout its range because it is both a source of leather and because it is South America's equivalent of the fox. Raids on chicken farms cost local people many eggs and birds. If caught, the lizards are themselves occasionally destined for the cooking pot.

Large tegus are terrestrial animals that are active predators, foragers, and scavengers. Their diet is extremely broad, taking in a great variety of invertebrates (insects, snails, spiders, worms) and vertebrates (birds, eggs, small mammals, other reptiles, frogs), as well as animal carcasses and leftovers from human meals. They will also feed on snakes, including some of the smaller venomous species. Because of their fondness for these items, they are commonly found around human settlements where trash, chickens, and eggs are in abundance. They are difficult to capture, though, because even large tegus are

199

Black tegus have variable personalities and strong jaws. Use thick gloves if you must handle one that appears aggressive or nervous.

Approximate natural range of *Tupinambis teguixin* (yellow) and *T. rufescens* (red).

extremely wary. The appearance of a human several dozen yards (m) away will generally cause a tegu to flee, at great speed, for cover.

Tegus are excellent at digging, running, and swimming, and young animals also climb well. They excavate burrows in slightly moist or clay-based soils and use the burrows as retreats from the sun and to lay eggs. A burrow may be several yards (m) in length. Black tegus prefer high humidity, in excess of 80 percent.

Jaw muscles in tegus are quite strong, allowing them to overpower many prey species, crack

eggs, and break small bones in carrion. Males have noticeable enlarged jaw muscles that, in adults, take on the appearance of jowls.

Captive Care: Similar to that of the Argentine tegu (*Tupinambis merianae*). These are comparatively intelligent lizards that will often become used to a schedule–they will expect to be fed at certain times and at a certain place. They are also very variable in temperament. In my early years, I kept adult specimens that roamed freely around my rooms, knew where food and water dishes were located, and were docile enough to allow handling. Other specimens may be quite aggressive, engaging in hissing, tail lashing, and biting. If a tegu bites, it often holds on and may attempt to twist. The late veteran lizard breeder Bert Langerwerf suggested that if you want a tegu that can be safely handled, you should obtain a young specimen and handle it regularly.

A tegu is a hardy animal that can live for many years–ten or more are possible–if well cared for. They will accept a wide variety of foods, including snails, crickets, locusts, and young mice (for young tegus), and mice or rats, boiled eggs, canned dog food, sausages, and chicks as adults.

Albino blue tegu. The true identity of blue tegus is puzzling–they could be a new species or a variety of *T. teguixin* or *T. merianae*.

Varanus salvadorii

9

ANGUIMORPHA

Sheltopusik photographed in the Balkans. The species ranges from this area to central Asia.

The Anguimorpha includes two superfamilies, the Diploglossa and Varanoidea. The term "anguimorph" comes from the Latin for "snake bodied" and refers to the many limbless and quite serpentine taxa in the superfamily Diploglossa. The two superfamilies are quite distinct in external appearance, and we must examine primarily internal skeletal and musculature features to understand their affinities. All species, however, possess opaque moving eyelids, round pupils, and ventral scales that form longitudinal series.

Superfamily Diploglossa

Diploglossans include American alligator lizards, legless lizards, xenosaurs, slow worms, galliwasps, and the Chinese crocodile lizard. Among the characteristics they share are a broad short protrusible tongue with a nicked tip, moveable opaque eyelids, and hard shiny scales. They are found on all continents except Africa, Australia, and Antarctica.

Family Anguidae

The Anguidae is distributed across the Northern Hemisphere and South America but is absent from Africa, Madagascar, and Australia. The name anguis is Latin for "snake" and refers to the small, limbless slow worms (*Anguis fragilis*) of Europe. Other limbless, as well as limb-reduced, species occur throughout the family's range and include the North American glass lizards (*Ophisaurus*) and Eurasian sheltopusik (*Ophisaurus apodus*). It is mainly among the limbless anguids that we find species that approach 1 yard (1 m) in length. Anguids have the power of caudal autotomy. Most species lay eggs, but several produce live young.

Although sheltopusiks are capable of eating rodents, they do best on a varied diet of arthropods, snails, and the occasional mouse.

Genus *Ophisaurus* Daudin, 1803

Members of this genus are known variously as glass lizards, snake lizards, or sheltopusiks. The body is elongated and protected by hard shiny scales. Eyelids, broad and barely nicked tongues, and external ear openings easily distinguish them from snakes, as does the extremely long tail. Found in temperate habitats across the northern hemisphere, including North America, Europe, and Asia.

Ophisaurus apodus (Pallas, 1775)
Sheltopusik

Etymology: *Ophisaurus* comes from the Greek ωφι, *ophi-*, snake, and σαυρω, *sauros*, lizard. *Apodus* comes from Latin *a-*, without, and *pod-*, foot. "Sheltopusik" is Russian and means "yellow belly."
Range: Eurasia from central Europe east through the Urals and central Russia.

Maximum Size: 57.8 inches (1,470 mm)
References: Campbell (1990); Obst et al. (1988).
Captive Suitability: 3
Natural History: The sheltopusik is a large-scaled lizard that looks like an armored snake. Although long known to Europeans and Asians, there has been relatively little fieldwork done on this species. There is no external sexual dimorphism.

Natural diet consists primarily of snails, slugs, and worms. Occasionally the sheltopusik may also consume small lizards, snakes (including vipers, whose fangs cannot penetrate the armored scales), and small rodents.

Autotomy is present, but regrown tails are poor copies of the original. Sheltopusiks are reluctant to drop the tail and will twist and bite a potential attacker rather than drop their tail and flee.

Mating occurs shortly after the lizards emerge from winter hibernation, from mid-March

BREEDING SHELTOPUSIKS, *OPHISAURUS APODUS*

By Bert Langerwerf

The sheltopusik is so different from other species of *Ophisaurus* (e.g., in having keeled scales and a very slow rate of tail regeneration) that it is sometimes given a genus name of its own, *Pseudopus* Blanford, 1876, with only one species, *Pseudopus apodus*.

The large natural range of this species contains a variety of habitats that roughly get drier to the east. The animals have adapted to this and choose the driest places in the habitat on the Balkans, while choosing the wetter places in western Asia. The table shows some important climatological data for several locales within the range.

	LOCATION	HOURS OF SUN/ DAY	LOWEST RECORDED TEMP. F (C)	AVERAGE LOW TEMP. F (C)	AVERAGE HIGH TEMP. F (C)	AVERAGE PRECIPITATION/ MONTH. INCH (CM)
JANUARY	Ankara (Turkey)	3	-13 (-25)	24 (-4.4)	39 (3.9)	1.3 (3.3)
	Ashgabat (Turkmenistan)	4	-9 (-22.8)	25 (-3.9)	38 (3.3)	1.0 (2.5)
	Thessaloniki (Greece)	4	13 (-10.6)	35 (1.7)	49 (9.4)	1.7 (4.3)
JULY	Ankara (Turkey)	12	44 (6.7)	59 (15)	86 (30)	0.5 (1.3)
	Ashgabat (Turkmenistan)	12	49 (9.4)	71 (21.7)	97 (36.1)	0.1 (0.3)
	Thessaloniki (Greece)	12	58 (14.4)	70 (21.1)	90 (32.2)	0.9 (2.3)

A climate comparable to Salt Lake City, Utah, is acceptable for sheltopusiks. Therefore, this lizard may be kept in outdoor vivaria in many parts of the U.S. In the southeast, you have to cover the hibernation terrariums with plastic to keep them dry enough. In the northern parts of the country, the lizards may be kept in unheated greenhouses. For breeding, they need to hibernate every year. They will go into hibernation at the start of October and emerge between mid-March and mid-April, depending on the latitude and climate of your locale.

It is not easy to recognize the sexes. One can try to evert the hemipenes; otherwise, males have longer tails compared to SVL than females. Males also tend to have slightly larger heads.

Eggs are always laid in a dugout burrow in loose soil under a large flat stone.

Females stay with the eggs to protect them. The number of eggs per clutch ranges from 5 to 12. On one occasion, I found two females protecting their communal eggs. The longest egg was 2.2 by 0.9 inches (55 by 22 mm), and a normal-sized egg was 1.8 by 0.9 inches (45 by 22 mm). Eggs were incubated at around 80°F (26.7°C) in moist sand and hatched 57 to 68 days later. Babies had a TL of about 9 inches (22.9 cm), while SVL was near 3.6 inches (9.1 cm). Baby sheltopusiks have a nice bluish-gray color with oblique olive-colored bands. This nice coloration fades gradually and is lost within a year. According to Russian literature, they reach sexual maturity in nature in their fourth year.

In nature, the most frequently eaten prey are slugs, snails, and beetles. In captivity, they eat pinky mice and rats, crickets, roaches, superworms and mealworms. They are very opportunistic, also taking bird eggs, young birds, small lizards, and small snakes. Once in the Netherlands, I noticed that one sheltopusik accidentally ate a fire salamander (*Salamandra salamandra*) without any ill effects, even though fire salamanders contain strong poison.

Their terrarium should have some bushes and a large flat stone upon soft soil. Lizards like to climb in bushes and to hide and make burrows under stones. An outdoor terrarium for a breeding pair could be 100 sq. feet (9.3 sq. m). A 4- by 4-foot (1.2- by 1.2-m) terrarium will do indoors, but don't expect much breeding in such a confined space.

Mating sheltopusiks. Like many other lizards (and snakes), the male bites the female on the nape while mating.

through early May. Females will lay up to 12 eggs under rotting logs, wooden debris, or rocks or other humidity-retaining cover. The eggs hatch after some 30 to 50 days, producing silver and black mottled young. This unusual coloring fades after about two years, when the lizards take on the ochre dorsal and pale yellow ventral coloration.

This species is sometimes called *Pseudopus apodus*, but taxonomists do not universally accept the name. The name *Ophisaurus* Daudin 1803 predates *Pseudopus* Merrem 1820, so the question revolves around whether the sheltopusik deserves a genus distinct from other "glass" lizards. Several contemporary authors consider the genera distinct enough to place the sheltopusik in *Pseudopus*. Some authors recognize three subspecies: *Ophisaurus apodus apodus* of the Caucasus and central Asia; *O. a. durvilli* of south-central Asia; and *O. a. thracius* of Europe, North Africa, and the Middle East.

Captive Care: A hardy but rarely kept lizard, the sheltopusik has a reputation for both extreme docility and a life span in captivity of 20 years or more. Provide sheltopusiks with a large terrarium filled with branches and rocks over which they may climb and bask. The lizards tolerate a range of humidity and temperatures. In the wild, they hibernate between October and March or April, so a cooling period is recommended.

Feed lizards three or four times per week, including small rodents, lizards, snails, slugs, worms, shrimp, and moistened chunk dog food in the diet.

Superfamily Varanoidea

Varanoids are lizards that share a host of characteristics, including a long protrusible bifid tongue, four well-developed limbs with five clawed digits on each, loss of caudal autotomy, moveable opaque eyelids, an elongated snout, and reproduction by eggs. Varanoids are found in North and Central America, Africa, Asia, and Australia, with fossils also known from Europe. There are three living genera (*Heloderma*, *Lanthanotus*, and *Varanus*) placed in two or three families, depending on authority.

Family Helodermatidae Gray, 1837

These are stout-bodied lizards of the arid regions of southern North America and Central America as far south as Guatemala. The tail is thick in well-fed individuals, serving as a fat reservoir. External ear openings are present, and there is no pineal eye. Helodermatids are crepuscular and primarily terrestrial in habits. The two living species in this family were long considered unique in being the only venomous lizards known. Their delivery system for venom, though, remains the most complex among living lizards. Unlike the venom apparatus of snakes, where toxin is pumped from an upper lip gland down through enlarged teeth in the upper jaw, helodermatids have both the glands and grooved teeth in the lower jaw. Furthermore, the lower teeth are not true fangs but are merely grooved, allowing venom to mix with saliva and flow into a wound. Because venom is passively rather than actively transferred, the lizard must maintain a strong grip until prey begins to succumb.

From this description and the ominous name given to the northern species as Gila monster, the lizards have gotten a reputation far more severe than is warranted by reality. Few people are ever bitten by the animals, and while those bitten suffer excruciating pain, human fatalities are extremely rare. Most deaths associated with Gila monster bites occurred in people who were also alcoholically intoxicated; alcohol exacerbates envenomation, for with increased heart rate comes quicker dispersal of venom throughout the body. There are no validated records of human fatalities caused by Mexican beaded lizard bites. Venom is principally neurotoxic, and a bite victim may have difficulty in breathing. The greatest risk of severe or fatal bites is in children and the aged. Nevertheless, *these are venomous animals and should not be kept in private homes except by the most experienced of keepers.* Antivenom for the bite of these lizards is available.

Helodermatids once ranged farther across North America and into western Europe and central Asia. Today their range is restricted to patches of land from extreme southern Utah and Arizona south to northern Guatemala.

The family and genus names derive from the Greek: ʻηλωσ, *helos*, studded, and δερμα, *derma*, skin. Gila monsters reach a maximum TL of only 28 inches (71.1 cm), so they do not qualify for inclusion here.

Although beaded lizards are venomous, there are no records of this species causing human fatalities.

Genus *Heloderma* Wiegmann, 1829
Data as for the family.

Heloderma horridum (Wiegmann, 1829)
Beaded Lizard/ Mexican Beaded Lizard/
Escorpión
Venomous
Etymology: From the Latin *horrid*, meaning
"prickly" or "horrible."
Range: Widely distributed from central Mexico
south into Guatemala. Absent from Baja
California.
Maximum Size: 40 inches (1,016 mm)
References: Beck (1991, 2004, 2005); Beck and
Ramírez-Bautista (1991); Bogert and Del Campo
(1960); Campbell and Lamar (2004); Campbell
and Vannini (1988); Sprackland (1992, 1993b).

Captive Suitability: 2
Natural History: This is a large, predominantly
terrestrial lizard that also climbs well and will
enter water if present. The large claws allow the
lizards to excavate long burrows in hard soils or
modify commandeered burrows made by small
mammals. Unlike Gila monsters, beaded lizards
have pink tongues, the head is solid black with
no light coloring, and the tail is longer than the
snout-vent length.

Four subspecies have been described based
primarily on color pattern. From northernmost to
southernmost these are *Heloderma h. exasperatum*,
H. h. horridum, *H. h. alvarezi*, and the Guatemalan
H. h. charlesbogerti. *H. h. alvarezi* is a melanistic
form from the forested regions of southern
Mexico, and it reaches the greatest length of any
subspecies.

Pair of Rio Fuerte beaded
lizards (*Heloderma horridum
exasperatum*). Sexing these
animals is difficult;
adult males are
generally larger and
bulkier than the
females.

Beaded lizards are residents of arid country but may be found in deserts and forests. They are adequate climbers, so it is not unusual to see one in a bush or on a low tree branch. They are typically crepuscular, avoiding the intensity of the daytime sun.

Captive Care: Beaded lizards are extraordinarily hardy animals if kept warm with appropriate seasonal and nighttime drops in temperature and given an adequate diet. Keep daytime summer temperatures at 86 to 95°F (30 to 35°C), and allow a nighttime drop of 10 to 15°F (5.6 to 8.3°C). Humidity should range from 50 to 90 percent. Beaded lizards are typically active at and after twilight, when they may actively forage. These clumsy-looking lizards are also adept climbers and will take to exploring and perching in low trees and thick bushes. Terrarium specimens will climb to get close to a heat bulb.

Beaded lizards feed on eggs, rodents, chicks, and turkey sausages. Lizards should be fed five times weekly and their foods supplemented with vitamin and calcium/phosphorus powders. Juveniles will take vitamin- and mineral-dusted crickets, roaches, and pinky mice. The lizards can be housed in small groups provided they are of similar size.

Provide animals you wish to breed in terrariums with at least 24 inches (61 cm) of substrate. Gravid females will excavate long, deep burrows in soil that is firm and can hold a steady humidity.

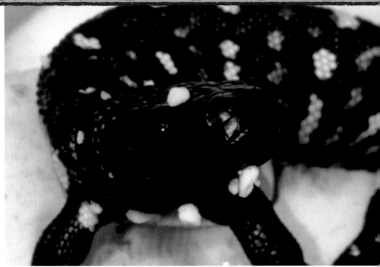

Freshly hatched Rio Fuerte beaded lizard. Captive breeding of beaded lizards and Gila monsters is still uncommon outside of zoos.

Family Varanidae Merrem, 1820

Monitor lizards all belong to a single genus, *Varanus*, which inhabits much of the Old World's Southern Hemisphere. Widely distributed through Africa, southern Asia, Australia, and Oceania, they are conspicuously absent from South America, Madagascar, and New Zealand. All prefer hot habitats, and the few species that range into temperate climates spend the cold months in a state of dormancy.

The family presents an excellent array of species for anyone engaged in comparative biology, whether the focus is evolution, morphology, behavior, or ecology. The lizards of the family are extremely similar to each other in several ways. The monitors all possess four strong pentadactyl limbs, with no sign of limb or digit reduction.

Although Gray's monitor is famous as a fruit-eating monitor, it still consumes crabs, snails, and other small animals occasionally.

The snout and body are elongated. Eyelids and external ear openings are always present, while autotomy is lacking. The tongue is long, narrow, and deeply bifid, resembling that of a snake. An elongated venom gland lies in the mandibular tissues, and secretions are emitted when the lower jaw is squeezed. The teeth are not grooved but show a complex system of vertical dentine infolding. A parietal eye is universal. Ventral scales are small and arranged in longitudinal rows. Monitors lack spines, crests, or frills seen in other lizard groups. The hyoid apparatus, that group of throat bones and cartilages that helps support the tongue, are highly mobile, allowing monitors to

consume comparatively much larger prey items than can other lizards. All are egg layers, are primarily diurnal, and eat other animals. (Even the famous Gray's monitor, a known fruit eater, takes snails as a major component of its diet.)

But for all the similarities, which are often noted by authors, the range of variation is impressive. They range in size from the tiny *Varanus brevicauda* (the shortest monitor at 8 inches [203 mm]) to the bulky Komodo dragon (at 122.5 inches [3,112 mm]). The tail may barely equal the snout-vent length or greatly exceed that measure, and it may be circular, oval, or quite compressed in cross section. Excepting *V. brevicauda* at the smallest level and *V. salvadorii* at the largest, the larger the monitor, the shorter the relative length of the tail compared to snout-vent length. All varanids have considerable control of tail muscles and can use the appendage as a whip or scull for swimming. Several species of tree monitor have fully prehensile tails capable of grasping tree branches.

The nostril may be a tiny pinhole or a slit half as long as the snout. The scales may be small and granular or large, rough, and widely spaced. The color may be dull tans and browns or bright yellow, green, or blue. Males may or may not have preanal pores. Even the relative length and shape of the claws are variable.

Considerable data have been obtained regarding the reproduction of monitors both in nature and captivity. Several of the larger species–from across the family's range–will dig into concrete-hard termitaria (termite nests) and deposit eggs. Termites repair the nest, providing protection

Several species of monitors (*V. albigularis* in this photo) excavate termite mounds to make their nests.

from predators and changing temperatures. The inner environment of a termite nest is often maintained to within less than 0.6°F (1°C). The female monitor will return at hatching time to free the otherwise trapped neonates. Species in which this behavior has been documented include the Nile, white-throated, Bengal, desert, and lace monitors. Incubation time is quite long, ranging, for giants, from 250 to 310 days.

The origin of the name "*Varanus*" is confusing. The Arabic word for the desert monitor (*Varanus griseus*) is ouran or arin, which in turn sounds similar to the German word warne, meaning "to warn." Another Arabic term for a large

burrowing lizard is *waral* ورل, which may have led to the German term *warane*. Legends from at least as far back as Herodotus tell that monitors eat crocodile eggs (true) and that their presence warns humans of the presence of crocodiles. The German word, therefore, seemed appropriate for the lizards, and when "to warn" is rendered into Latin, it becomes the infinitive verb form *monere*, from which we get "monitor." Meanwhile, *Varanus* is the Latinized version of *ouran*. Varanids are also the subject of a new research journal, *Biawak*, published by the International Varanid Research Society.

MAXIMUM KNOWN SIZES (TOTAL LENGTHS) FOR GIANT MONITORS

Species marked with an asterisk (*) have only been discovered and described since 1990; species marked with a double asterisk (**) have been described much earlier but not recognized as valid again until after 1990.

MONITORS	SIZES	MONITORS	SIZES
Komodo dragon *Varanus komodoensis*	122.5 inches (3,112 mm)	Rough-necked monitor *Varanus rudicollis*	63 inches (1,600 mm)
Tree crocodile monitor *Varanus salvadorii*	111 inches (2,820 mm)	Clouded monitor ** *Varanus nebulosus*	63 inches (1,600 mm)
Water monitor *Varanus salvator*	110 inches (2,794 mm)	Gould's monitor *Varanus gouldii*	63 inches (1,600 mm)
Nile monitor *Varanus niloticus*	108 inches (2,743 mm)	Red sand monitor *Varanus rubidus*	63 inches (1,600 mm)
Perentie *Varanus giganteus*	96 inches (2,438 mm)	Philippine water monitor ** *Varanus cumingi*	59 inches (1,500 mm)
Bengal monitor *Varanus bengalensis*	80.5 inches (2,045 mm)	Argus monitor *Varanus panoptes*	58 inches (1,448 mm)
Lace monitor *Varanus varius*	74 inches (1,880 mm)	Mangrove monitor *Varanus indicus*	56.5 inches (1,435 mm)
Mabitang black monitor * *Varanus mabitang*	68.9 inches (1,750 mm)	Mertens' monitor *Varanus mertensi*	54.3 inches (1,380 mm)
White-throated monitor ** *Varanus albigularis*	65 inches (1,651 mm)	Savannah monitor *Varanus exanthematicus*	53 inches (1,350 mm)
Gray's monitor *Varanus olivaceus*	64 inches (1,626 mm)	Ornate Nile monitor ** *Varanus ornatus*	51 inches (1,300 mm)

MONITORS	SIZES	MONITORS	SIZES
Duméril's monitor *Varanus dumerilii*	50 inches (1,270 mm)	Long-tailed rock monitor *Varanus glebopalma*	39.4 inches (1,000 mm)
Spencer's monitor *Varanus spenceri*	49.2 inches (1,250 mm)	Blue tree monitor * *Varanus macraei*	39.4 inches (1,000 mm)
Peach-throat monitor ** *Varanus jobiensis*	48.5 inches (1,231 mm)	Seram monitor * *Varanus ceramboensis*	38.7 inches (984 mm)
Blue-tailed monitor ** *Varanus doreanus*	47.4 inches (1,204 mm)	Black tree monitor *Varanus beccarii*	37.2 inches (945 mm)
Yemeni monitor *Varanus yemenensis*	45.3 inches (1,150 mm)	Yellow monitor *Varanus flavescens*	36.2 inches (920 mm)
Desert monitor *Varanus griseus*	44.8 inches (1,140 mm)	Gold-speckled tree monitor * *Varanus boehmei*	35.4 inches (900 mm)
Tri-colored monitor * *Varanus yuwonoi*	44 inches (1,118 mm)	Yellow savanna monitor ** *Varanus ocellatus*	34.4 inches (875 mm)
Quince monitor * *Varanus melinus*	44 inches (1,118 mm)	Green tree monitor *Varanus prasinus*	34.4 inches (874 mm)
Blue-spotted monitor * *Varanus caerulivirens*	43.3 inches (1,100 mm)	Mourning monitor *Varanus tristis*	33.5 inches (850 mm)
Heath monitor *Varanus rosenbergi*	40 inches (1,020 mm)	Teri's monitor *Varanus keithhornei*	30.2 inches (767 mm)
Bismarck monitor ** *Varanus finschi*	39.4 inches (1,000 mm)		

215

Genus *Varanus* Merrem, 1820

Monitor lizards are the true giants of the lizard clan, with several species passing the 78.7 inch (2-meter)length. The official record still stands with the Komodo dragon for 122.5 inches (3,112 mm), but credible reports of tree crocodile monitors reaching or exceeding that length have been common. Among the species that are known to reach a maximum length of 96 inches, or 8 ft, (2,438 mm) are the Komodo dragon, Asiatic water monitor, Nile monitor, tree crocodile monitor, and perentie. A list of the giants, in order of maximum known sizes, is given in the accompanying table.

Because of the range of variation seen among the species in this family (see table), several authors have recognized subgenera to further put the lizards into categorical subgroups. The subgenera are predominantly geographical enclaves, and while such recognition may be useful for certain analytical studies, they are not yet well defined or widely accepted, and their use is of only marginal relevance to the needs of herpetoculturists. Complicating things further is the rate at which new monitors are being discovered and named, particularly as Indonesian animal dealers search previously unexplored islands for species that will fetch high prices with European, Japanese, and American buyers. Many islands contain endemic species, and no doubt many varanids will come to light as "new" species in the coming years. As this manuscript was being written, a new member of the tree monitor group was described, and I have data on another two species that may be described shortly.

Monitors are known as biwaks and biawaks in parts of Asia, goannas in Australia, and leguaans in southern Africa. Because the general natural history and care of several species are so similar, I have grouped the giants by geographic region.

The Komodo dragon undoubtedly is the most famous of the monitors.

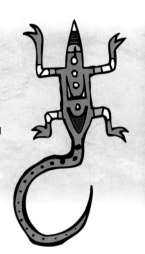

White-throated monitor basking on a dirt road in Serengeti National Park, Tanzania.

Africa: Savanna Monitor Group

These large terrestrial lizards have a blunt head, stout body, comparatively short limbs and claws, and a tail that in adults is less than 1.8 times SVL. Most of the tail is laterally compressed. Dorsal and ventral coloring are little differentiated from each other. For taxonomic review, see Bayless and Sprackland (2000, 2000a).

Varanus albigularis Daudin, 1803
White-Throated Monitor/Cape Monitor/
Black-Throated Monitor

Etymology: (Latin) *alba*, white, and *gularis*, throat.
Range: Sub-Saharan and eastern Africa, from southern Sudan to South Africa.
Maximum Size: 65 inches (1,651 mm)
References: Balsai (1997); Bayless and Sprackland (2000, 2000a); Böhme and Ziegler (1997a, 1997b); Hudson et al., (1994); Phillips and Millar (1998); Sprackland (1992, 2001a); Sprawls et al. (2002);

Summers (2003); Switak (2002).
Captive Suitability: 3
Natural History: White-throated monitors are widely distributed along Africa's eastern forests and savannas, but generally they do not stray far from permanent water sources. They are somewhat arboreal, especially when young, and have been observed both perching and hunting in trees. The monitors are also adept burrowers that engineer long, deep chambers into which they can retreat from the African sun. Chambers may also retain considerable humidity and moisture, thereby attracting potential prey species as well. The lizards are not adverse, however, to claiming a mammal's burrow if the opportunity presents itself.

Prey and jaw anatomy alter radically as the lizards age. Juveniles have skulls that are similar to the savanna monitor (*Varanus exanthematicus*), with uniform long, sharp teeth. Juveniles and subadults feed on a variety of insects, centipedes, scorpions,

V. albigularis is a highly variable animal. Here are two views of the "ionidesi" form, commonly called the black-throated monitor.

and smaller reptiles. Young adults have stouter teeth than the young, and the posterior teeth begin to take on a broader and more blunted configuration. Diet then shifts predominantly to other vertebrates, including mammals, birds and their eggs, and snakes. Both cobras and vipers are included in the diet of white-throated monitors, and the lizards are immune to the effects of the snakes' venom. As the lizards mature, the posterior teeth alter again, becoming longer and broader at the base and much more flattened at the tips. In the final configuration, there is considerable resemblance to mammalian molars but with only a single flat surface instead of a pair of ridges. Prey items of adults include birds' eggs, snails, fresh water mussels and clams, and other hard-bodied animals.

The different vernacular names given to this species reflect the variation seen in the patterns of the lizards across their great range. All young

specimens of *Varanus albigularis* normally have a black gular region, and although this may fade to light gray in adults, it persists with age. The lower lips may be pale gray or creamy white in some specimens but is not a consistent characteristic. Pattern variation is extremely variable among hatchlings and young monitors, even from the same clutch of eggs, but tends to develop toward a more nearly uniform adult form.

One variant occurs in which the dorsal-most light spots meet and fuse into a vertebral series of very large spots has been dubbed the "Ionides" phase, after a purported subspecies, *V. a. ionidesi*. The describer of that subspecies has since decided that the subspecific status is unwarranted, and the full details of the elimination of all subspecies of white-throat monitor is provided in Bayless and Sprackland (2000, 2000a). In short, those authors plotted all available locality data for

Juveniles and subadults should be fed mice, young rats, sausages, raw or boiled eggs, and large insects on alternate days. Adults require a single large meal each week–mainly fresh killed or thawed rodents–especially if they do not have the opportunity to be very active. Inactive monitors have a tendency to become obese quite rapidly.

Mating occurs in the spring, and egg laying follows about a month later. Females lay up to 50 eggs per clutch, and these take 110 to 150 days to hatch. Neonates may either all express a similar color pattern or a variety of patterns. They generally take food after their first week.

Here is a *V. albigularis* that matches the description of the nominate, or "true *albigularis*" form.

white-throat monitors in Africa and discovered that color pattern was closely correlated to rainfall and elevation. Their conclusion held that pattern variation of the "subspecies" was an ecotypic effect, and no subspecies could be warranted. The Ionides variant, originally attributed to Tanzanian populations, has subsequently been found throughout the range of the species, from Tanzania and Angola south to South Africa.

Captive Care: Hardy and long lived, this is an excellent display animal for a facility that has adequate space to properly house it. They require large terrariums with individual hiding areas. Best results are obtained when animals are kept on deep soil, allowing them to dig burrows and nests. If carefully handled, this species can make an excellent display and demonstration animal that is reluctant to bite.

Approximate natural range of *V. albigularis*.

219

KEEPING AND BREEDING *VARANUS ALBIGULARIS*

By Robyn Markland and Chad Brown

We have worked with *Varanus albigularis* since 1990, and they have always been among our favorite monitors. They are hardy, easy to care for, and have a great monitor personality.

The vast majority of baby white-throats on the reptile market are farmed animals from Tanzania. These babies actually have black throats and bands of spotting down the back. They are no longer recognized as a subspecies (Bayless and Sprackland, 2000), but these animals have been known in the past as *ionidesi*, or "Ionides" black-throated monitors. The Ionides dominate the white-throat market and are visually different from the "true" *V. albigularis*, or banded cape monitor, a white-throat monitor with distinct solid banding down the back.

Banded cape white-throats are beautiful monitors but much rarer (coming largely from South Africa) in the captive market than the Ionides black-throats. The banded capes vary in adult size from just over 2 feet (61 cm) long in total length to 6 feet (1.8) or more. The Ionides becomes a 6-foot (1.8-m) animal as a healthy adult, and we regularly see babies reach 4 feet (1.2 m) in the first year.

We strongly believe that black-throats are the best choice for a giant lizard in a captive environment. They reach a visually impressive size, but they are not as massive as an adult water monitor, which may reach 65 to 70 pounds (29.5 to 31.8 kg). A large black-throat will weigh about 25 pounds (11.3 kg). That makes the black-throat a more easily handled species, one that is simpler to interact with and ultimately easier to house.

Try to acquire any new monitor species as a hatchling. This is especially important if breeding is your ultimate goal. Starting with hatchling monitors, you will be able to address socialization issues, as well as provide ideal husbandry throughout the life of the monitor.

You can breed white-throats as a pair (one male and one female) or as a trio (one male and two females). If you keep more than three animals in a single cage, the cage size requirement becomes too massive to be realistic (except for zoos), and the socialization and group dynamic become exponentially more complicated. For a pair of adult Ionides, 30 sq. feet (2.8 sq. m) of cage space should be considered a minimum starting size.

Gravid female white-throated monitor; gravid monitors increase greatly in girth over the course of gestation.

We use soil that allows lizards to dig and burrow in our breeding monitor setups. A good soil is the key to achieving significant breeding events and other natural behavior. We use cypress mulch for short-term hatchling setups. Lack of a good, usable substrate can be the biggest obstacle to getting healthy, viable eggs.

Under ideal conditions, we have had Ionides breed at 12 to 14 months of age. If a well-socialized group of Ionides is kept properly, with great temperatures (daytime ambient of 85°F [29.4°C], basking spot of 130°F (54.4°C]), a sensible, nutritious diet (rodents and commercially raised feeder insects like crickets and roaches), and a properly set up cage, breeding actually comes naturally.

After mating, the next step is to actually obtain strong, viable eggs (as opposed to dead eggs, slugs, or unfertilized ova), a hurdle that many keepers have not overcome. A proper substrate is one of the key details to reaching this goal. A female without a suitable substrate is likely to retain her eggs longer than necessary, resulting in much lower viability. If she deposits eggs on time, the likelihood of successful hatching is substantially increased. Ionides females will dig a specific egg-laying burrow when oviposition is near. This chosen spot must meet the moisture and temperature requirements of proper egg incubation, for as far as the female is concerned, this spot must provide the ideal conditions until the babies hatch out.

However, we incubate most monitor eggs in a separate, thermostatically controlled incubator, and we must also provide an ideal situation for the eggs to go full term and successfully hatch. Incubating in a Perlite medium at 82 to 84°F (27.8 to 28.9°C) results in hatching in 140 to 160 days. Hatchlings may take two or even three additional days to fully absorb their yolk and emerge from the shell. At this point they can be housed in a hatchling-specific setup. We typically use one 10-gallon (37.9-l) glass aquarium tank per hatchling. Our baby rooms have ambient room heating (set to the mid 80s°F [roughly 29 to 30°C]) and basking spots of 120 to 130°F (48.9 to 54.4°C).

Lack of a suitable nesting site is one of the major reasons keepers fail to breed their white-throats. This situation can cause a female to either retain her eggs for too long or to scatter them about the enclosure—either behavior usually leads to dead eggs.

We feed hatchlings six days a week—four days on insect feeders and two days of thawed rodents. Assuming proper temperatures and setup, it is actually very difficult to overfeed your Ionides babies at this fast-growth stage. This is also the perfect time to start assembling social groups for future breeding projects.

The savanna monitor is probably the most commonly kept monitor in the U.S. hobby. They are prone to becoming obese when kept as pets.

Varanus exanthematicus (Bosc, 1792)
Savanna Monitor/Bosc's Monitor

Etymology: From the Greek εξάνθημα, *exanthema*, a rash, in reference to the pebbly scalation. Louis Augustin Guillaume Bosc d'Antic was the scientist who described the species in a very brief paper in 1792.

Range: A broad band across central sub-Saharan Africa, from Senegal (type locality) in the west to Sudan and Kenya in the east.

Maximum Size: 53 inches (1,350 mm); generally much smaller

References: Balsai (1997); Bayless (1997, 2002); Bayless and Sprackland (2000, 2000a); Bennett (1998); Bennett and Thakoordyal (2003); Böhme and Ziegler (1997a, 1997b); Coiro (2007); Spawls et al. (2002); Sprackland (1992, 2001a)

Captive Suitability: 5

Approximate natural range of *V. exanthematicus.*

Female savanna monitor digging a nest. Despite being common in the hobby, this species is rarely captive bred.

diet and temperature regime. They need to be kept in the 85 to 100°F (29.4 to 37.8°C) range during the day. Captives must be given access to clean drinking water; in a large enough container, they will frequently lie completely immersed, although they almost never submerge. Although they dig in the wild state, captive animals do not require soil substrate if they are given adequate shelters in which to completely hide. Young will climb if given the opportunity, but this species is primarily terrestrial in habits. They do well in terrariums where they may excavate their own burrows. Savanna monitors easily become docile if properly and regularly handled. They often learn to recognize their keepers.

Natural History: Savanna monitors have been staples in the pet trade for more than 40 years, once having come behind the Bengal, water, and Nile monitors in availability. Despite this access, very little has been known about the lizards in the wild until quite recently, largely through the independent work of Daniel Bennett and Mark Bayless. The lizards are residents of grasslands and forests that border savannas. They may excavate or appropriate deep burrows, where they will retreat during the long dry season.

Like white-throated monitors, savanna monitor dentition varies with age. Young lizards have uniformly pointed teeth, but the posterior dentition becomes broader, lower, and blunted as the lizards get larger.

Captive Care: Savanna monitors can be hardy captives provided they are given an appropriate

Approximate natural range of *V. ocellatus.*

223

Varanus ocellatus Heyden, 1830
Yellow Savanna Monitor

Etymology: (Latin) *ocellus*, eye.

Range: Southern Sudan and along the Nile north into Egypt.

Maximum Size: 34.4 inches (875 mm)

References: Bayless and Sprackland (2000, 2000a).

Captive Suitability: 4

Natural History: This species is very similar to the savanna monitor in morphology, size, and habits, and it is distinguished from that species largely by features of the skull and in having a lighter yellow-tan dorsal color. The posterior process of the premaxilla bone is thinner and without a flattened table, and there are paired nasal bones, unlike the broad process and single nasal seen in *Varanus exanthematicus*. The tongue is pink in *V. ocellatus* and purple or dark blue in *V. exanthematicus*.

Captive Care: Similar as for the savanna monitor.

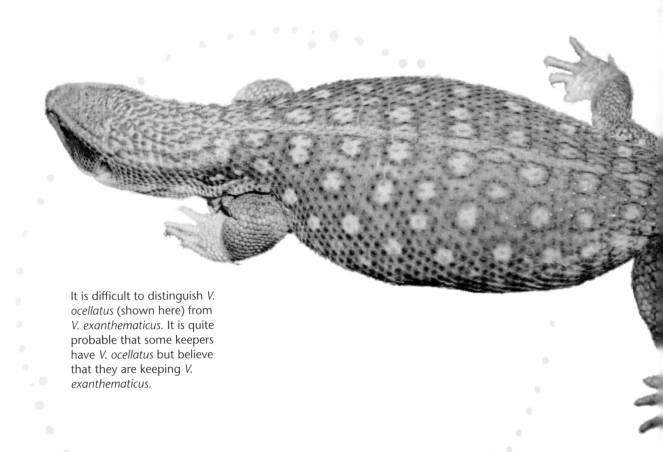

It is difficult to distinguish *V. ocellatus* (shown here) from *V. exanthematicus*. It is quite probable that some keepers have *V. ocellatus* but believe that they are keeping *V. exanthematicus*.

The Nile monitor is the most aquatic monitor species in Africa. This one was photographed in Kruger National Park, South Africa.

Africa: Nile Monitor Group

These are large to very large lizards that are primarily aquatic and arboreal as young and terrestrial and slightly aquatic as adults. Most of the tail is laterally compressed. The snout in adults is moderately elongated, the limbs slender, and the tail up to 1.8 times SVL. Dorsal and ventral coloration are distinct from each other. For taxonomy, see Bayless and Sprackland (2000, 2000a) and Böhme and Ziegler (1997b).

Varanus niloticus (Linnaeus, 1766)
Nile Monitor

Etymology: Named for the Nile River in eastern Africa.

Range: Widely distributed in eastern Africa from Egypt south to South Africa and south of the Sahara as far west as Senegal.

Maximum Size: 108 inches (2,743 mm)

References: Balsai (1997); Bayless (1997, 2002); Bayless and Sprackland (2000, 2000a); Böhme and Ziegler (1997a, 1997b); Cowles (1930); Lentz (1995); Spawls et al. (2002); Wright (2007).

Captive Suitability: 4

Natural History: If the desert monitor proves to represent three distinct species (which is possible–see the discussion of *Varanus griseus*), then the

Approximate natural range of *Varanus niloticus* (yellow) and *V. ornatus* (red).

Nile monitor will hold the record for the greatest range of any varanid. Along with the desert monitor, this species is perhaps the monitor with the longest written history in Western cultures. It is this species that provides the story of the monitor as a creature that warns humans of the presence of crocodiles. Nile monitors are large and opportunistic meat eaters, readily digging up the nests of Nile crocodiles to gorge on the eggs. They also feed on snakes (they are impervious to the bites of many venomous species), lizards, young crocodiles, reptile and birds' eggs, small mammals, fish, clams, snails, and carrion. As in related species–the white-throated, ornate, and savanna monitors–Nile monitors undergo tooth modification as they age. Young lizards have sharp, pointed, slightly curved teeth, while adults convert the rearmost teeth into lozenge-shaped molars. These broad teeth are then used for crushing the shells of mollusks, large eggs, and presumably young crocodiles.

Although generally reaching a maximum adult length of about 6 feet (1.8 m), at least one reliable report from South Africa documents a 9-foot (2.7-m) specimen.

It was a young Raymond B. Cowles who first documented the extraordinary nesting behavior of Nile monitors, observing them tear into tall terrestrial termite nests (termitaria) and then deposit eggs. The termites would repair the nest, in turn protecting the eggs from predators while also keeping them in an incubator with a nearly constant temperature and humidity level. We now know that several large varanids use termitaria as incubators.

Juvenile Nile monitors are one of the most commonly available monitors in the U.S.–unfortunate given their eventual enormous size and often aggressive disposition.

Captive Care: Nile monitors are commonly imported and are among the least expensive of varanids to acquire. However, they are also the most aggressive of the monitors so that, with very few exceptions, they are unsuitable for private collectors. Stories of "dog-tame" Nile monitors refer to extraordinarily unusual individuals.

Terrarium considerations must account for the large size, active habits, ability to dig and swim well, and strength to find and exploit any weakness in a cage. Because Nile monitors occur in seasonally variable habitats, they may be kept under a range of temperature and humidity conditions with no ill effect.

Two views of the ornate Nile monitor, *V. ornatus*. The ornate Nile monitor was long considered a subspecies of *V. niloticus*, but it tends to be more docile and does not grow as large.

Varanus ornatus Daudin, 1803
Ornate Nile Monitor

Etymology: (Latin) *ornata*, decorated or colorful.

Range: Forests of central and west-central Africa.

Maximum Size: 51 inches (1,300 mm)

References: Bayless (1997, 2002); Bayless and Sprackland (2000, 2000a); Böhme and Ziegler (1997b); Sprackland (2001a); Sprawls et al. (2002).

Captive Suitability: 3

Natural History: *Varanus ornatus* was long considered a subspecies of the Nile monitor, but further comparison of the animals has shown them to be distinct and valid species. The ornate monitor differs from the Nile monitor in having a yellow (versus purple) tongue, six broad rows of yellow dorsal spots (versus several indistinct cream-colored rows), and in features of skull and hemipenial anatomies.

Captive Care: Same as for the Nile monitor, although this species is reportedly more docile in captivity.

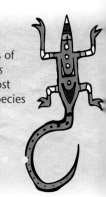

Of the three subspecies of desert monitor, *Varanus griseus griseus* is the most well studied. The subspecies may quite possibly be recognized as three full species in the future.

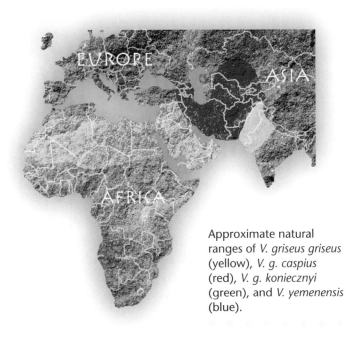

Approximate natural ranges of *V. griseus griseus* (yellow), *V. g. caspius* (red), *V. g. koniecznyi* (green), and *V. yemenensis* (blue).

Africa to South Asia: Desert Monitors

These are medium-sized lizards with a dorsally depressed body. They have short strong limbs, very long and only slightly recurved claws, and a tail more than 1.8 times SVL that is completely or nearly completely round in cross section. Unlike the African monitors, teeth in desert monitors do not undergo major ontogenetic changes with age. Desert monitors are apparently close to the ancestral varanid type and have no closely related species. Their closest relatives are the Nile and savanna monitors.

Varanus griseus (Daudin, 1803)
Desert Monitor/Gray Monitor

Etymology: (Latin) *griseus*, gray.
Range: Northeastern Africa east through the

Arabian Peninsula to western India.

Maximum Size: 44.8 inches (1,140 mm)

References: Auffenberg et al. (1990); Bayless (2000); Mertens (1954); Perry et al. (1993); Stanner (1999); Stanner and Mendelssohn (1987, 1991); Vernet (1977); Vernet et al. (1988); Vogel (n.d.).

Captive Suitability: 4; CITES Appendix I

Natural History: This is the species of monitor with the longest written association with the Western world. Populations have been intensely studied, and African and Arabian specimens were once extremely common in the live animal trade. Despite this long familiarity, however, there are major gaps in our knowledge of desert monitors because three distinct subspecies–very possibly full species–are involved.

Varanus g. griseus (Daudin, 1803) has the widest continuous range of any varanid, extending from north central Africa's Atlantic coast east to Iran and the entire Arabian Peninsula. This form has an indistinct and variable pattern of light markings on a gray dorsum. The large spots on the back are irregular and unequal, not forming a distinct pattern. The tail is round in section, and the subcaudals are slightly larger than the dorsal and lateral caudals. Most of the published accounts for "*Varanus griseus*" are based on this taxon.

Varanus g. caspius (Eichwald, 1831) occupies the circum-Caspian area of western Asia, from Iran east to central Pakistan. The back is marked by distinct, sharp-edged dark crossbands that are not bordered by light spots. The predominant background color is pale sandy white to light gray. The tail is compressed so that it is nearly triangular in section. This is the largest form.

Superficially, the Yemeni monitor resembles *V. albigularis*. However, it has numerous internal differences, warranting its recognition as a full species.

Varanus g. koniecznyi Mertens, 1954, ranges from central Pakistan east through the northwestern third of India. The body may be yellowish, orange, brick red, or brown, with a series of broad, jagged-edged dark bands. Each band is bordered by equal-sized light round spots. The tail is similar to *V. g. griseus*, except all caudal scales are subequal, forming distinct rings all the way around. This is the smallest subspecies.

Captive Care: This species is a resident of some of the driest and most inhospitable desert terrain on the planet. They are excellent burrowers, capable of digging long, deep tunnels into cooler, moist sand. The terrarium should take into account this behavior and be set up in a similar manner as for white-throated monitors.

Varanus yemenensis Böhme, Joger, and Schätti, 1989
Yemeni Monitor

Etymology: Named for the country Yemen on the southern Arabian Peninsula.

Range: The southwestern corner of the Arabian Peninsula.

Maximum Size: 45.3 inches (1,150 mm)

References: Böhme et al. (1989).

Captive Suitability: 3

Natural History: Poorly studied but known to frequent valleys and regions where sparse vegetation is prevalent, providing places for perching and attracting the large insects and millipedes that make up the bulk of its prey. Yemeni monitors are similar in morphology to the African savanna and white-throated monitors, and they represent the easternmost range for the African varanid clade.

This species came to light when German herpetologist Wolfgang Böhme saw the then-unknown lizard on a television documentary about Yemen. Following up on the lead, he and his colleagues soon collected and named specimens. This method of discovery is similar to that related for finding Fiji's crested iguana (q.v.) by John Gibbons.

Captive Care: Similar as for the savanna monitor.

Approximate natural ranges of *V. boehmei* (red), *V. macraei* (green), *V. prasinus* (yellow; range extends off this map), and *V. beccarii* (blue).

Indo-Australia: Subgenus *Euprepiosaurus*

A large assembly of two ecologically very different types of lizards that inhabit humid tropical forests, mangroves, and places near permanent water. The mangrove monitor branch includes nine species of large animals that are terrestrial and partially to highly aquatic and partially arboreal. They have an elongated snout, shiny and slightly keeled scales, and a laterally compressed tail. The other branch contains the tree monitors, highly elongated, thin-bodied tree dwellers with a highly prehensile tail that is round in section and more than two times SVL.

When the first edition of *Giant Lizards* was published in 1992, the lizards in this group were among the least studied, and only about six species were recognized. Of the nine named

HALMAHERA

SERAM

NEW GUINEA

ARU ISLANDS

Wild-caught adult black tree monitor (left) and a captive-bred hatchling (right). This species–along with most other tree monitors–is nervous and flighty, requiring a large cage with plenty of cover.

mangrove species, three (*V. caerulivirens, V. ceramboensis,* and *V. juxtindicus*) are controversial and may represent only normal variation within *Varanus indicus*. Regarding the tree monitors, three of the named seven have been described only since 1995. Two of those species (*V. reisingeri* and *V. zugorum*) do not quite meet the size requirement for giant lizards. A third, *V. rainerguentheri*, may be a color variation of a previously named mangrove monitor species.

Varanus beccarii (Doria, 1874)
Black Tree Monitor

Etymology: Named for Italian naturalist-explorer Odoardo Beccari, an authority on birds and one of the first European explorers to make extensive collecting and mapping trips into the interior of New Guinea in the late 1800s.

Range: The Aru Islands group south of West Papua (Irian Jaya), Indonesian New Guinea.
Maximum Size: 37.2 inches (945 mm)
References: Eidenmüller (1997); Sprackland (1991c, 1991a, 1994a).
Captive Suitability: 3
Natural History: Very poorly known from the wild. This species is found only on the Aru Islands, well south of the Indonesian half of New Guinea. The habitat is a variety of lowland wet forests and swamps. Lizards spend virtually all their time in the trees, where they feed upon a range of invertebrates, particularly ornithopteran insects. Distinct and consistent differences serve to distinguish this species from the similar green tree monitor (*Varanus prasinus*) of the New Guinea mainland and islands close to New Guinea. Hatchlings are black with transverse rows of

light green spots that gradually fade within the first year of growth. A similar but smaller species, *Varanus bogerti*, is known only from two islands of the D'Entrecasteaux Islands of eastern Papua New Guinea.

Captive Care: Black tree monitors have become fairly common among reptile dealers, bringing the cost down considerably since 1990. However, although zoos and some private breeders have gotten the species to reproduce in terrariums, such successes are still relatively rare. Of interest is the fact that neonates are predominantly black but sport a series of tiny green spots on the head, body, and tail. In coloration they are similar to green tree monitors, but the green quickly fades as the lizards grow.

These are notoriously active lizards, given to frequent dashes across the terrarium and often rubbing their snouts raw. They need plenty of space in a tall terrarium that allows climbing on fairly stout objects, such as natural logs. They also require a variety of hiding places. Keep the temperature in the 85 to 95°F (29.4 to 35°C) range, but allow it to drop to about 70°F (21.1°C) at night.

Varanus boehmei Jacobs, 2003
Gold-Speckled Tree Monitor

Etymology: Named for German herpetologist Prof. Dr. Wolfgang Böhme, a leading contemporary student of varanid lizard biology at the Alexander Koenig Museum in Bonn.

Range: Waigeo, West Papua (Irian Jaya), Indonesian New Guinea.

Maximum Size: 35.4 inches (900 mm)

References: Jacobs (2004); Reisinger and Reisinger-Raweyai (2007).

Captive Suitability: 3

Natural History: This New Guinea endemic is very similar in form and coloration to the canopy monitor (*Varanus keithhorni*) of northern Australia, although healthy adults of *V. boehmei* are slightly stouter. In general morphology, the gold-speckled tree monitor is similar to the green tree monitor, differing mainly in coloration. This species is black with tiny yellow speckles on the back, some of which form nebulous ring shapes. The anterior third of the belly is light gray, the remainder similar to the dorsum. This species has not yet been studied in the wild.

Captive Care: Care is very similar as for the black tree monitor. Lizards require a large terrarium with plenty of room to climb and run without easily bumping into terrarium walls. Provide them with a vertical heat gradient that's hottest near the top of the enclosure, and be sure that there are adequate sources to produce shade on the ground and lower climbing objects. They require a variety of large insects and occasional offerings of chopped prawns, bananas, and young mice.

Teri's monitor is an arboreal monitor that is stockier than *V. prasinus* and other tree monitors. It has rarely been kept in captivity, but it did well at the Australia Zoo when fed like other monitors of its size.

Varanus keithhornei Wells and Wellington, 1985
Canopy Monitor/Teri's Monitor
Etymology: Named for an acquaintance of the describers.
Range: Australia's Cape York Peninsula, Queensland.
Maximum Size: 30.2 inches (767 mm)
References: Engel (2004); Sprackland (1991a); Wilson and Swan (2003).

Captive Suitability: 3
Natural History: Largely unknown. The species is known only from areas of the southeastern forests of Cape York, but lack of suitable access to other areas means that this may simply reflect collecting bias for accessible areas. The lizards are found in the canopy and upper branches of the forest's tallest trees.

In general appearance and morphology, Teri's monitor closely resembles the gold-speckled tree monitor.
Captive Care: Same as for the green tree monitor, *Varanus prasinus*. The only legally held captives were observed and bred at the Australia Zoo in the late 1990s. The parents and resulting young were released into the wild in 2000.

The blue tree monitor is very poorly studied; however, it is sporadically available in the pet trade.

Varanus macraei Böhme and Jacobs, 2002
Blue Tree Monitor

Etymology: Named for Duncan Macrea, an Indonesia-based animal collector and dealer.

Range: Known only from Batanta Island to the extreme northwest of West Papua, Indonesia.

Maximum Size: 39.4 inches (1,000 mm)

References: Böhme and Jacobs (2002); Dedlmar (2007); Jacobs (2004).

Captive Suitability: 2

Natural History: Largely unknown. However, this is a remarkable varanid, having a black body covered with large blue ocelli. Like other tree monitors, the snout tip is pale, there is a light postocular streak, and the nostril is situated in a slight fleshy prominence near the snout tip. It can be described simply as a very blue version of the green tree monitor.

Captive Care: Same as for *Varanus beccarii* and *V. prasinus*. Provide a tall, roomy terrarium with a vertical thermal gradient. Offer a variety of foods, including insects, chopped boiled egg whites, small lizards (geckos or anoles), baby mice, chopped bananas, and finely diced cooked turkey sausages. Be sure that there is always a large dish of clean drinking water. Lizards do best in cages with some airflow. At least one herp dealer has offered captive-bred hatchlings of this species, but there are no published reports on this subject.

Close-up view of a typical green tree monitor's face (left). The animal on the right is a very blue individual.

Varanus prasinus (Schlegel, 1839)
Green Tree Monitor

Etymology: (Latin) *prasinus* is a leek, a bright green form of onion.

Range: New Guinea generally and several offshore islands.

Maximum Size: 34.4 inches (874 mm)

References: Cogger (2000); Sprackland (1989a, 1991a, b, c, 1994a).

Captive Suitability: 2

Natural History: A widespread species that is almost totally arboreal. It has, along with its closest allies, the most prehensile tail of any varanoid, using the rounded appendage as a fully functional grasping limb. The monitors are thus able to suspend themselves from a branch with just the tail.

These are speedy, wary, active lizards that seem to be forever foraging. Their diet consists mainly of large stick insects, supplemented with grasshoppers, beetles and their grubs, and large moths. Green tree monitors are reportedly seasonally active, being most conspicuous just after the rains and becoming secretive during the dry season. The only notes on reproduction in the wild were made by ornithologists from the University of California, Berkeley, who noted eggs found in a tree stump (H. Greene, pers. comm.).

Although the subspecies *Varanus prasinus kordensis* was considered a color variation of *V. prasinus* by Sprackland (1989), recent authors believe that evidence exists to support elevation of *Varanus kordensis* to species level.

Captive Care: All tree monitors are nervous, active species that respond to any disturbance by rushing around the terrarium. Green monitors are much more inclined o acclimate over time to human activity than are the black relatives, but they should still be given large and tall facilities.

Breeding green tree monitors in captivity is uncommon. The hatchlings have a different pattern than the adults.

Juvenile blue-tailed monitor.

Provide solid vertical climbing materials with stout horizontal branches. Hide boxes on the "tree" will simulate natural tree hollows, a favored refuge and nest area for the lizards.

A great many specimens arrive with bruised or bleeding snouts, whether captive bred or wild caught. This is because the lizards are so active that they tend to crash into enclosure walls. Treat all new specimens with care, and treat injuries carefully. New acquisitions should be quarantined for at least 30 days.

Tree monitors–all species–are hyperactive animals that burn a lot of calories and easily become dehydrated. They do best if fed daily, and there must always be a source of clean drinking water. Although tree monitors rarely soak in a large container, they have been known to do so prior to shedding or if they are dehydrated. It is advisable to lightly spray the terrarium each morning; lizards tend to drink the "dew" while basking.

There are many published accounts of tree monitors being successfully maintained on a diet of small mice. I suggest using freshly killed juvenile mice, as adults put up sufficient struggle as to generally cause jaw injuries to the lizards. Preferable would be a diet made up of gut-loaded adult crickets and other soft-bodied insects. Captives have also eaten small banana pieces and earthworms, but they generally reject slugs and snails.

Captive breeding incidents are rare. Females will lay eggs in holes excavated in moist (not wet) soil or in soft wood in rotting logs. Juveniles should be fed small crickets, wax worms, and mealworms.

Adult blue-tailed monitor. These monitors have been offered for sale under the name Kalabeck's monitor in the past.

Varanus doreanus (Meyer, 1874)
Blue-Tailed Monitor

Etymology: Named for the village of Doré (also spelled "Doreh") in what is now West Papua in Indonesian New Guinea, where the original specimens were collected.

Range: Throughout New Guinea and adjacent islands, particularly near the western portion of the island (West Irian, now known as West Papua).

Maximum Size: 47.4 inches (1,204 mm)

References: Böhme et al. (1994); Sprackland (1999e, 1999f, 1998, 1995); Sprackland and Sprackland (1999).

Captive Suitability: 2

Natural History: This species very nearly resembles the widespread mangrove monitor (*Varanus indicus*) but has a pale yellow tongue, a noticeably rounded snout, and usually blue or pale blue-gray bands around the tail. There are alternating irregular dark and light bars on the lips. Beyond that, there is considerable variation in color pattern.

Blue-tailed monitors are also considerably more arboreal than mangrove monitors, rarely spending time foraging on the ground. Food in nature includes tree frogs, large insects (especially stick insects and orthopterans), and birds' eggs.

Captive Care: Similar as for the closely related mangrove monitor but requiring a taller terrarium and plenty of vertical and horizontal objects on which to climb and bask. During the hottest part of the day, lizards prefer to retreat under palm fronds, loose bark, and other light shelter. Provide them with seasonal humidity variation, from a

Blue-tailed monitor showing off its most notable feature.

Varanus finschi Böhme and Ziegler, 1994
Bismarck Monitor
Etymology: (Latin) named in honor of a German, Otto Finsch (1839-1917), a curator at several museums in Holland and Germany and an anthropologist who specialized in the region of eastern New Guinea and northern Australia.
Range: Definitely known only from the island of New Britain in the Bismarck Archipelago, Papua New Guinea, although reports of specimens from other localities across New Guinea and into Australia's Cape York Peninsula have recently been published.
Maximum Size: 39.4 inches (1,000 mm)
References: Böhme and Ziegler (1994); Sprackland (1995, 1998, 1999e, 1999a); Sprackland and Sprackland (1999).
Captive Suitability: 3, possibly 2
Natural History: No studies of this species in the wild have been reported. The name *Varanus doreanus finschi* was first applied by Böhme et al. in 1994, but the taxon was subsequently elevated to species status by Sprackland (1995, 1998), a position later corroborated by Ziegler et al. (1999).
Captive Care: In recent years, several animal dealers have claimed to offer *Varanus finschi* for sale. However, there is no legal export of reptiles from Papua New Guinea, and this species is restricted to some poorly known areas, so in many cases the dealers are–presumably unintentionally–not offering this lizard. Two suppliers have relayed that their animals come from Kei and the Aru Islands to the southwest of New Guinea, but the species is not definitely known to occur there. A very brightly patterned mangrove monitor

dry season low of 30 percent to a rainy season high near 100 percent. Also, give them a vertical thermal gradient with the highest temperatures near the top of the terrarium and the lowest on the ground.

Feed blue-tailed monitors a variety of large insects, especially roaches, grasshoppers, crickets, and locusts. Supplement with small mice, boiled eggs, and canned dog food.

V. finschi is an active and nervous lizard that requires a tall cage with plenty of hiding places and climbing branches. It is not known to be in the pet trade at this time.

first described by Robert Mertens as *Varanus indicus rouxii* came from Kei Island but has been subsequently determined by several authors to be synonymous with *V. indicus*. There is an interesting taxonomic puzzle to be resolved with this species.

Although similar in appearance to mangrove monitors, the Bismarck monitor is far more arboreal. Their care should be similar as for *Varanus doreanus*, but the terrarium should have many hiding places and vertical objects on which lizards may climb. This species tends to stay more nervous than *V. doreanus*, and they are very active; an owner must provide a large terrarium so that the lizards will not race into the glass or walls.

Provide humidity between 50 and 70 percent, and allow adequate ventilation; avoid a terrarium with still, humid air. They will feed on a variety of insects, small eggs (such as quail or gecko eggs), boiled egg whites, and small lizards.

239

Juvenile (left) and adult (right) mangrove monitors. This species is very variable and has a large range; it is quite likely a complex of multiple species.

Varanus indicus (Daudin, 1802)
Mangrove Monitor

Etymology: (Latin) The name *indicus*, meaning "Indian," was incorrectly applied because the describer thought that the lizard was taken in the East Indies.

Range: This species has arguably the broadest distribution for any varanid, ranging from New Guinea and Palau east through the Solomon Islands and south into northern coastal Australia.

Maximum Size: 56.5 inches (1,435 mm)

References: Böhme et al. (1994); Buden (1995); McCoy (1980, 2000); Philipp et al. (1999); Sprackland (1999e, 1999f, 1998, 1995); Sprackland and Sprackland (1999); Wilson (1987); Wilson and Knowles (1988); Wilson and Swan (2003).

Captive Suitability: 3

Natural History: This species is a dark-bodied

lizard with small yellowish spots, and for many decades, any monitor that fit the description was labeled "*Varanus indicus*." Today we know that *Varanus indicus* is part of a larger species complex that includes at least twelve species (commonly grouped into a subgenus, *Euprepiosaurus*). Eight of these (so far) are members of the tree monitor group (*Varanus prasinus* group), and the remainder are "mangrove monitors." True mangrove monitors are distinguished from their similar relatives by possession of a dark purple tongue.

Mangrove monitors serve well to illustrate how widespread is the misconception that large lizards must necessarily be formidable hunters. Prior to World War II, the Japanese allegedly introduced mangrove monitors into Palau and the Caroline and Mariana Islands in an attempt to control the growing rat populations there. (The rats, too,

Varanus juxtindicus. Whether this species is indeed valid or just a variation of the mangrove monitor remains a question for further study.

had been introduced, although unintentionally.) The monitors had no appreciable effect on the rodents, feeding instead on their preferred prey: invertebrates, small eggs, and the occasional nestling bird (Losos and Greene, 1988; Sprackland, 1995).

Mangrove monitors are typically found in groups, with lizards climbing trees and foraging on the ground near water. Although common in mangroves and quite capable of swimming in the ocean, they also occur considerable distances inland along riverbanks.

Captive Care: These are active lizards that require a large pool in which to swim. They may spend hours basking on dry land near a pool, but when active will forage through the entire terrarium. Because they become so large and bulky (compared with their lithe tree-dwelling kin), these lizards need very large terrariums, at least 9.3 feet (3 m) to a side. They climb, swim, and dig well; take these factors into account when setting up the enclosure.

These lizards require daytime temperatures of 85 to 100°F (29.4 to 37.8°C) and humidity in excess of 80 percent. Provide a diet of shrimp, raw fish, turkey sausages, lean chopped beef or thin steak strips, large insects, small lizards, and small rodents.

Captive breedings are rare, probably because this species is still not widely kept and because adults require so much space. Females typically lay two to six large eggs per clutch. Eggs are buried in holes or under leaf litter near permanent water. Hatchlings are large enough to eat most of the same foods as adults.

Varanus jobiensis Ahl, 1932
Peach-Throated Monitor

Etymology: Named for the type locality, Jobi Island, north of Indonesian New Guinea.

Range: Broadly distributed in lowland New Guinea, excepting the eastern island groups.

Maximum Size: 48.5 inches (1,231 mm)

References: Bayless and Dwyer (1997); Böhme et al. (1994); Eidenmüller (1997); Sprackland (1995, 1998, 1999e, 1999f, 2007); Sprackland and Sprackland (1999).

Captive Suitability: 4

Natural History: This species can appear very

Juvenile (opposite) and adult (above) peach-throated monitors. It can be easy to confuse this species with either mangrove or blue-tailed monitors. The pink tongue, dark stripe through the eye, and light-colored (off-white to peach to bright pink) throat are only seen in the peach-throats.

similar to the mangrove monitor but is readily distinguished in having a dark head with no upper markings, a pink tongue, and a pronounced longitudinal stripe through the eye. The eye is comparatively larger than that of other monitors, and the throat and temples may be pale to intense pink. Many populations of peach-throat monitors

242

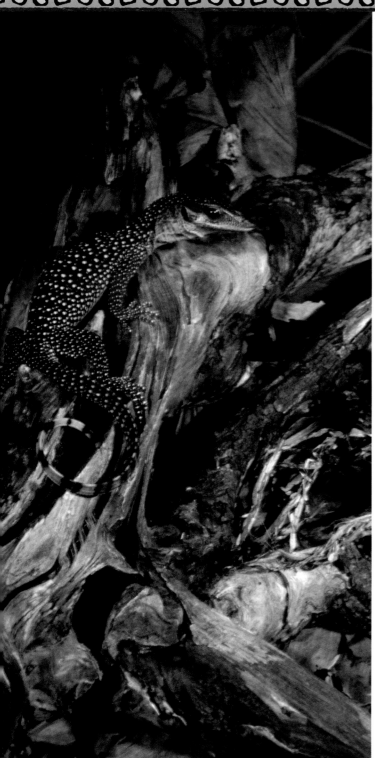

sport pale or bright turquoise blue spots on the limbs and bands on the tail. Most specimens, though, have grayish markings instead of blue. Juveniles are more brightly colored versions of the adults.

Peach-throated monitors are generally leaner and more active then the closely related mangrove monitors, and they are considerably more arboreal, too. Unlike mangrove monitors, which may be common near brackish water, peach-throated monitors prefer habitats near fresh water. Prey includes primarily grasshoppers, crickets, and katydids (orthopterans) and stick insects, but they also take small skinks on occasion.

Ernst Ahl first described the peach-throated monitor as a subspecies of *Varanus indicus* in 1932, based on a young, alcohol-faded specimen in the Berlin museum. In 1951, Robert Mertens described similarly faded adults from the Field Museum as *Varanus karlschmidti*, but in 1994, several researchers determined that Ahl's name was correct but the lizards deserved to be ranked as a species.

Captive Care: Similar to that for the tri-colored monitors, although they are much less aggressive. They should only be housed with their own species and require strong materials on which to climb.

Varanus melinus Böhme and Ziegler, 1997
Yellow Monitor/Quince Monitor

Etymology: (Latin) *melinus*, the yellow fruit known as quince.

Range: The Sula archipelago, Indonesia, including the islands of Mangole, Taliabu, Bowokan, Banggai and possibly Sanana.

Maximum Size: 44 inches (1,118 mm)

References: Böhme and Ziegler (1997).

Captive Suitability: 4; CITES Appendix I

Natural History: Not yet studied.

Captive Care: This beautiful yellow and black monitor is one of the more colorful surprises that came from the considerable number of new varanid species described between 1990 and 2001. Quince monitors are very similar in form and habits to the mangrove monitors, but they are considerably more arboreal. They require similar terrarium conditions to those required for mangrove monitors. Quince monitors are much less hyperactive than other members of the mangrove monitor group, and they may allow handling and use in live animal lectures.

They tend to be active at any time as long as there is daylight but rarely forage for more than 20 to 30 minutes at a time. They will bask on tree trunks or on large rocks and otherwise stay in semi-concealment. Quince monitors swim well and will spend considerable time submerged. In this regard, they most closely resemble mangrove monitors rather than any of the several other closely related species.

Keep the terrarium warm (80 to 86°F [26.7 to 30°C]), with humidity above 80 percent; a warmer

The quince monitor is both more arboreal and more docile than the mangrove monitor. It has been captive bred by hobbyists and professional breeders.

basking site near the top of the enclosure is fine but not required. Provide plenty of shelter, as these lizards like to be well concealed when not basking or foraging.

Captives may lay from 2 to 12 eggs per clutch, and if incubated at 80 to 86°F (26.7 to 30°C) will hatch after 165 days. Incubate eggs in a 1:1 ratio of vermiculite or perlite to water.

Lizards of all age groups should be fed live insects, preferably daily. Supplement the diets of adults with a weekly offering of small freshly killed mice.

Head and full body views of the tri-colored monitor. These lizards tend to be aggressive to keepers and will not hesitate to eat other lizards, including other tri-colored monitors.

Varanus yuwonoi Harvey and Barker, 1998
Tri-Colored Monitor

Etymology: Named for Indonesian animal dealer/collector Frank Bambang Yuwono, who provided the specimens for the type description.

Range: The eastern Indonesian island of Halmahera.

Maximum Size: Unknown but grows to at least 45.3 inches (1,150 mm)

References: Harvey and Barker (1998).

Captive Suitability: 4

Natural History: Largely unknown. This beautiful forest lizard was unknown to science until 1995, and it was soon named as a new species. It is one of the largest predators on its island home and feeds upon any smaller animal it can overpower and consume. Although they can overpower rodents and other lizards, preferred prey consists of insects, other large invertebrates, and small eggs. Adults closely resemble young Komodo dragons in proportions and general morphology; they resemble the *Velociraptors* of *Jurassic Park* in temperament and behavior!

They prefer hot temperatures (85 to 105°F [29.4 to 40.6°C) in shaded forest environments but are known to forage on beaches and swim in the ocean. Tri-colored monitors are very active lizards that can dig, climb, and swim with equal ease.

Captive Care: There are few specimens of this species in captivity, and very little is known about them in the wild. These beautiful lizards require the facilities you would supply both a tree monitor and mangrove monitor. They are excellent climbers that may spend days on vertical perches, such as tree trunks, and then retire to a large pool for a day or two. They swim and climb

245

with equal facility, and although not as skittish as tree monitors, they are still prone to bursts of quick speed. This is an aggressive species that's quite prone to biting and clawing both keepers and other monitors, so they are best handled carefully and housed singly. A large terrarium is a must, preferably one with at least 10 x 6.5 feet (3 x 2 m) of floor space and that is 6.5 feet (2 m) or more tall. The upper areas should be allowed to get in the 85 to 105°F (29.4 to 40.6°C) range, but the substrate area should stay below 85°F (29.4°C). Let nighttime temperatures drop 5 to 10°F (2.8 to 5.6°C).

Tri-colored monitors feed on small rodents, large insects (roaches, adult crickets, and locusts are good choices), canned and packaged dog foods, and turkey sausages.

This species is one of the most aggressive of monitors, and a warning display is as likely to lead to an attack as a careful retreat. *Do not house these monitors with other lizards*, and keep only tri-color monitors of similar size in an enclosure. I have observed one of these monitors kill and consume a slightly smaller mangrove monitor.

The blue-spotted monitor appears occasionally in the U.S. hobby. It may be a variant of the mangrove monitor rather than a valid species.

Varanus caerulivirens Ziegler, Böhme, and Philipp, 1999
Blue-Spotted Monitor

Etymology: (Latin) *caerulea*, blue, and *virens*, greenish
Range: Halmahera Island, Indonesia.
Maximum Size: 43.3 inches (1,100 mm)
References: Delisle (2007); Dieter (1999); Eidenmüller at www.monitor-lizards.net; Ziegler, Böhme, and Philipp (1999)
Captive Suitability: 3
Natural History: If this is indeed a valid species– there are some data to question its validity–then it represents another endemic from Halmahera, a relatively small island between western New Guinea and Sulawesi. Similarly, *Varanus ceramboensis* (see next entry) is also so similar to

Varanus indicus that its validity is also in question. Since 1995, several species have been described from that island. In appearance it resembles the mangrove monitor but has more and smaller light markings, giving it its blue-green coloring. The preserved materials in Germany closely resemble *Varanus rainerguentheri*, another species named by the same team, also from Halmahera. There have been no field studies to date.

Captive Care: There have been sporadic shipments of these lizards during the past several years under various names. Care is essentially the same as for mangrove monitors.

Very little is known of the Seram monitor in nature because it has long been confused with the mangrove monitor. It feeds mainly on large invertebrates, lizards, and eggs.

Approximate natural ranges of *V. caerulivirens* and *V. yuwonoi* (red), *V. melinus* (blue), and *V. ceramboensis* (yellow).

Varanus ceramboensis **Philipp, Böhme, and Ziegler, 1999**
Seram Monitor
Etymology: Latin for the Indonesian island of Ambon.

247

Range: Known only from Ambon (type locality), Seram, Banda, Buru, and Obi.
Maximum Size: 38.7 inches (984 mm)
References: Eidenmüller at www.monitor-lizards. net; Philipp, Böhme, and Ziegler (1999).
Captive Suitability: 3
Natural History: Another of the ever-increasing numbers in the mangrove monitor group allied to *Varanus indicus*, this species escaped notice because of the difficulties of ascertaining several characteristics from preserved specimens. Although the Seram monitor has not knowingly been studied in the wild, it is possible that at least some reports regarding *Varanus indicus* may actually refer to this cryptic species. Like the mangrove monitor, *Varanus ceramboensis* is a dark lizard with tiny yellow or cream-colored dorsal spots. The spots, though, form indistinct crossbands, a pattern also known from many populations of *V. indicus*. In the wild, the lizards feed on similar prey, including large insects, centipedes, crabs, spiders, smaller lizards, and small eggs.
Captive Care: The same as for *V. indicus*.

Southeastern Asia: Indian Monitors

These are medium to large, primarily terrestrial lizards found in dry, open habitats from India east to central Indonesia. They parallel the African monitors in many features of anatomy, ecology, and behavior. Like the African species, the tail in adults is under 1.8 times SV and laterally compressed. The posterior teeth become molar-like as the lizards age. Although they can swim, they tend to avoid entering the water.

Varanus bengalensis (Daudin, 1802) Bengal Monitor/Indian Monitor

Etymology: From Latin, meaning "of Bengal."
Range: Widespread from Pakistan and India south to Sri Lanka and east to Singapore and Java.
Maximum Size: 80.5 inches (2,045 mm)
References: Auffenberg (1994); Böhme and Ziegler (1997c); Sprackland (1992).
Captive Suitability: 4; CITES Appendix I
Natural History: The Bengal monitor is one of the best studied of all lizards, being the subject of a major ecological monograph (Auffenberg, 1994) and many shorter studies ranging from mating behavior to hormone activity. As a common large lizard in India, it is the subject of many medical and physiological studies, and the reports often erroneously use the name "*Varanus monitor*" in reference to the species (Sprackland, 1982a).

Juveniles up to about 20 inches (50.8 mm) long are largely arboreal but will come to ground to hunt. Subadults and adults are predominantly terrestrial, and they may excavate deep, long burrows to use as daytime retreats and in search of prey. Although Bengal monitors can swim well,

The Bengal monitor preys on the venomous snakes that occur within its range and is immune to their venom.

they will avoid entering the water if an option to do so exists, even when being pursued by predators.

Captive Care: In the 1960s, Bengal monitors were the most inexpensive and commonly available varanids in the pet trade. They are hardy and tractable, and they don't require many of the difficult-to-provide materials of other large monitors. Terrarium setups can be kept simple with a wooden, glass, or laminated floor and a box large enough for the lizard to take refuge.

Daytime temperatures should be in the 85 to 95°F (29.4 to 35°C) range, with seasonal increases to 103.5 to 113°F (39.7 to 45°C); the temperatures may be lowered considerably at night. Humidity should be low–30 to 50 percent–and a large dish of clean water always available. These lizards will drink frequently. Natural diet includes almost any manner of animal food (including venomous snakes, the bites of which have no apparent effect), from eggs to carrion. They will hiss and lash the tail, putting on an excellent facade of aggression, but they rarely bite even if seized.

THEN AND NOW

I recall purchasing a 13-inch (33 cm) Bengal monitor for $12.50 in July 1969. Subsequently, as the species was listed on CITES Appendix I, availability dried up for more than two decades. When specimens became available again in the 1990s, the numbers in the price were similar, although the decimal point was gone!

Clouded monitors have long been considered a subspecies of the Bengal monitor. The two species are very similar in appearance and life history.

Varanus nebulosus (Gray, 1831)
Clouded Monitor/Indian Monitor

Etymology: (Latin) *nebulosus*, cloudy or clouded.
Range: Pakistan east to Java and western Borneo and south to Sri Lanka.
Maximum Size: 63 inches (1,600 mm)
References: Auffenberg (1994); Böhme and Ziegler (1997c).
Captive Suitability: 5
Natural History: A well-studied species, although universally mixed with *Varanus bengalensis*, with which most authors still consider it a subspecies. Although Auffenberg (1994) noted the considerable mixing of traits in central Indian lizards, I consider the region a hybrid zone, on either side of which the lizards hold a consistent set of distinctive features. For example, in clouded monitors, the snout is more elongated, the supraocular scales are larger than the surrounding scales, the head has a distinct yellow coloring (at least in young animals), and the body has distinct, often tricolor bands (that tend to fade with age). In contrast, Bengal monitors have a truncated snout, lack distinctly enlarged supraoculars, and have simple bands only in the young.
Captive Care: Same as for either the Bengal or white-throated monitors.

Golden monitors are critically endangered, mostly because of habitat loss. They are also hunted for food and leather.

threat to golden monitors has been habitat loss. They are normally residents of flat floodplains near rivers, lakes, and other fairly stable water sources, all of which are ideal for agricultural use by humans. Their diet is made up largely of creatures associated with watery habitats: worms, frogs, tadpoles, reptile and bird eggs, large insects, and crustaceans.

The summer months produce extreme heat in many areas of the golden monitor's range, and they are, along with mastigures, among the most heat tolerant of reptiles. Daytime temperatures may reach 113°F (45°C), at which time lizards have been observed to be basking.

Coloration is variable and recalls that of the red tegu. Adults are generally black with pronounced yellow markings but may also sport red bands. Young are often black with red and orange dorsal markings.

Mating takes place in June and July, and females will lay up to 30 eggs between August and October. Hatchlings emerge after an incubation period of 28 to 35 weeks.

Captive Care: Very little has been written about this species in captivity, although the few reports relate that golden monitors are relatively docile and lethargic. They should be fed three to four times weekly, generally need vitamin supplements, and may live for more than a decade.

Varanus flavescens (Hardwicke and Gray, 1827)
Golden Monitor/Yellow Monitor

Etymology: (Latin) *flavescens*, golden.
Range: Northern India east through southern Nepal and Bangladesh.
Maximum Size: 36.2 inches (920 mm)
References: Auffenberg et al. (1989); Bennett (1998); Sprackland (1992); Visser (1985).
Captive Suitability: 3; CITES Appendix I
Natural History: This is both a poorly known species and an endangered one. Although they have been hunted as sources of food and leather, the major

Southeastern Asia: Water Monitors

These are the true giants among lizards, reaching lengths up to 9 feet (2.7 m). Water monitors are found in areas with permanent or dependable seasonal water sources, ranging from ponds and rivers to mangroves and beaches, being among the few lizards that actually swim at sea. Young lizards are equally comfortable in water, trees, or on land, but adults are less likely to climb.

Although some water monitors superficially resemble Nile monitors, the former have a longer, more attenuated snout, smaller and more anterior nostrils, and a comparatively longer tail.

Varanus cumingi Martin, 1838
Philippine Water Monitor

Etymology: Named for Hugh Cuming, a wealthy shipping merchant of the 19th century, who provided the first specimens for the British Museum (Natural History).
Range: Philippine islands of the Greater Mindanao region, including Mindanao, Basilano, Bohol, Leyte, and Samar.
Maximum Size: 59 inches (1,500 mm)
References: Bayless and Adragna (1997); Gaulke (1992, 1992a).
Captive Suitability: 3
Natural History: These beautiful bumblebee-patterned monitors were totally unknown except as preserved museum specimens until Dr. Maren

The Philippine water monitor was long considered a subspecies of the common water monitor. It is less tied to bodies of water than the common water monitor.

Gaulke of Germany began a long series of studies on the herpetofauna of the Philippines. This distinctive species contains two geographically distinct color varieties. Most of the populations are more similar in coloring to other water monitors, being dark gray with grayish-yellow heads and napes. The lizards from Mindanao are the bright yellow and black animals that are generally taken to represent the species.

Unlike the other water monitors of the Philippines, this species is much more of a loner, rarely found in small groups. They are far more

terrestrial, traveling far inland, away from water. Also, adults are almost as likely to climb trees as juveniles, something larger water monitors almost never do.

Captive Care: Philippine water monitors are rarely encountered outside of zoos because of their size requirements, cost of care, and hefty price tags. Because they are more active than the larger water monitor species, they require extremely large terrariums, at least 12 feet (3.8 m) to a side and about as tall. Provide a distinct hot spot for basking (113°F [45°C]), and have a variety of hiding places–hollow logs, boxes, artificial caves–to provide privacy and an escape from the heat. Although wild lizards are not as linked to the water as their name implies, captive animals do spend considerable time soaking, and if the pool is large enough, swimming.

Feed the lizards daily, providing live or fresh prawns, fish, rats, and chicks; also offer large roaches and other large insects to adults and smaller insects to juveniles. Males tend to be more robust, particularly behind the eyes, than females.

This is an unusual species of animal because the relationship of color pattern to age is the opposite of what is seen in the vast majority of animals. In Philippine water monitors, the young hatch with drab brown coloration and slowly acquire the bright yellow bands as they mature.

Captive Philippine water monitors may mate at any time of year, and eggs are laid about a month later. Two or three clutches of up to 12 eggs may be laid each year, and incubation takes 190 to 220 days if kept between 80 and 86°F (27 and 30°C).

Superficially, the water monitor bears a strong resemblance to the Nile monitor. In the water monitor, the nostril is on the tip of the snout, while in the Nile, it is closer to the eye.

Varanus salvator (Laurenti, 1768)
Asiatic Water Monitor/Banded Monitor/
Kabara-Goya (Sri Lanka)/Biawak (Borneo)

Etymology: (Latin) *salvator*, savior or rescuer, in accord with ancient belief that the presence of large monitors warned people of the presence of crocodiles. This species is often still called– incorrectly–either *Varanus cepedianus* or *Varanus monitor* in literature from Asia. Both names were declared invalid by the International Commission on Zoological Nomenclature (ICZN) long ago.
Range: Widespread from Burma (Myanmar), eastern India, and Sri Lanka east to Sulawesi (Celebes), Indonesia, and north through the

There are several subspecies and local variants of *V. salvator* known. From left to right: *V. s. marmoratus* from the Philippines; *V. s. komaini* from northern Thailand; *V. s. togianus* from the island of Togi, Indonesia; and a darkly colored *V. s. salvator* from an unknown locality.

Philippines and southern China; also found on the Nicobar and Andaman Islands.

Maximum Size: 110 inches (2,794 mm)

References: Biswas and Sanyal (1980); Dieter (1999a); Ditmars (1933); Dwyer and Perez (2007); Gaulke (1989, 1992, 1992a); Pandav and Choudhury (1996).

Captive Suitability: 3

Natural History: This species is second in mass only to the Komodo dragon. A large, well-fed adult may weigh 150 pounds (68 kg). Although known as the water monitor, this species is very much a generalist capable of digging and climbing as well as swimming. Specimens have been seen swimming many miles (km)from land, and no doubt they are able to swim among the islands of Southeast Asia. A water monitor was the first

nonflying vertebrate recorded from the remnant islet after the eruption of Krakatau. They are encountered in most habitats near standing water but are absent from dry grasslands and deserts.

Throughout much of their range, people use water monitors as a food source, and monitors are both trapped and hunted for the pot and for their valuable hides. Natives of many Asian countries believe that the monitors–which are also scavengers–consume human corpses and thus provide a home for the souls of departed people. The lizards were long the predominant varanid exported to the world's live animal dealers, but the popularity of other species has sometimes eclipsed the water monitor. Young specimens are particularly susceptible to virulent respiratory infections they contract during the period of

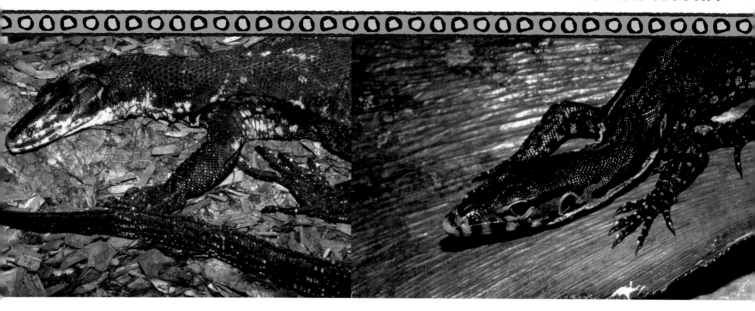

confinement in Asia, and few juveniles that survive the trip to Europe, Japan, or America live long.

This species almost certainly represents a species-complex, meaning there are probably several very closely related taxa that will be formally recognized once the different populations are better studied (such as happened with the mangrove and tree monitor groups). Several subspecies have been named over the years, and their validity is highly questionable. *Varanus salvator cumingi* has been considered a species in its own right. (See *Varanus cumingi* in this chapter.) *V. s. marmoratus* (Wiegmann, 1834) and the white-headed *V. s. nuchalis* (Günther, 1872) are found in the Philippines. In both taxa, the nuchal scales are larger than the dorsals, but only *V. s. nuchalis* has nuchals that are also larger than the occipital scales. I have examined the holotype and other specimens of *V. s. togianus* and find little that distinguishes it from *V. s. salvator*; it is from the small island of Togi east of

Sulawesi (Celebes), Indonesia. The entirely black form known as the Komaini phase, *V. s. komaini* Nutphand, 1987, is from upper Thailand and is morphologically very similar to *V. s. salvator* except in color. There is also a bright powdery yellow color morph that showed up at dealers' shops around 2000 and is sold under the name "sulfur phase" water monitor. Many questions await systematists, taxonomists, ecologists, and zoogeographers who tackle the water monitor group. Because of the similarity in names, water monitors are sometimes mistaken for New Guinea's tree crocodile monitor–the Asian is *Varanus salvator* and the New Guinean is *Varanus salvadorii*.

Captive Care: Obtain captive-bred juveniles if at all possible because they are much more likely to be healthy and survive into adolescence than wild-caught specimens. If you must acquire a wild-caught animal, avoid specimens under 9.8 inches (250 mm) SVL. Subadults are more likely to be in

Water monitors mating in a Sri Lankan river.

KEEPING AND BREEDING VARANUS SALVATOR

By Paul Rodriguez

Unlike most monitor enthusiasts who fell in love with monitors upon seeing a Komodo dragon, I did not become passionate about them until I saw a photo of a crocodile monitor at age 13. I was in love, although it would be a long time before I acquired a monitor. I bought my first, a Nile monitor, at age 20. Over the following several years, I raised savannas, Argus monitors, Timor monitors, and water monitors. I bred Nile monitors in 1998, water monitors from 1999 to 2004, and Timors in 2004.

Gravid water monitor.

Due to the size of water monitors, only individuals who can maintain large enclosures should keep these animals. Although water monitors are known for being "tame," some turn out to be very skittish and defensive. Large animals have the potential to inflict damaging bites, so care and common sense are critical to prevent accidents. Carelessness with a water monitor can cause ripple effects for other monitor enthusiasts and lead to bans on the keeping of larger varanids.

It is important to keep in mind that the following approach to breeding worked for me with one pair of water monitors over several years. The information should be viewed as a guide, not as law. The key to breeding any animal is to be observant and modify conditions as necessary.

HOUSING

Water monitors need a large enclosure, and using an entire room is not excessive. Several hiding and basking spots to each animal will reduce aggression between individuals.

Further, whenever two animals are kept together, a second enclosure should be ready in case aggression necessitates separation temporarily or permanently. In captivity, it is possible that one animal may not be receptive to living with another animal.

A deep substrate is required. It might be best to build a large box and fill it with dirt. Approximately 24 inches (61 cm) of soil seems to be the minimum depth required for nest building. The ideal substrate clumps and holds its form, and a mixture of plain dirt and cypress mulch achieves this ideal. If the nesting substrate is dry and dusty, water should be added to return it to a condition that allows clumping. Don't make the dirt too wet, as such a substrate will not be usable by the monitor.

Basking temperatures should range from 107 to 120°F (41.7 to 48.9°C), although some keepers provide higher-temperature basking sites. The ambient temperature of the enclosure should provide a gradient for the animal to use, including cooler temperatures. Make clean water available at all times. Captive animals may benefit from water containers that allow them to fit in completely, but excessive soaking may indicate that an enclosure is too dry. The monitors should be fed frequently. I provide a rodent-based diet, but I do not count the number of rodents per feeding or feed on a set schedule.

A cattle watering trough serves as a nesting box for this female. It is almost impossible to give these giant lizards too much space for living and breeding.

258

REPRODUCTION

Females cycle without exposure to a male and can produce a clutch of eggs approximately every three to four months. Cycling is indicated by increased girth in the abdomen. No special procedures are required to induce breeding. Prior to mating, the female allows the male near her. Mating usually occurs during the night hours in total darkness and may take place over seven days. At the end of the breeding period, the female may resume some aggression toward the male. The male should be removed from the enclosure, as female aggression toward him can be fatal.

Egg deposition occurs 28 to 45 days after the last mating. It appears that the ideal time for egg deposition is closer to 28 days. Later egg deposition time may be the result of the female holding the eggs until the male is removed or because of an excessively dry nesting substrate.

The female begins egg laying by digging a pit in the substrate. She may spend a day or two digging the nest. Lengthier diggings seem to reflect a substrate that is too dry. Egg deposition occurs entirely at night, and the pit is covered by the morning.

The following data reflect 64 eggs in five different clutches. The average clutch size ranges from 11 to 15 eggs. Eggs can be incubated on a mixture of vermiculite or perlite and water at a 1:1 ratio by volume. Excessive water causes eggs to swell and break open. Eggs should be incubated at approximately 80 to 85°F (26.7 to 29.4°C). Higher temperatures may shorten the incubation period but seem to result in smaller hatchlings and higher mortality rates. Average egg weight ranges from 1.4 to 2.7 ounces (40 to 76.5 g).

Hatchlings emerge after approximately 195 days, although I have experienced a range of 177 to 206 days. Hatchlings range in size from approximately 13 to 17 inches (33 to 43.2 cm) and weigh approximately 1.5 ounces (42 g).

Newly hatched babies should be set up in aquariums and provided access to a basking spot and hide areas. I allow the neonates to remain in the incubator for two days and then move them to an aquarium with a cypress mulch substrate. I offer food after several days, but feeding often does not occur until about seven days after hatching. Once the hatchlings begin to feed, I offer food on a near daily basis. Young monitors will eat readily and constantly. Well-fed, well-kept babies will grow quickly and will need larger enclosures within a few months.

tolerable health. Any wild-caught water monitor should be kept in isolation and subjected to a full veterinary examination for parasites, injuries, and diseases.

Expect water monitors to grow rapidly if properly fed and housed. Juveniles should double in length during each of their first three years of life. Young require copious amounts of live foods on a daily basis. Provide gut-loaded crickets, roaches, grasshoppers, earthworms, pinky mice, small pieces of cooked sausages, and diced boiled eggs. As lizards grow, provide larger food items. Once the monitors exceed 9.8 inches (250 mm) SVL, feed three or four times per week; when SVL exceeds 15.7 inches (400 mm), they should be fed no more than twice weekly.

Although juveniles are apt to climb if given a tall enough terrarium and some branches, this species tends to be primarily terrestrial. They spend the days alternately foraging for food–they are quite good at finding buried meals, such as turtle eggs–basking on a log near water, or resting in a hollow tree or burrow. With frequent handling, water monitors can become incredibly docile, and I have witnessed a specimen that would allow small children to ride on its back (not recommended, I hasten to add).

Reports of captive breeding are much more common today than they were in the 1980s but are by no means common. The biggest drawback to regular captive breeding is that the adults are large and require more room than most herpetoculturists can provide.

Southeastern Asia: Forest Monitors

Lizards in this group are related to water monitors but have quite different biologies. All are largely arboreal, but there the similarities end. Each species in this group is morphologically and ecologically distinct from the others, including the only monitors that feed primarily on crabs or fruits. The species in this group include the monitors with the most solidly ossified skull and another with the longest skull. These lizards are distributed from Myanmar (Burma) east through Borneo and Sumatra and north to the Philippines.

Varanus dumerilii (Schlegel, 1839)
Duméril's Monitor
Etymology: Named for André Marie Constant Duméril (1774-1860), a prolific French herpetologist at the National Museum of Natural History in Paris, whose contributions included the first major catalog of the reptiles of the world.
Range: Southeastern Asia, from central Burma (Myanmar) east to Borneo and Sumatra.
Maximum Size: 51.2 inches (1,300 mm)
References: Krebs (1979); Hauschild (2001); Radford and Paine (1989); Sprackland (1977, 1992, 1993, 1995a); Ziegler and Böhme (1996).
Captive Suitability: 5
Natural History: Duméril's monitor is riparian in habits, being both an excellent burrower and swimmer. The nostrils are equipped with passive valves that shut as the lizard submerges its head. While in repose, these monitors may stay submerged for as long as four hours. They excavate long burrows in the moist riverbank soil, into which they may flee if threatened while

too far from the water to dive to safety. They also climb well but are not principally arboreal except when young.

Duméril's monitor is much more colorful as a hatchling than as a subadult or adult. Hatchlings have intensely bright orange heads and subdued orange crossbands on a black dorsum. By six weeks of age, the orange is already fading into what will become a dull earthy tan, while the black becomes a chocolate brown. Presumably, the juvenile color serves to make these harmless lizards look like the lethally venomous kraits (genus *Bungarus*) with which they are sympatric in Southeast Asia.

Adult Duméril's monitor feeding on a crab. In some areas of its natural range, Duméril's monitor may feed heavily on crabs.

Hatchling Duméril's monitor in hand, showing both the bright colors of the juveniles and the size at hatching.

Duméril's monitors take a variety of live foods, including large insects–orthopterans such as locusts, and katydids are preferred–worms, centipedes, frogs, other lizards, and small eggs. They also consume crabs, which might make up the staple diet for populations of monitors in mangrove swamps and ocean beach habitats. Krebs (1979) reported the systematic manner in which the monitors capture crabs and then tear off the legs, saving the carapace for consumption last.

Along with the ability to overpower crabs come the massive jaw muscles that make crushing crab

Adult Duméril's monitor feeding on a large roach. Always use tongs or other tools for feeding large lizards, never your bare hands.

shells possible. The upper temporal openings of the skull are much smaller in this species than any other varanid, the added bone providing much more anchoring space for the muscles. As the monitors age, the posterior teeth become slightly blunted and broader at the base, facilitating the cracking of hard shells.

Although two subspecies were named, it has been demonstrated (Sprackland, 1993) that there is no justification for them. No characteristic serves to reliably distinguish one form from another.

Captive Care: This is one of the best varanid species for the novice giant lizard keeper to maintain. Duméril's monitors are less active than many other varanids, and although they will actively prowl a terrarium, they are also inclined to become more sedate in their surroundings with time.

These monitors require a large container of water in which they can fully immerse themselves, and ideally, swim or walk along the bottom. The water must be cleaned at least daily, as lizards will defecate and shed there.

The bright colors of hatchling Duméril's monitors fade to the adult colors after six weeks or so.

Duméril's monitors acclimate well to captivity and will generally allow handling without attempting to bite. The claws are extremely sharp and may cause serious scratches, so gloves and long sleeves may be useful when handling these lizards. Although they are disinclined to bite, new arrivals may display hissing and tail lashing with considerable intensity. They may inflate the body and tilt it at a 30-degree angle toward the perceived aggressor. If touched, the lizard may assume an unusual warning posture, with the body held rigid and the head and neck arched back and upward. Presumably, this posture makes the lizard appear too large or difficult to swallow to would-be predators.

Mating of captive animals generally occurs in July and August, and egg deposition follows in October or November. Eggs incubate well in a mixture of vermiculite to water ratio of 5:6, by volume. Incubate eggs at 80 to 86°F (26.7 to 30°C), and expect hatching in 200 to 240 days. Feed young a variety of insects, such as adult crickets and grasshoppers, and supplement with crawfish tails, shredded crabmeat, and young mice. Juveniles should be fed daily during the first six months of life, then four times weekly.

BREEDING AND REPRODUCTION OF *VARANUS DUMERILII*

By Ben Aller and Michaela Manago

Copulation of captive Duméril's monitors can occur year round when lizards are kept in ideal conditions. Having a common area such as an outdoor enclosure so monitors can be "rotated" in and out can help stimulate breeding behaviors. Duméril's monitors do not require any specific photoperiod changes or drop in temperature to stimulate reproduction. The most important factor in breeding Duméril's is providing excellent nesting options well before ovulation and subsequent copulation.

Males and females can be housed together year round as long as you provide enough space. Housing multiple males and especially females together in any enclosure is not recommended, as the fighting between females tends to be much more vicious and damaging then the ritualized combat seen between males.

A gravid female will show signs of bloating and digging, and may refuse food a few days to a week before oviposition. Nesting sites should be provided soon after copulation because females will pick out nest spots weeks prior to egg-laying. Proper nesting sites should have deep substrate and security, as well as maintain moisture without flooding. Females will often use elevated nesting boxes and providing several nesting boxes in different locations within the enclosure aids in successful laying. Female Duméril's tend to nest where soil temperatures are around 85°F (29.4°C) and have enough moisture. Sandy loam, various ratios of sand, dirt, coconut shell bedding, sphagnum moss, and leaf litter work well as nesting media. In the wild, they often lay eggs in river banks or in rotting logs.

Duméril's monitor nest created within its enclosure (left). Hatching clutch of Duméril's incubated on coarse vermiculite (right).

Generally eggs will be deposited in the middle of the night or in the early morning. Carefully remove and mark the top of each egg, in the position in which you found it, with a simple pencil marking. Eggs should be kept in this position during the entire incubation process. Incubate eggs in vermiculite or perlite, though greater success has been found while using perlite, with a water ratio of 1:1 by volume at 83 to 86° F (26.5 to 30°C). Expect hatching in 179 to 240 days. The moisture level and temperature in your egg containers should be kept constant; to do this an initial weight of the 1:1 ratio of water to substrate should be recorded. Check the eggs weekly and correct for any loss of water. Water bottles can be placed in empty spaces inside the incubator to help maintain the temperature.

Hatchlings should be kept warm and very moist, as they dehydrate quickly. They generally feed a few days to three weeks after hatching, consuming adult crickets, cockroaches, cut-up whole-bodied crawfish, and shrimp (with heads). It is crucial to provide whole-bodied prey items throughout the life of the monitor. Juveniles should be fed daily

Cage setup for hatchling Duméril's monitors. Note the sphagnum moss, which helps maintain the high humidity these lizards need.

Hatchling (left) and subadult (right) *V. rudicollis*. The juveniles are often brightly marked in black and green, while adults become mostly black with traces of gray and green.

Varanus rudicollis (Gray, 1845)
Rough-Necked Monitor

Etymology: (Latin) *Rudi-*, rough or keeled, and *collis*, neck.

Range: Heavily forested regions of Southeast Asia, including Burma (Myanmar), Thailand, Malaysia, Borneo, and the extreme southern Philippines.

Maximum Size: 63 inches (1,600 mm)

References: Sprackland (1992).

Captive Suitability: 4; 3 if recently imported

Natural History: This is a sleek black lizard with an extremely long snout and long slit of a nostril. The body is relatively short and the tail long. The nape is covered with large pyramid-like keels. Despite its

truly unique appearance, many people still confuse rough-necked monitors with the stouter, longer-bodied, brown and tan Duméril's monitor.

These lithe lizards are primarily arboreal, spending most of their time in the forest trees. Their body proportions–a long snout and tail and short, squat body–make them resemble huge anoles, and like the small American lizards, they spend much of the daytime on tree trunks looking

V. mabitang is a large arboreal monitor of the Philippines about which little is known.

for invertebrate prey and keeping watch for potential predators.

Captive Care: These are beautiful display animals, but the main drawback to keeping them is that most specimens are still wild caught, arriving with heavy infestations of internal and external parasites. Prognosis for such animals is dismal. By all means, get freshly acquired wild-caught specimens to a veterinarian and have a complete set of tests for parasites. Keep new specimens in strict quarantine for at least 30 days and until veterinary exams show no pathogens.

Captive-bred specimens, although rare, are hardy and adapt well to proper housing conditions if given a varied diet of invertebrate foods and both vitamin and mineral supplements. The few

studies of the gut contents of wild rough-necked monitors show prey to include mostly stick insects and large katydids, and these possibly contain vitamin or mineral sources not reproduced in regularly available insect sources. Feed lizards a variety of large insects, especially roaches, and baby mice. Supplement with boiled eggs.

These large lizards require very tall enclosures and plenty of vertical surfaces to climb. Use natural logs when possible. Provide a large enough water dish to allow lizards to soak. Daytime temperatures should be in the 85 to 95°F (29.4 to 35°C) range and humidity between 40 and 60 percent.

This species becomes docile and allows handling. They rarely attempt to bite, but their sharp claws can cause serious cuts.

V. mabitang is an oddity among monitors in that it seems to be completely herbivorous.

Varanus mabitang Gaulke and Curio, 2001
Mabitang Black Monitor

Etymology: Mabitang is the local name used by the people of Panay for this species.

Range: Panay Island, Philippines.

Maximum Size: 68.9 inches (1,750 mm)

References: Gaulke and Curio (2001)

Captive Suitability: 1

Natural History: Nature has presented the world with a truly unusual monitor. Almost all members of the larger grouping Varanoidea are made up of carnivorous species. One large Philippine monitor, Gray's monitor, surprised herpetologists when it was found to feed largely upon fruits, but its diet was seasonally based, and so it ate snails during much of the year. The Mabitang black monitor, however, is the first known fully frugivorous varanid. They consume figs and the fruit and leaves of the screw palm but have not yet been observed feeding on any animal matter. The caecum is unusual in that it is more similar in form to that of other plant-eating lizards than to the closely allied monitors.

Like *Varanus olivaceus*, the Mabitang black monitor is primarily arboreal, found where the fruits are in the forest canopy. This species is extremely similar to Gray's monitor in morphology and size but differs in being almost entirely black. A few tiny yellow spots are found on the extremities and on the soft skin between some scales. The tongue is pink.

Captive Care: Unknown, although specimens may have been kept in the Philippines.

Gray's monitor is rarely kept in captivity. It requires a large enclosure with sturdy climbing branches and a large water bowl.

Varanus olivaceus Hallowell, 1856
Gray's Monitor/Butaan

Etymology: (Latin) *olivaceus*, olive colored. For nearly a century, this species was incorrectly called *Varanus grayi* because the description by Hallowell was not understood to go with the Philippine species. Only when there were sufficient specimens available for comparison in the 1980s was the error noted and the original name restored.

Range: Northern parts of the Philippines, notably on Luzon Island.

Maximum Size: 64 inches (1,626 mm)

References: Auffenberg (1976, 1979, 1982, 1988).

Captive Suitability: 4

Natural History: This remarkable lizard managed to escape the eyes of scientists–excepting a skull and two small preserved examples–from 1855 until 1978, even though it exceeds 5 feet (1.5 m) in length and lives near a major urban population center. When rediscovered by Walter Auffenberg, it was soon learned that this arboreal forest monitor feeds upon large fruits that grow in the trees. Subsequently, the lizard became famous as a frugivorous varanid, although it actually makes up most of its diet by consuming the large tree snails with which it lives.

Many large monitors undergo ontogenetic tooth change, meaning that the typical curved, sharp teeth of the young lizards convert to broader, blunter molar-like teeth in adults. This occurs in the African species (except *Varanus griseus*), Bengal, Indian, and golden monitors. In *Varanus olivaceus*, the teeth also change but at an

earlier age than in the other varanids; this is most likely linked to the predominance in the lifelong diet of snails, crabs, hard-shelled beetles, and fruits.

Captive Care: These lizards require large enclosures with stout branches and plenty of climbing space on broad trunks. Basking and resting are done in trees, but foraging, feeding, and swimming bring them to the ground. Temperatures should be kept high (77 to 103°F [25 to 39.4°C]), with adequate clean water and hiding places for the lizards to escape direct heat. Humidity should vary between 70 and 100 percent.

Terrarium animals will consume rodents, large insects, turkey sausages, fresh fish, shrimp, snails, slugs, and fruits such as figs, mangos, plums, grapes, and bananas.

Mating may take place anytime during the summer months, with egg deposition in late summer to early fall. Females use burrows, hollow tree trunks, or nest boxes for deposition of 4 to 11 eggs. Incubation takes 270 to 300 days.

Australia: Sand Monitors

Sand monitors are large to very large primary predators found widely across Australia, its offshore islands, and into New Guinea.

Varanus giganteus (Gray, 1845) Perentie

Etymology: (Latin) *gigant-*, a giant. At the time this species was described, it was believed to be the largest lizard in the world. "Perentie" is an Aboriginal Australian name for the species.

Range: Dry, interior Australia, from the Western Australian coast and nearby islands east to central Queensland and New South Wales.

Maximum Size: 96 inches (2,438 mm)

References: Bennett (1998); Irwin (1997); Macdonald (2007); Murphy (1972); Vincent and Wilson (1999); Wilson (1987); Wilson and Knowles (1988); Wilson and Swan (2003).

Captive Suitability: 3

Natural History: Perenties are inhabitants of the hottest and most inhospitable places the Australian Outback has to offer. Their eyesight is reportedly excellent, allowing them to spot prey or predator equally well from considerable distances. Unlike most other large monitors, perenties are generally gracile and lithe unless they have recently fed.

Habitats include sandy areas across the northern third of Australia, from open flatland to rocky ravines. Perenties are wide-ranging foragers that may travel considerable distances to find prey in particularly inhospitable terrain. Survival in the desert Outback has required perenties to become excellent burrowers and predators, with

Hatchling (left) and an adult (right) perentie. The hatchlings are about 14.5 inches (36.8 cm) in total length. The adult is covered in dirt from burrowing.

superb long-distance eyesight. As a consequence of the habitat, the monitors feed on all manner of animal food, from invertebrates to vertebrates to eggs and carrion. Among the vertebrate prey are many venomous snakes, which the lizards grasp quickly, then shake until the prey's back is broken. They also consume small marsupials and other monitors. Perenties living near beaches will consume turtle eggs and hatchling sea turtles when available.

Captive Care: There is little useful information on the care of perenties outside of facilities in or near their native homes in Australia. They are prone to respiratory infections, allegedly induced if they become chilled. Their native habitats are extremely low-humidity areas, generally below 30 percent. Because many bacteria thrive in higher-humidity and temperature environments,

it is possible that perenties in captivity become susceptible to infections because of the higher humidity in terraria. Captives do best if kept at temperatures above 110°F (43.3°C) and given several options to escape the heat. Shelters should include large hide boxes or deep sand in which the monitors will excavate long burrows. Perhaps best of all is a buried hide box. Sand should contain enough moisture to allow excavation of burrows, and within burrows or boxes the humidity should be around 75 percent.

Perenties are among the widest ranging of reptiles, and their need for extremely large areas makes them poor candidates for captivity. Several Australian zoos and private breeders have successfully bred perenties, but overseas efforts have been less fortunate.

They are as catholic in their tastes as captives as

Perentie climbing a tree in the Northern Territory. Despite their size, perenties may be quite arboreal in certain habitats.

Varanus gouldii (Gray, 1838)
Gould's Monitor/Sand Monitor

Etymology: Named for John Gould, noted ornithologist of the 19th century who specialized in naming the birds from Australia and New Guinea.

Range: Broadly distributed throughout Australia's drier habitats; notably absent in humid forests and riparian environments.

Maximum Size: 63 inches (1,600 mm)

References: Balsai (1997); Card (1995); Cogger (2000); Ehmann (1992); International Commission on Zoological Nomenclature (ICZN) (2000); Mitchell (1990); Shine (1986); Sprackland et al. (1997); Trembath (2000); Vincent and Wilson (1999); Weigel (1988); Wilson (1987); Wilson and Knowles (1988); Wilson and Swan (2003).

Captive Suitability: 4

Approximate natural range of *V.g. gouldii* (yellow) and *V.g. flavirufus* (red).

they are in the wild, so feed them prawns, crabs, fresh fish, eggs, large arthropods, smaller lizards, rodents, or small birds. Because these lean lizards are so active, they should be fed daily. They do bask in small pools, but opportunities to do so should be limited for specimens kept indoors because they may spend too much time in the pools causing various health issues.

On the left, a Gould's monitor from New South Wales covered in reddish dirt from digging. The animal on the right is the questionable *flavirufus* subspecies and was photographed near Pannawonica, Western Australia.

Natural History: This is one of the most broadly distributed of varanids, ranging across mainland Australia and apparently absent only from part of southeastern Western Australia, southern Victoria and central Queensland. Gould's monitors are found in arid deserts, xeric scrub forests, and near human settlements. Although long confused with the Argus monitor, Gould's monitors are readily characterized by the pure yellow distal third of the tail. In Argus monitors, the tail tip is mottled. In addition, a putative subspecies, *Varanus gouldii flavirufus* Mertens, 1958, has been recognized and is distinguished largely by its more intense yellow and orange coloring. Professional taxonomists have not adequately addressed the status of *V. g. flavirufus*, although the amateur and commercial communities retain the name for the higher-priced color variety.

Although quite similar in appearance to Argus monitors, Gould's monitors differ in both appearance and natural history. Gould's monitors are less cold tolerant, spending cold days in deep burrows or rocky crevices.

Like other species in its group, Gould's monitors can stand upright on the hind legs and tail, assuming a tripod stance. This is sometimes used as part of a threat display but seems more common as a simple periscope attempt to see a greater field of vision. Angered lizards rise on the hind limbs, arch the head and neck downward, and hiss slowly and ominously. Although they may lash with the tail, they rarely attempt to bite unless seized.

This species will eat almost anything of animal nature that it can swallow. Large prey is twisted and wrenched into bite-sized pieces. Typical foods

273

include lizards, small marsupials, large arthropods, and eggs. Insects make up the majority of the diet by mass.

Wild lizards tend to mate in the spring (September through November) and lay up to 11 eggs per clutch in December through January. Young emerge in October through November.

Captive Care: Because this species is generally more active than Argus monitors, the cage area should be larger than for the latter species. Basking sites that allow lizards to reach temperatures of 112°F (44.4°C) should be provided, along with adequate individual refugia from the heat and light. House males singly or with one or two females. Feed these lizards daily or on alternate days. Captives do well on a diet of freshly killed rodents, precooked sausages, large insects, and lizards.

Argus monitor standing on its hind legs. A number of monitor species perform this behavior, both to get a better view of the surrounding area and during threat displays.

***Varanus panoptes* Storr, 1980**
Argus Monitor
Etymology: (Latinized) named for the Greek god Argus, who had 1,000 eyes all over his body. From *pan*, all, and *ops*, eyes.
Range: Much of the northern half of Australia and lowland New Guinea.

Head and full-body images of Argus monitors. The animal on the left is from New Guinea, while the animal on the right was photographed in Kakadu National Park, Northern Territory.

Maximum Size: 58 inches (1,448 mm)
References: Alles and Charlson (2007); Balsai (1997); Böhme (1988); Cogger (2000); Dieter (2000); Dwyer and Bayless (1996); Ehmann (1992); Eidenmuller (1997, 2007); Houston (1978); International Commission on Zoological Nomenclature (ICZN) (2000); Lenk et al. (2005); Sprackland (1992, 2001a); Sprackland et al. (2004); Storr (1980); Storr et al. (1983); Swan et al. (2004); Wilson (1987); Wilson and Knowles (1988); Wilson and Swan (2003).
Captive Suitability: 5
Natural History: Argus monitors may reside in a wide range of habitats, from islands in the Great Barrier Reef to open outback to muddy riverbanks. Their primary criterion for a residence seems to be having ample heat, as they are rarely, if ever, observed when the air temperature is lower than

90.5°F (32.5°C). They are equally likely to be found around the noisy power generator near a station as in the remote and pristine outback.

These are large and wide-ranging lizards, typically foraging over an area 2 to 2.5 miles (3.2 to 4 km) in diameter. Foods include almost anything of animal origin that they can find, from carcasses of road-killed mammals to eggs to snakes. Although they are often seen patrolling along beaches on the Great Barrier Reef–Lizard Island is named for this species–Argus monitors seem to loathe actually entering the water.

Although swift and wary, these lizards allow humans to come quite close if approached slowly. Once the distance is shortened to about that where you could stretch and actually touch the animal, it moves quickly out of range. When disturbed, it rises up on stiffened legs and slowly

and ominously hisses, occasionally lashing the tail at the intruder. However, even if grabbed, these lizards are reluctant to bite.

A New Guinea subspecies was named based primarily on the presence of ventral dark spots, but subsequent examination of lizards from New Guinea and Australia has yielded such specimens from across the range. As no other diagnostic characteristics were found that could be used to distinguish the lizards from each other, no subspecies are presently recognized.

Captive Care: This is a hardy species that has been successfully maintained and repeatedly bred by many herpetoculturists. They almost never climb, so these are lizards for which horizontal floor space is of paramount concern. Because they are expert diggers, there should be a deep substrate of slightly moistened sand so that they can excavate tunnels used for refuge.

Keep temperatures above 90.5°F (32.5°C), with a hot spot near 120°F (48.9°C). Humidity is not a major concern and may safely range from 30 to 100 percent. If gently and regularly handled, Argus monitors become docile and are good animals to use in educational shows and presentations.

Captive breeding is now common to the point that there is no justification for collecting from wild populations. This is the first species of varanid for which parthenogenetic reproduction has been recorded (Lenk et al., 2005).

Varanus rosenbergi Mertens, 1957
Rosenberg's Monitor/Heath Monitor

Etymology: Named in honor of Hans Rosenberg, wildlife photographer for the Senckenberg Museum and Frankfurt Zoo during the 1930s and 1940s.

Range: This species has a disjunct distribution along southern Australia in regions of dense vegetation and high humidity, from the Perth area of Western Australia east to central coastal New South Wales; absent from the Nullarbor region.

Maximum Size: 40 inches (1,020 mm)

References: Case and Schwaner (1993); Christian and Weavers (1994); Eidenmüller (1997); Green and King (1993); Greer (1989); Houston (1978); Rismiller et al. (2007); Swan et al. (2004); Wilson (1987); Wilson and Knowles (1988); Wilson and Swan (2003).

Captive Suitability: 4

Natural History: This is perhaps the most cold tolerant of the monitors, for although it does not occur as far south as the white-throated monitor of Africa, it is nevertheless active at lower temperatures along Australia's southern coast and wind-lashed offshore islands. The dark gray to black dorsal coloration may help it absorb sunlight and thus heat up quickly.

Heath monitors are found in flat rocky areas with sparse vegetation and in valleys with large boulders. They have been the subjects of physiological studies (see Green and King, 1993) but have otherwise not drawn the attention of many herpetologists. With the captive breeding of the species came the discovery that hatchlings are beautifully marked with black, ash, and

Head and full-body images of heath monitors. They are closely related to *V. gouldii* but are much darker in color, possibly an adaptation to their colder habitat.

orange bands, possibly mimicking local venomous snakes.

Captive Care: Similar as for the Argus and lace monitors. There have been few kept in captivity, and published accounts of captives are almost nonexistent.

Approximate natural range of *V. panoptes* (red) and *V. rubidus* (green) and *V.rosenbergi* (yellow).

277

Red-tailed monitors from near Paynes Find, Western Australia. The animal above is puffed up in a defensive display.

Varanus rubidus Storr, 1980
Red Sand Monitor/Red-Tailed Monitor

Etymology: From Latin, *rubidus*, reddish.
Range: Ranges through much of Western Australia, from the coast to near the South Australia border. Absent from the Nullarbor and northern regions of the state.
Maximum Size: 63 inches (1,600 mm)
References: Ehmann (1992); Storr (1980); Storr et al. (1983); Wilson (1987); Wilson and Knowles (1988); Wilson and Swan (2003).
Captive Suitability: 4
Natural History: Very poorly studied; presumably similar to that of *Varanus panoptes*. (*V. rubidus* was first described as a subspecies of *V. panoptes*.) Unlike *V. panoptes*, *V. rubidus* has a distinct yellow

tail tip with faint darker bands. In *V. panoptes*, there are thin dark bands.

The hottest and driest deserts of Western Australia are home to *Varanus rubidus*. Because the sands of these deserts are often reddish, the monitors acquire dust that gives them, too, a red coloring. After a fresh shed, the skin looks considerably more tan and yellow. To escape the extreme heat, which may reach or exceed 104°F (40°C), the monitors dig long, deep burrows into cooler, moist sands. Alternately, they "borrow" the burrow of another animal.
Captive Care: Probably similar as for the Argus and lace monitors. There is very little information about this species in the literature at present.

Varanus spenceri Lucas and Frost, 1903
Spencer's Monitor

Etymology: Named for Sir Walter Spencer (1860-1929), former curator at the South Australian Museum.

Range: East central Northern Territory and central Queensland in spare, arid habitats.

Maximum Size: 49.2 inches (1,250 mm)

References: Cogger (2000); Ehmann (1992); Hoser (1989); Peters (1970); Wilson (1987); Wilson and Knowles (1988); Wilson and Swan (2003).

Captive Suitability: 4

Natural History: This species is another enigma among monitors: It is large and has been known to science for more than a century, yet there is very little known about its natural history. They are residents of extremely harsh terrain but prefer harder-packed soil than perenties do. The claws are particularly long and thick for varanids and can be used to burrow into the baked clays of its habitat. From September to early November, females dig deep burrows in which they deposit up to 31 eggs. Hatching follows in five to six months.

Most information about the biology of Spencer's monitors is anecdotal. Along with the black-headed pythons (*Aspidites melanocephalus*) that share their range, the reptiles are believed to retreat into deep fissures in the earth to escape the most intensely hot part of the austral summer. Because the preferred habitats are largely devoid of trees and other shade-producing cover, lizards tend to stay in hiding during the hottest parts of the day, being active in the morning and afternoon.

V. spenceri inhabits harsh deserts in central to eastern Australia; this captive adult is obviously not in naturalistic housing.

Given their habitat, Spencer's monitors are opportunistic carnivores, feeding upon any animal they can overpower and consume.

Captive Care: Again, little is known about Spencer's monitors. They require roomy terrariums but do not need climbing areas or a large water dish. Given deep enough substrate, they will burrow. In lieu of substrate, provide each lizard with its own hide box. Be sure to provide both UV and high-heat sources, giving the lizards a basking site that reaches 113 to 130°F (45 to 54.4°C) with retreats so that they can cool down when they desire. The only known captive breedings occurred at Sydney's Taronga Zoo. Of 18 eggs laid, only 11 hatched after 120 days.

Australia: Rock Monitors

Rock monitors are sleek, active, hyperactive lizards that are found in rocky areas or near trees. Most are too small to be considered giants, but two make the cut.

Varanus glebopalma Mitchell, 1955 Long-Tailed Rock Monitor

Etymology: (Latin) *Glebo-*, pebble-like, and *palma*, palm or sole.

Range: Scattered across the northern quarter of Australia in rocky habitats.

Maximum Size: 39.4 inches (1,000 mm)

References: Bennett (1998); Christian (1977); Cogger (2000); Ehmann (1992); Eidenmüller (1997); Glasby et al. (1993); Greer (1989); Sprackland (2001); Sweet (1999); Wilson (1987); Wilson and Knowles (1988); Wilson and Swan (2003).

Captive Suitability: 4

Natural History: These beautiful lizards are part of the mourning, or *Varanus tristis*, monitor group. This unusual varanid is largely, if not primarily, active at dusk. It also has the second longest tail length in proportion to its body of any monitor. (The tree crocodile monitor, *Varanus salvadorii*, has the longest, and it may tie in second place with the Kimberley rock monitor, *Varanus glauerti*).

These lithe, active lizards are found in rocky terrain in dry forest areas near rocky ridges and ranges. Males of this species explore and defend well-defined territories, a behavior possibly unique among monitors. Unlike most monitors, long-tailed rock monitors rarely forage for prey, using a sit-and-wait strategy instead. This way, they are always in or near the protection offered by rocky crevices. The diet is

Long-tailed rock monitors are sit-and-wait predators, unlike most other monitors. They seem to feed heavily on lizards and frogs in nature.

Varanus tristis (Schlegel , 1839)
Mourning Monitor/Black-Headed Monitor

Etymology: (Latin) *tristis*, sad or in mourning.

Range: Most of Australia except for the southern quarter, most of New South Wales, and the southeastern third of Queensland.

Maximum Size: 33.5 inches (850 mm)

References: Cogger (2000); Storr (1980); Storr, et al. (1983); Swan and Wilson (2003); Wilson (1987); Wilson and Knowles (1988); Wilson and Swan (2003).

Captive Suitability: 4

Natural History: This species was first described in 1839, and subsequent authors have erroneously believed that the holotype was lost. It is in the National Museum of Natural History in Leiden, the Netherlands (RMNH 3858, male, Swan River, Australia), and clearly represents the black-headed form. *Varanus tristis* is a very variable lizard that almost certainly represents a species complex. In the past, the *Varanus tristis* and *V. timorensis* groups have been considered subspecies of each other, and a host of subspecific names has yet to be resolved. L. A. Smith, Graham Thompson, and I have independently been working on the systematics of the two groups for several years without a reasonable resolution as yet.

There are two subspecific entities generally allied as *Varanus tristis*. One is the nominate form, with its distinctive black head and tail, which is found over much of Western Australia, the Northern Territory, South Australia, and New South Wales. The freckled monitor, *Varanus tristis orientalis* Fry, 1913, is similar in form and pattern, save it lacks the black head and tail. It inhabits northern New South Wales and Queensland.

seasonally regulated and includes large insects during the dry months, switching to smaller lizards and frogs during the wet season.

Captive Care: Long-tailed rock monitors require a very roomy terrarium with plenty of cover, preferably made of overlapping flat stones and with some vertical props for climbing. They need a dedicated hot spot where temperatures may approach 122°F (50°C), but you must provide a considerably cooler area for retreat (81°F [27°C]). Because they prefer waiting for prey to approach them, live foods are preferred. Feed them a variety of insects and supplement with small feeder lizards (such as anoles) and baby mice.

This species has been bred in captivity with some regularity, although published accounts are still lacking.

There are two subspecies of the mourning monitor: the darkly colored *V. tristis tristis* (right), often called the black-headed monitor, and *V. tristis orientalis* (below), commonly called the freckled monitor.

There are several reasons for considering the two subspecies as distinct species.

Both forms favor xeric forest habitats, where tree hollows provide ample shelter and the prey comprises a variety of insects. Most of the diet is made of small lizards, followed by grasshoppers, katydids, and stick insects. They can run long and fast on open land but will climb the first vertical object that could provide shelter. Although they can swim, they are averse to entering the water.

Juveniles of both forms are remarkably similar. The bodies are pale gray with tiny dark spots arranged in transverse bands. The head is pale, ranging from yellow to pinkish, becoming darker after about six weeks of age. Males develop an enlarged circle of scales on either side of the tail posterior to the vent.

Captive Care: These are active climbing lizards;

give them a roomy, tall terrarium with plenty of cover in the form of branches or hide boxes. They require daily feedings of insects and pinky- or hopper-sized mice.

Mating occurs in spring, with eggs laid three to five weeks later. Clutches number up to 17 eggs, and these should be incubated at 80 to 86°F (26.7 to 30°C) at 65 to 70 percent humidity. Hatching follows after 110 to 135 days.

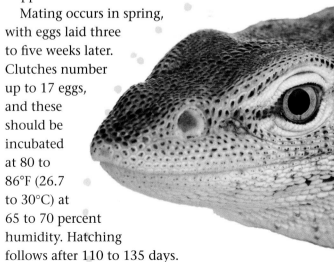

282

Male Mertens' monitors develop a bluish coloration on their lips during the breeding season.

Specialized Australian Monitors

These are very large, robust animals that are distinct from their kin because of habits and habitat preference. Mertens' monitor is primarily aquatic, and the lace monitor has complex breeding behaviors.

Varanus mertensi Glauert, 1951
Mertens' Monitor

Etymology: Named for Prof. Dr. Robert Mertens, former herpetologist and director of the Senckenberg Museum in Frankfurt, Germany, and one of the most prolific and influential herpetologists of the 20th century.

Range: Across the northern quarter of Australia in freshwater courses, lakes, and billabongs.

Maximum Size: 54.3 inches (1,380 mm)
References: Blamires (1999, 2000); Brotzler (1965); Christian et al. (1996); Cogger (2000); Ehmann (1992); Eidenmüller (1990, 1995, 1997); Eidenmüller and Stein (1991, 1998); Glasby et al. (1993); Hermes (1981); Hudson et al. (1994); Murphy (1972); Polleck (1999); Schürer and Horn (1976); Vincent and Wilson (1999); Wilson (1987); Wilson and Knowles (1988); Wilson and Swan (2003).
Captive Suitability: 3
Natural History: This is one of the most aquatic of living monitors. Although there is nothing unusual in a monitor having a compressed tail, Mertens' monitors have a somewhat taller tail than other species, which makes the appendage

283

an excellent aquatic propulsion device. This species has dorsal nostrils, a situation known in only one other type of monitor. When the lizard submerges, a soft white layer of tissue passively rises in the nasal cavity, closing the nostrils. While foraging underwater, these lizards are capable of extruding and flicking their long tongues without opening the mouth.

Mertens' monitors are resident of hot (81 to 104°F [27.2 to 40°C]) regions near permanent fresh water. They will spend considerable time basking on logs, rocks, and other perches that provide a broad view of the nearby area. At any sign of danger, the lizards will flee into the water, where they may remain submerged for more than 20 minutes. The natural diet includes all manner of animals found in or near the water, including frogs, crabs, crawfish, bird and reptile eggs, and fish.

There are populations of this large lizard across Australia's top end, and notable geographic variation can be observed. Females from the western two-thirds of the range have orange or pink facial coloring that is reportedly brighter during the breeding season. The snout is more blunt in eastern populations than western. So far there has been no detailed study of these variations. In some cases, the lips of males become blue during breeding season.

Captive Care: The overriding factor required in properly housing Mertens' monitors is to provide them with considerable water. Animals will use

Basking Mertens' monitor. Note the flattened, rudder-like tail, an adaptation to its highly aquatic lifestyle.

water as shelter, when foraging, to soak, and for sleeping. Juveniles seem to be more aquatic than the adults. The length of an aquatic area should be as large as possible but certainly no shorter than twice the total length of the lizard. Provide a dry area for basking and climbing, and give lizards a spot under a high-intensity heat lamp.

Breeding and oviposition may occur at any time of year. Eggs should be placed in a vermiculite and water mixture and incubated at 82 to 85.5°F (27.8 to 29.7°C); they should hatch in 180 to 330 days.

The two color phases of the lace monitor were once regarded as separate species. However, both patterns can occur in hatchlings of the same clutch.

Varanus varius (Shaw, in White, 1790)
Lace Monitor

Etymology: (Latin) *Varius*, variable or lace-like.
Range: Much of eastern coastal Australia in forest habitats ranging from riparian to scrub, from which it is absent only in the extreme south and Tasmania.
Maximum Size: 74 inches (1,880 mm)
References: Carter (1990, 1992, 1999); Cogger (2000); Green and King (1993); Greer (1989); Horn (1980); Horn and Visser (1989); Hoser (1989, 2003); Houston (1978); McDowell and Bogert (1954); Sprackland (1989a, 1992); Swan et al. (2004); Weigel (1988); Wilson (1987); Wilson and Knowles (1988); Wilson and Swan (2003).
Captive Suitability: 4

Natural History: This is a remarkable lizard in that it is still relatively poorly studied despite being the largest lizard distributed throughout the thickest human population regions of Australia. On a very basic level, the status of the two major color phases was only recently clarified. Shaw described the more common spotted phase in 1790, and a handsome yellow and black banded form was described as *Varanus bellii* by Duméril and Bibron in 1836. Robert Mertens considered the two forms to be mere color variants and not subspecies when he produced his monograph on the varanids (1941). Another German researcher first claimed that the banded, or "Bell's," pattern was due to sex linkage, and such animals were all males (Horn, 1980). Further examination showed

Even large adult lace monitors are adept climbers. When threatened, lacies will dash up the nearest tree.

this hypothesis to be invalid. Fieldwork by myself and a team working for the Australian Herpetological Society (AHS) in 1999 collected specimens of both color phases at the Yathong Nature Preserve in central New South Wales, leading us to conclude that the pattern was merely within the normal variation of the species, possibly from within a single clutch. Confirmation of this hypothesis was published by Hoser (2003), based on direct evidence of the production of both color morphs from the same clutches of captive-produced eggs. Assertions that the banded phase is restricted to the populations west of the Great Dividing Range are also unfounded; I have observed banded specimens at three eastern locations in Queensland.

Lace monitors are found in a variety of forest habitats, from moist southern forests to dry spinifex scrubs. They are common in flat terrain and in rocky hills as long as there are

ONE SPECIES OR TWO?

"The" lace monitor may actually represent two species. Specimens from different regions have different tongue colors; i.e., a population will either have dark purple tongues or pale yellow tongues but not both. Tongue color is not correlated with sex or pattern (so it is not a color variant linked, say, to the banded phase). All species of varanids, save one (the tree crocodile, which is aberrant in several ways from other monitors), have species-specific tongue colors, which leads me to suspect that there is more than one lace monitor species out there.

stout trees for the lizards to climb. The monitors are among the true generalists among lizards, being able to run, burrow, swim, and climb with near-equal proficiency. They feed upon all manner of animal foods, from carrion to other reptiles. They are also fond of eggs and regularly prey upon those of the emu.

Like the Nile monitor, "lacies" excavate part of termitaria, and the female lays eggs there. These are sealed into the repaired nest by the insects, providing concrete-like protection and near constant temperatures and humidity for the embryos. The female excavates the nest again when the young hatch. There is no confirmation that hatchling lizards prey upon their termite hosts.

Lace monitors and heath monitors range into some of the coldest Australian environments in Victoria and New South Wales. During the winter months, the lizards take shelter in deep burrows or rocky crevices and caves and wait for the return of warmer weather. They have been observed to be active on days when the air temperature is just 60°F (15.6°C), able to do so because of phenomenal thermoregulating ability. The body temperature of such an animal may exceed 95°F (35°C).

Captive Care: Similar as for the water monitor, *Varanus salvator*. There is no need for constant high humidity, and lacies can tolerate cooler temperatures both at night and as seasonal lows (to 50°F [10°C]).

Komodo dragons are the most massive of all the lizards and are known to feed on prey as large as water buffalo.

Indonesia-New Guinea: True Giant Monitors

These two species, although very different in biology, have long vied for the record for world's longest living lizard. The tree crocodile monitor allegedly grows to 15 feet (4.6 m) in total length, but no record of a specimen much longer than 8 feet (2.4 m) exists. Almost nothing is known of its natural history, and most of what we do know has been based on observing captives since about 1990. In contrast, Komodo dragons have become icons of reptilian endangered species and are among the most thoroughly studied of lizards.

Varanus komodoensis Ouwens, 1912
Komodo Dragon/Ora

Etymology: Named for the central Indonesian island Komodo.

Range: Limited to Komodo, Padar, Rintja, and western Flores Islands in central Indonesia's Lesser Sunda Archipelago.

Maximum Size: 122.5 inches (3,112 mm)

References: Auffenberg (1970, 1981); Diamond (1992); Lange (1989); Minton and Minton (1973); Murphy et al. (2002); Pfeffer (1965); Shnayerson and Plotkin (2002); Tennesen (2006); Walsh et al. (1993); Watts et al. (2006).

Captive Suitability: 2; CITES Appendix I

Komodo dragons are mostly solitary, although many individuals will gather at the feeding stations set up for tourists wishing to view the lizards.

Komodo dragons have an extremely acute sense of smell. The scent of carrion may draw dragons to feed from miles (km) away.

Natural History: The Komodo dragon may well be the only monitor species familiar to the majority of nonzoologists. It has been the subject of several books, magazine articles, nature television shows, and in April 2005 gave its name to a blend of Starbuck's coffee. The history of the relationship between the Komodo dragon and Western science could well have served as the inspiration for the 1933 film *King Kong*. The lizard was known to local peoples and seafaring traders–some from as far away as China–for centuries, perhaps inspiring some material for dragon legends. It wasn't until a Dutch Air Force officer had to ditch on Komodo that a European first laid eyes on the lizards. That officer's report resulted in orders being dispatched from the capital to collect specimens for scientific examination.

From that time onward, dragons have been among the most intensely studied of lizards, being one of the very few lizard species with several scholarly books written about them. Expeditions to observe and capture oras occurred in the years between the World Wars, bringing a host of ill-fated specimens back to zoos and museums in Europe and America. Captives quickly languished and died, and studies after 1945 were primarily field studies on Komodo and nearby islands. As a result, there is a considerable body of literature for this species, which in turn led to successful captive husbandry. (See "Captive Care.")

Oras from Komodo are quite distinct from those on the larger island Flores that lies to the east. Komodo-based animals are gray and largely

The dragons found on Flores may differ from those from the smaller islands. One difference is that the Flores dragons have yellow, orange, and/or greenish colors on their head.

Shnayerson and Plotkin (2002) have demonstrated that the lizards do possess a virulent bacterial "cocktail" in the saliva that is the result of carrion and other foods they eat, but this cocktail is found among many carrion-eating animals. Work by Bryan Fry and colleagues (Fry et al., 2005) have demonstrated that Komodo dragons–and other varanids–do indeed possess mandibular venom glands but lack fangs or grooved teeth. They are, therefore, technically and morphologically venomous. People working with large varanids would still be prudent to remember that even without venom, the bite from an adult lizard can still have serious health implications.

Captive Care: The first 80 years of attempts to keep Komodo monitors in zoos met with extremely limited success. By the 1980s, zookeepers had pretty much worked out the essentials of proper husbandry, and by the early 1990s, captive breeding–pioneered by Trooper Walsh and his associates at the U.S. National Zoo in Washington, D.C.–was achieved. Today, the animal that was rarely seen alive outside its Indonesian home is now featured at many zoos around the world. In fact, the ease with which Komodo monitors can be bred has led some zoos to a moratorium on further reproductive efforts because of space limitations for growing families! Despite these phenomenal successes, Komodo dragons are not legally available for private ownership.

unmarked as adults, while specimens from Flores are patterned with yellow, orange, and green on the head and dorsum. Minor morphological differences are also seen, and the two populations warrant further systematic study. Flores is also home to the large water monitor (*Varanus salvator*). It remains to be seen if the two taxa occur in the same areas or have distinct habitats. Another large monitor, the extinct *V. hoojeri*, is also known from Flores.

Because the bites from Komodo dragons fester and often lead to severe infections, there has been supposition that the bite might be venomous.

Varanus salvadorii (Peters and Doria, 1878) Tree Crocodile Monitor

Etymology: Named for Italian ornithologist Count Tommaso Salvadori (1835-1923). He was vice-director of the zoology museum at the University of Turin and authored two volumes of the Catalogue of Birds in the British Museum (Natural History) in 1890-1891.

Range: Throughout New Guinea

Maximum Size: Unknown; specimens up to 111 inches (2,820 mm) have reliably been measured, and credible suggestions have been advanced that the species may reach 144 to 192 inches (3,658 to 4,877 mm).

References: Sprackland (1992).

Captive Suitability: 1

Natural History: Unknown. However, according to Canadian herpetoculturist Steve Blaine, tongue color is sexually indicative in this species, with males having yellow tongues and females having pink with yellowish tones, making this the only known species of varanoid lizard (the group that includes monitors, the earless monitor, and venomous lizards) in which more than one tongue color is found in a single species.

This monitor has a number of peculiar characteristics. First, it has the longest tail to body ratio of any large monitor and of any monitor excepting *Varanus pilbarensis*. This is odd because in monitor lizards, as adult body size increases, the relative length of the tail decreases. Yet here is

Juvenile crocodile monitors (opposite) are among the most brilliantly colored lizards. Although the color fades somewhat as the lizard ages, most adults (left) retain some bright yellow markings.

arguably the longest of monitors with the longest of tails.

Second, the teeth are unlike that seen in any other lizard. Instead of being slightly curved and conical, tree crocodile teeth are compressed elongated triangles that resemble stilettos. When the mouth closes, the upper teeth intermesh with the lower, causing a shearing bite. Also, the teeth of a tree crocodile are longer–not proportionately but in actual measure–than those of an equal-sized Komodo dragon.

Third, here is a giant among lizards that is primarily arboreal. Again, in large monitor species, they become less arboreal as they get larger. Tree crocodiles, though, take to the trees as juveniles and then stay there. Tree crocodiles are

predominantly arboreal lizards that spend most of their time high in the canopy or exploring hollow trees. Because these are also important refuges for bats, the flying mammals may well make up the primary diet of the lizards.

Finally, juveniles have been observed to engage in a remarkable behavior: When jumping from a tree to a branch or the ground, they expand the ribs (as monitors do when presenting a threat display) and launch into the air. The combination of a small, wide, flat body and extremely long, thin tail allows the lizards to slow their descent. It's not quite parachuting, but it's certainly breaking their fall.

The people who live near crocodile monitors have a variety of names for them, but many

Crocodile monitors are highly arboreal, and it is rare to see one on the ground in nature. However, they are known to drop out of a tree onto unsuspecting prey below.

Tooth of a crocodile monitor. Note the serrations on both sides; crocodile monitors have a very bad bite.

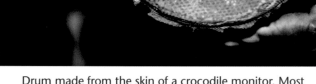

Drum made from the skin of a crocodile monitor. Most monitors are hunted for their skins.

translate into one version or another of "tree crocodile" or "death from above." The latter comes from the lizards' tendency to drop from a tree and kill hunting dogs and to sometimes attack humans.

Captive Care: This species is hardy in captivity, and although expensive, is readily available through specialty reptile importers. However, tree crocodile monitors rate a captive suitability rating of 1 because they are extremely dangerous animals. Their teeth are like those of no other living animal, and even a small lizard is able to bite with both ferocity and the ability to be very damaging. Cage, heat, and food requirements are similar to those of the water monitor, but the terrarium must be quite high because these are climbing lizards. Although some specimens allow handling,

there are many stories of lizards that suddenly turned and seriously bit their handler.

Captives require a varied diet of mammals (from rats to rabbits, depending on size), boiled eggs, and birds. They will spend time soaking in a large pool and should always have a clean source of drinking water. Do not house other species or tree crocodiles of different sizes together.

295

Ctenosaura sp.

GLOSSARY

acclimation: The adjustment by an animal to its surroundings when brought into captivity

agonistic display: Any social interaction between two animals, including actions to induce mating, threaten competitors or potential enemies, mark out territorial claims

allantois: The embryonic membrane into which the developing embryo secretes waste materials; from the French word for "sewer."

allopatric: Two or more species whose natural ranges do not overlap

alveolus (plural alveoli): The small, dead-end, spherical, and microscopic spaces inside lungs where respiratory gas exchange occurs

amnion: The embryonic sac that surrounds the embryo and allantois, retaining water inside the egg. The amnion is surrounded by a thicker protective membrane called the chorion and may be further surrounded by a calcium-based shell.

analogous: Anatomical features, such as bones, muscles, and nerves, that are not derived from common embryological tissue; e.g., wings of insects (derived from tissues of the back) and birds (derived from the forelimbs) are analogous organs.

anorexia: A symptom that involves the cessation of feeding. It may be caused by a number of factors, including stress, incorrect foods, disease, injury, or parasites.

antibiotic: A drug that is used to combat pathogenic bacteria that have infected an animal. They have no effect on viral infections.

arboreal: living in or on trees.

articulate: To join one bone to another. Loose articulation via tendons results in a movable joint; solid articulation such as through bone-to-bone fusing produces an immovable joint.

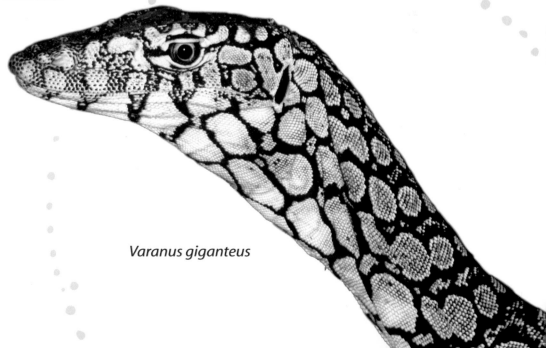

Varanus giganteus

autotomy: The ability to lose and then regrow a replacement tail. The new tail lacks bones, however, and lacks the flexibility of the original.

axilla: The armpit

chorion: The outermost membrane of an amniotic egg unless a shell is present. This is a fibrous, waterproof sac that surrounds the embryo, yolk sac, amnion, and allantois.

CITES: The Convention on International Trade in Endangered Species. This is a set of regulations that governs any trade in wildlife and its products among countries that have signed the convention.

cloaca: The ventral slit immediately posterior to the hind limbs. Both excrement (feces and uric acid) and eggs or young emerge from this combined orifice. Birds, reptiles, amphibians, many fishes, and monotreme mammals possess cloacas; mammals have separate anuses, urinary tracts, and (in females) vaginas. From the Latin for "sewer."

complement: A protein carried in the blood that helps body cells recognize invading cells. If complement binds to a cell, the body's defensive cells attack the marked cell. Because the complement proteins of each species vary, the degree to which the body's attack cells respond to complement can be used to calculate the degree of relationship between different species.

condyle: Smooth, knob-like surface at the end of a bone that forms part of a joint

conspecific: Of the same species

crepuscular: Active at dawn or dusk, the twilight hours of the day

deoxygenated: Literally, without oxygen. The term is used to describe blood that has a reduced oxygen content and is being returned to the lungs via the heart, where it will exchange high carbon dioxide load for oxygen. Deoxygenated blood is carried in veins, with the exception of the pulmonary vein, which brings oxygenated blood back to the heart.

dewlap: The thin, longitudinal throat fan of a lizard, such as seen in green iguanas

diapsid: The condition in a terrestrial vertebrate skull characterized by the presence of two temporal openings. Diapsids include tuatara, lizards, snakes, crocodilians, dinosaurs, birds, and possibly turtles.

digit: A finger or toe

discrete characters: Anatomical features that can be defined as either present or absent, e.g., moveable eyelids, caudal autotomy, limbs present, or tongue color. In contrast are meristic characters or meristics.

diurnal: Active during the daytime

dorsal: Pertaining to the top of the body, including the top of the head, back, and upper tail

ectoparasite: Invertebrates such as mites, ticks, and fleas that live on the skin of a host animal and penetrate the skin with complex sucking mouthparts

ecotypic: Variation in a species across populations that is due to environmental, rather than strictly genetic, factors

endemic: Native to only one place; e.g., marine iguanas are endemic to the Galápagos Islands.

etymology: The study of the origins of words

extinct: The termination of a species or population. The most serious condition of extinction occurs when all the members of a species are deceased, as is the case for

dodoes and Cape Verde giant skinks. Local extinctions are situations where a species no longer inhabits one part of its natural range but may still be found in the wild elsewhere. An example is the heath monitor that was a recent resident of some islands in the Bass Straits between the Australian mainland and Tasmania; it is extinct on the islands but is still common on the mainland. Technical extinction or extinct in the wild means that a species is no longer found in nature but only in captivity. The Guam rail (a bird) is now to be found only in a few zoos.

fenestra: A naturally occurring hole formed in the skull where adjacent bones do not meet

fossorial: An animal that is a burrower or that prefers to dwell underground.

gular: the throat region.

herptile: A casual term coined to refer to both reptiles and amphibians; often further shortened to "herp."

herpetoculture: The practice of the captive care and breeding of reptiles and amphibians

herpetofauna: A term that refers to the reptiles and/or amphibians in a region

herpetology: The branch of the science of zoology that deals with the biology of reptiles and amphibians

herpetologist: A person who scientifically studies the biology of reptiles and amphibians

homologous: Anatomical features, such as bones, muscles, and nerves, that are derived from common embryological tissue; e.g., wings of birds and bats are homologous, both being derived from the same structures of the front limbs. Features that are homologous to each other are termed "homologues."

holotype: The specimen that is used as the basis of the original description of a species when it is named by the describer

hot: Herpetological slang, referring to a reptile that is venomous and potentially dangerous to humans

intraspecific: Within a single species; the frill of frilled lizards is an intraspecific feature that all frilled lizards possess.

Lacey Act: A U.S. law that regulates the transportation of living things across state lines

lecithotrophic: Reference to an embryo that derives nourishment from a yolk instead of directly from its mother

matrotrophic: Reference to an embryo that is nourished directly by its mother's body until birth

melanophore: A cellular organelle (like the nucleus or mitochondria) that contains the pigment melanin. The apparent color of the skin is determined by the degree to which the melanin is dispersed or concentrated in the skin cells. Lizards that can alter the melanin dispersal, such as chameleons, will be able to change color.

mental scale: The scale of the lower jaw that is centrally located in the foremost position

meristics: Anatomical characteristics that can be measured mathematically, such as numbers of scales around the body, ratio of tail length to snout-vent length, and number of ventral scales in a row. Meristics reflect variable characters, in contrast to discrete characters.

metabolism: The net biochemical activity, called physiology, of a living organism. It includes respiration, digestion, oxidation, nerve impulse generation, thinking, moving, excreting, and growth.

neonate: A newly born or hatched reptile

neurotoxin: A venom or poison that acts on a victim by disabling the nervous system, usually by destroying nerve cells or their ability to function

nocturnal: Active at night or in the dark

nuchal: The back of the neck; nuchal scales are the scales on the back of the neck.

occipital: The large plate-like bone at the very rear of the skull; also, the region of the back of the head.

orthopteran: Insects that include grasshoppers, katydids, locusts, crickets, and their kin

osteoderm: A small bit of bone that grows external to the skeleton. Osteoderms may fuse to the roof of the skull or may be embedded in individual scales, providing protective armor to the lizard.

oviparous: Egg-laying

ovoviviparous: An animal that retains the developing egg inside her body until the offspring is ready to hatch

oxygenated: The term for oxygen-rich blood, coming from the lungs to the heart and then to the cells of the body. Oxygenated blood is carried in arteries, excepting the pulmonary artery that carries deoxygenated blood to the lungs.

paratype: One or more specimens other than the holotype designated by the describer of a new species when the species is named in a publication

parietal eye: See pineal eye

parsimony: The philosophical principal that states that the simplest explanation for a problem is most likely to be correct (or closest to reality).

parturition: The production of either live offspring or fertilized eggs containing embryos

pathogen: A disease-causing substance or organism, such as viruses, bacteria, or parasites

pentadactyl: Having five digits (fingers or toes) on each limb

phylogenetics: The branch of systematics that studies organisms in an effort to determine their relationships to each other and their paths of evolutionary history

pineal eye: The third partially or nonfunctional eye that lies in the pineal foramen (on top of the skull). The organ contains the same structures as other eyes but lacks a working lens or complete retina. It is sensitive to ultraviolet radiation.

Heloderma horridum

301

poikilothermic: Blood physiology in which blood temperature is controlled by external factors, such as sunlight or air and water temperature. Mammals and birds, in contrast, control blood temperature by producing heat within their bodies (called homeothermic).

preanal pores: A series of one to five enlarged circular structures, usually forming a V-shape, immediately in front of the cloaca in some lizards, notably male geckos

prehistoric: Literally, "before history," meaning any time prior to about 12,000 years ago

riparian: Living along the banks of streams or rivers

sagittal: In a direction that follows the spine, i.e., from the front to the back of the animal. The opposite of transverse. Stripes are sagittal, bands are transverse.

saxicollis: Living among rocks

subadult: The equivalent of an adolescent; an animal that is nearly completely grown but not yet of normal reproductive age.

sympatric: Refers to the range of two or more species whose ranges overlap

systematics: The branch of biological science that deals with determining the evolutionary relationships among and between organisms

systematist: A biologist who studies the relationships among and between evolutionary histories of organisms

taxon (plural: taxa): Any group of organisms that can be assigned a single name. A species is a taxon; a genus is a taxon.

taxonomy: The branch of systematics that involves the scientific classification and naming of organisms. In zoology, taxonomists are bound by the International Code of Zoological Nomenclature (ICZN) for how names must be prepared, used, and published.

third eye: See pineal eye

transverse: Going from left to right across the body; bands are transverse, stripes are sagittal.

UV light: Ultraviolet light. This is light that comes from the sun in the far purple wavelength range and is invisible to human eyes. Birds, insects, and many reptiles can see these wavelengths, and the pineal (parietal) eye of lizards is particularly sensitive to this light. UV light is largely responsible for both tanning and sunburn in humans but is essential for people as a precursor in being able to convert dietary calcium into new bone cells. Its value for reptiles is still equivocal.

vagile: Highly mobile, able to successfully traverse distances and establish new populations

venomous: An animal that produces a toxin that must actively be injected through a bite or sting into another animal

vent: The body opening that leads from the reproductive and urinary tracts and the anus. In lizards and snakes, the cloaca is a transverse slit, while in crocodiles, it is longitudinal.

ventral: Pertaining to the underside of the body, including the throat, belly, and vent

viviparous: Live-bearing; production of offspring without a self-contained egg, where the mother provides food in place of a yolk.

zoögeography: The study of the distribution of animals and the causes and patterns of those distributions

zoönosis: A disease that is carried by animals and can be transferred to humans

THE GREEK ALPHABET

The accompanying chart provides both upper and lowercases for the Hellenic (classical) Greek alphabet, along with a pronunciation key. Note that for the letter sigma, the lowercase version σ is used at the start or inside a word, while ς is only used when it is the last letter of a word.

A	α	alpha	al-fah		N	ν	nu	noo
B	β	beta	bay-tah		Ξ	ξ	xi	kzie (rhymes with "die")
Γ	γ	gamma	gam-mah		O	o		oh-muh-kron
Δ	δ	delta	del-tah		Π	π	pi	pie
E	ε	epsilon	ep-suh-lon		P	ρ	rho	roe
Z	ζ	zeta	zay-tah		Σ	ς, σ	sigma	sig-muh
H	η	eta	ay-tah		T	τ	tau	tow, as the first part of "tower"
Θ	θ	theta	thay-tah		Y	υ	upsilon	oop-suh-lon
I	ι	iota	ee-oh-tah		Φ	φ	phi	fie (rhymes with "die")
K	κ	kappa	kop-pah		X	χ	chi	kie (rhymes with "die")
Λ	λ	lambda	lam-duh		Ψ	ψ	ypsilon	yip-suh-lon
M	μ	mu	moo		Ω	ω	omega	oh-may-gah

Varanus tristis

REFERENCES

Ackerman, Lowell (ed.). 1997. *The Biology, Husbandry and Health Care of Reptiles*. 3 volumes. TFH Publications, Neptune, NJ.

Alberts, A., R. Carter, W. Hayes, and E. Martins (eds.). 2004. *Iguanas, Biology and Conservation*. University of California Press, Berkeley.

Alles, J., and A. Charlson. 2007. The Argus monitor. *Reptiles* 15(7): 68-73.

Allison, Allen. 2006. Reptiles and amphibians of the Trans-Fly region, New Guinea. *Contribution 2006-039, Pacific Biological Survey*, Bernice P. Bishop Museum.

Arnett, J. R. 1979. Breeding the Fiji banded iguana *Brachylophus fasciatus* at Knoxville Zoo. *International Zoo Yearbook* 19: 78-80.

Arnold, E. N. 1973. Variation in the cloacal and hemipenial muscles of lizards and its bearing on their relationships. Pp. 47-85. In: Ferguson, Mark (ed.). *The Structure, Development, and Evolution of Reptiles*. Zoological Society of London Symposia number 52.

ASIH, no date. *Career Opportunities for the Herpetologist*. American Society of Ichthyologists and Herpetologists, Washington, D.C.

Asma, Stephen. 2001. *Stuffed Animals and Pickled Heads: The Culture and Evolution of Natural History Museums*. Oxford University Press, Oxford.

Avila-Peres, T.C.S. 1995. Lizards of Brazilian Amazonia (Reptilia: Squamata). *Zoologische Verhandelingen*, Leiden 299: 1-706.

Auffenberg, Walter. 1994. *The Bengal Monitor*. University of Florida Press, Gainesville.

—, 1988. *Gray's Monitor Lizard*. University of Florida Press, Gainesville.

—, 1982. Catch a lizard, use a lizard. *International Wildlife* 12(6): 16-19.

—, 1981. *Behavioral Ecology of the Komodo Monitor*. University of Florida Press, Gainesville.

—, 1979. A monitor lizard in the Philippines. *Oryx* 15(1): 39-46.

—, 1976. First description of an adult *Varanus grayi*. *Copeia* 1976(3): 586-588.

—, 1970. A day with number 19. *Animal Kingdom* December: 18-23.

—, H. Rahman, F. Iffat, and Z. Perveen. 1990. Notes on the biology of *Varanus griseus koniecznyi* Mertens, Sauria Varanidae. *Journal of the Bombay Natural History Society* 87(1): 26-36.

—, 1989. A study of *Varanus flavescens* (Hardwicke & Gray) (Sauria: Varanidae). *Journal of the Bombay Natural History Society* 86(3): 286-307.

Avise, John. 1994. *Molecular Markers, Natural History and Evolution*. Chapman & Hall, NY.

Ax, Peter. 1987. *The Phylogenetic System*. John Wiley & Sons, NY.

Badger, David. 2002. *Lizards, a Natural History of Some Uncommon Creatures—Extraordinary Chameleons, Iguanas, Geckos, & More*. Voyageur Press, Stillwater, MN.

Baird, Irwin. 1970. The anatomy of the reptilian ear. pp. 193-276. *Biology of the Reptilia. Volume 2. Morphology B*. Academic Press, NY.

Balouet, Jean. 1990. *Extinct Species of the World*. Barron's Educational Services, Hauppauge, NY.

Balsai, Michael. 1997. *General Care and Maintenance of Popular Monitors and Tegus*. Advanced Vivarium Systems, Santee, CA.

Barbour, Thomas. 1911. A contribution to the zoogeography of the East Indian Islands. *Memoirs of the Museum of Comparative Zoology* 44(1).

Barthel, Tom. 2007. The hydration equation. *Reptiles* 15(7): 58-63.

—, 2004. Cold-blooded careers. *Reptiles* 12(12): 64-75.

Bartlett, Richard. 2003. *Spiny-Tailed Agamids: Uromastyx and Xenagama*. Barron's, Hauppauge, NY.

Bartlett, Richard and P. Bartlett. 1999. *Terrarium and Cage Construction and Care*. Barron's, Hauppauge, NY.

—,1997. *Lizard Care from A to Z*. Barron's, Hauppauge, NY.

Bayless, Mark. 2004. The local names of Pacific monitor lizards (Sauria: Varanidae), of Oceania & Indo-Malaysia, excluding Australia. *Micronesica* 37(1):49-54.

—, 2002. Monitor lizards: a pan-African check list of their zoogeography (Sauria: Varanidae: Polydaedalus). *Journal of Biogeography* 29:1643-1701.

—, 1997. The distribution of African monitor lizards (Sauria: Varanidae). *African Journal of Ecology* 35: 374-377.

Bayless, Mark and John Adragna. 1997. Monitor lizards in the Philippine Islands: a historical perspective (Sauria: Varanidae). *Asia Life Sciences* 6(1 & 2): 39-50.

Bayless, Mark and Ben Aller. 2004. Duméril's monitor lizard (*Varanus dumerilii*). *Reptiles* 12(3): 42-46.

Bayless, Mark and Quetzal Dwyer. 1997. Notes on the peach-throated monitor. *Reptile & Amphibian Magazine* 47: 26-30.

Bayless, Mark and Robert Sprackland. 2000. African monitor lizards, part I. *Reptiles* 5(6): 76-85.

—, 2000a. African monitor lizards, part II. *Reptiles* 5(7): 40-47.

Beck, Daniel. 2005. *Biology of Gila monsters and Beaded Lizards*. University of California Press, Berkeley.

—, 2004. Venomous lizards of the desert. *Natural History* 113(6): 32-37.

—, 1991. Ecology of the beaded lizard, *Heloderma horridum*, in a tropical dry forest in Jalisco, México. *Journal of Herpetology* 25(4): 395-406.

Beck, Daniel and Aurelio Ramírez-Bautista. 1991. Combat behavior of the beaded lizard, *Heloderma h. horridum*, in Jalisco, México. *Journal of Herpetology* 25(4): 481-484.

Becker, H., W. Böhme, and S. Perry. 1989. Die Lungenmorphologie der Warane (Reptilia: Varanidae) und ihre systematisch-stammesgeschichtliche Bedeutung. *Bonner Zoologische Beitr.* 40(1): 27-56.

Bedford, Gavin and Kieth Christian. 1996. Tail morphology related to habitat of varanid lizards and some other reptiles. *Amphibia-Reptilia* 17: 131-140.

Bedford, Gavin and Grant Husband. 2003. Captive breeding of the lemon throated monitor *Varanus baritji*. *Herpetofauna* (Sydney) 33(2): 105-108.

Bell, Thomas. 1843. Part V. Reptiles. pp. 1-72. In: Darwin, Charles (ed.). *The Zoology of the Voyage of H.M.S. Beagle, Under the Command of Captain Fitzroy, R.N., During the Years 1832 to 1836*. Smith, Elder and Co., Cornhill, England.

Bellairs, Angus. 1970. *The Life of Reptiles*. Two volumes. Universe Books, NY.

—, 1960. *Reptiles: Life History, Evolution, and Structure*. Harper Tourchbooks, NY.

Bennett, Daniel. 2007. Aspects of the ecology and conservation of frugivorous monitor lizards. *Biawak* 1(1): 43-44.

—, 2002. Diet of juvenile *Varanus niloticus* (Sauria: Varanidae) on the Black Volta River in Ghana. *Journal of Herpetology* 36(1): 116-117

—, 1998. *Monitor Lizards: Natural History, Biology & Husbandry*. Edition Chimaira, Frankfurt.

Bennett, Daniel and Lim Boo Liat. 1995. A note on the distribution of *Varanus dumerilii* and *V. rudicollis* in peninsular Malaysia. *Malayan Nature Journal* 49: 113-116.

Bennett, Daniel and Ravi Thakoordyal. 2003. *The Savannah Monitor Lizard—the Truth About* Varanus exanthematicus. Viper Press, Aberdeen.

Bernard, Susan. 1996. *Reptile Keeper's Handbook*. Krieger, Malabar, FL.

Biswas, S., and D. Sanyal. 1980. A report on the reptilia fauna of Andaman and Nicobars Islands in the collection of Zoological Survey of India. *Records of the Zoological Survey of India* 77: 255-292.

Blackburn, Daniel. 2000. Classification of the reproductive patterns of amniotes. *Herpetological Monographs* 14: 371-377.

Blair, David. 2004. Iguanidae: keeping it in the family. *Reptiles USA 2005 Annual*: 52-63.

—, 2004a. The rhinoceros iguana; take an in-depth look at *Cyclura cornuta*. *Reptiles* 12(2): 70-79.

—, 1994. Rock iguanas. *Reptiles* 1(4): 40-63.

Blamires, Sean. 2004. Habitat preferences of coastal goannas (*Varanus panoptes*): Are they exploiters of sea turtle nests at Fog Bay, Australia? *Copeia* 2004(2): 370-377.

—, 2000. Some habitat and behaviour observations of varanids in the Northern Territory. *Herpetofauna* (Sydney) 30(2): 42-45.

—, 1999. An observation of a possible wild mating attempt for the water monitor, *Varanus mertensi*. *Herpetofauna* (Sydney) 29(1): 55.

Bogert, C., and R. Del Campo. 1960. The Gila monster and its allies. *Bulletin of the American Museum of Natural History*, 109: 1-238.

Böhme, Wolfgang. 1988. The Argus monitor, *Varanus panoptes* Storr 1980, on New Guinea. *Salamandra* 24(2/3): 87-101.

Böhme, Wolfgang, H. G. Horn, and T. Ziegler. 1994. Zur Taxonomie der Pazifikwarane (*Varanus-indicus*-Komplex): Revalidierung von *Varanus doreanus* (A. B. Meyer, 1874) mit Beschreibung einer neuen Unterart. *Salamandra* 30(2): 119-142.

Böhme, Wolfgang, U. Joger, and B. Schätti. 1989. A new monitor lizard (Reptilia: Varanidae) from Yemen, with notes on ecology, phylogeny, and zoogeography. *Fauna of Saudi Arabia* 10: 433-448.

Böhme, Wolfgang, H. Meinig, and M. Rödel. 1996. New records of amphibians and reptiles from Burkina Faso and Mali. *Bulletin of the British Herpetological Society*, 56: 7-26.

Böhme, Wolfgang, and U. Sieling. 1993. Zum Zusammenhang zwischen Genitalstruktur, Paarungsverhalten und Fortpflanzungserfolg bei squamaten Reptilien: erste Ergebnisse. *Herpetofauna* 5(82): 15-23.

Böhme, Wolfgang, and T. Ziegler. 1997. *Varanus melinus* sp. n., ein neuer Waran aus der *V. indicus*-Gruppe von den Molukken, Indonesien. *Herpetofauna* 19(111): 26-34.

Böhme, Wolfgang , 1997a. Großwarane im Museum Koenig, mit Bemerkungen zu Afrikas größter Echse. Tier und Museum 5(3): 65-74.

—, 1997b. A taxonomic review of the *Varanus (Polydaedalus) niloticus* (Linnaeus, 1766) complex. *Herpetological Journal* 7: 155-162.

—, 1997c. On the synonymy and taxonomy of the Bengal monitor lizard, *Varanus bengalensis* (Daudin, 1802) complex (Sauria: Varanidae). *Amphibia-Reptilia* 18:207-211.

Boulenger, George. 1885. *Catalogue of the Lizards in the British Museum (Natural History)*. Vol. I-III. Taylor and Francis, London.

Boylan, Terry. 1989. Reproduction of the Fijian crested iguana *Brachylophus vitiensis* at Taronga Zoo, Sydney. *International Zoo Yearbook* 28: 126-130.

—. 1985. Captive management of a population of rhinoceros iguanas, *Cyclura cornuta cornuta*, at Taronga Zoo, Sydney. Pp. 491-494. In: Grigg, G., R. Shine, and H. Ehmann (eds.). *Biology of Australasian Frogs and Reptiles*. Surrey Beatty & Sons, Chipping Norton, NSW.

Brotzler, A. 1965. Mertens-Wasserwarane (*Varanus mertensi* Glauert 1951) züchteten in der Wilhelma. *Freund Kölner Zoo* 8(3):89.

Brown, James and Mark Lomolino. 1998. *Biogeography*. Second edition. Sinauer Associates, Sunderland, Mass.

Buckley, L., and R. Axtell. 1990. *Ctenosaura palearis* Stejneger. *Catalog of American Amphibians and Reptiles* 491: 1-3.

Buden, Donald. 1995. Reptiles, birds, and mammals of Mokil and Pingelap Atolls, Eastern Caroline Islands. *Micronesica* 28(1): 9-23.

Buhlmann, Kurt. 2007. Understanding the acronyms: what species regulations and rankings mean for herps, hobbyists and conservation. *Reptiles* 15(4): 68-71.

Burbrink, Frank, R. Lawson, and J. Slowinski. 2000. Mitochondrial DNA phylogeography of the polytypic North American rat snake (*Elaphe obsoleta*): a critique of the subspecies concept. *Evolution* 54(6): 2107-2118.

Burcaw, G. Ellis. 1975. *Introduction to Museum Work.* American Association for State and Local History, Nashville.

Burghardt, G., and A. Rand (eds.). 1982. *Iguanas of the World.* Noyes Publishing, NJ.

Bush, B., B. Maryan, R. Browne-Cooper, and D. Robinson. 2007. *Reptiles and Frogs in the Bush: Southwestern Australia.* University of Western Australia Press, Crawley, WA.

Campbell, J., and D. Frost. 1993. Anguid lizards of the genus *Abronia*: Revisionary notes, descriptions of four new species, a phylogenetic analysis, and key. *Bulletin of the American Museum of Natural History* 216: 1-121.

Campbell, J., and W. Lamar. 2004. *The Venomous Reptiles of the Western Hemisphere.* 2 volumes. Comstock Publishing, Ithaca, NY.

Campbell, J., and J. Vannini. 1988. A new subspecies of beaded lizard, *Heloderma horridum*, from the Motagua Valley of Guatemala. *Journal of Herpetology* 22(4): 457-468.

Campbell, Matthew. 1990. Scheltopusik: a fascinating lizard with a strange name. *Reptile and Amphibian Magazine* 4: 12.

Campbell, T. 2003. Species profile: Nile Monitors (*Varanus niloticus*) in Florida. *Iguana* 10(4): 119-120.

Canepuccia, Alejandro. 2000. *Tupinambis merianae*, the black tegu. *Reptilia* 10: 48-55.

Card, Winston. A fruit-eating monitor: research and conservation of Gray's monitor lizard in the Philippines. *AZA Communique* May 2005: 19-21.

Card, Winston.1995. Captive maintenance and reproduction of Gould's monitor lizard (*Varanus gouldii*). *Reptiles* 3(3): 84-91.

Card, Winston, and A. Kluge. 1995. Hemipeneal skeleton and varanid lizard systematics. *Journal of Herpetology* 29(2): 275-280.

Carpenter, Charles. 1966. The marine iguana of the Galápagos Islands, its behavior and ecology. *Proceedings of the California Academy of Sciences* 34(6): 329-376.

Carter, David. 1999. Nesting and evidence of parental care by the lace monitor *Varanus varius*. *Mertensiella* 11: 137-147.

—. 1992. Reproductive ecology of the lace monitor, *Varanus varius*, in southeastern Australia. Ph.D. Thesis, Australian National University.

—. 1990. Courtship and mating in wild *Varanus varius* (Varanidae: Australia). *Memoirs of the Queensland Museum* 29(2): 333-338.

Case, T., and T. Schwaner. 1993. Island/mainland body size differences in Australian varanid lizards. *Oecologica* 94: 102-109.

Cato, P. and C. Jones (eds.). 1991. *Natural History Museums: Directions for Growth.* Texas Tech University Press, Lubbock.

Christian, A., and T. Garland. 1996. Scaling of limb proportions in monitor lizards (Squamata: Varanidae). *Journal of Herpetology* 30(2): 219-230

Christian, Keith, and Brian Weavers. 1994. Analysis of the activity and energetics of the lizard *Varanus rosenbergi*. *Copeia* 1994(2): 289-295.

Christian, Keith, B. Weavers, B. Green, and G. Bedford. 1996. Energetics and water flux in a semiaquatic lizard, *Varanus mertensi*. *Copeia* 1996(2): 354-362.

Christian, T. 1977. Notes on *Varanus glebopalma*. *Victorian Herpetological Society Newsletter* 6: 11-13.

Christy, Bryan. 2008. *The Lizard King: the True Crimes and Passions of the World's greatest reptile smugglers*. Twelve Publishing, New York.

Cogger, H. 2000. *Reptiles and Amphibians of Australia*. Sixth edition. Ralph Curtis Books, Sanibel Island, FL.

Cogger, H. , and R. Sadlier. 1985. Population size and structure in the Fijian crested iguana. pp. 507-512. In: Roek, Z. *Studies in Herpetology: Proceedings of the European*

Herpetological Meeting (3rd ordinary general meeting of the Societas Europaea Herpetologica) Prague 1985. Societas Europaea Herpetologica, Prague.

Coiro, Jarrett. 2007. Captive breeding of *Varanus exanthematicus*. *Biawak* 1(1): 29-33.

Colli, G., A. Péres, and H. da Cunha. 1998. A new species of *Tupinambis* (Squamata: Teiidae) from central Brazil, with an analysis of morphological and genetic variation in the genus. *Herpetologica* 54(4): 477-492.

Cope, Edward. 1900. The crocodilians, lizards, and snakes of North America. *Annual Report of the Board of Regents of the Smithsonian Institution, Part II*. Pp. 155-1294.

Cowles, Raymond. 1930. The life history of *Varanus niloticus* (Linneaus) as observed in Natal. *South African Journal of Entomology and Zoology* 22(1): 1-31.

Cracraft, Joel and Michael Donoghue (eds.). 2004. *Assembling the Tree of Life*. Oxford University Press.

Dalrymple, George. 1979. On the jaw mechanism of the snail-crushing lizards, *Dracaena* Daudin, 1802. *Journal of Herpetology* 13(3): 303-312.

Darwin, Charles. 1859. *On the Origin of Species by Means of Natural Selection*. 1st Edition. Murray, London.

Das, Indraneil. 1998. *Herpetological Bibliography of Indonesia*. Krieger, Malabar, FL.

—. 1996. *Biogeography of the Reptiles of South Asia*. Krieger, Malabar, FL. Daudin, François. 1802. *Histoire Naturelle, Reptiles*. Tome 3. Paris.

Daugherty, C., A. Cree, J. Hay and M. Thompson. 1990. Neglected taxonomy and continuing extinctions of tuatara (*Sphenodon*). *Nature* 347(6289): 177-179.

Dedlmar, Armin. 2007. Keeping and breeding the blue tree monitor, *Varanus macraei*. *Reptilia* 50: 25-27

Delisle, Harold. 2007. *Varanus caerulivirens* (turquoise monitor). Reproduction. *Biawak* 1(1): 39-40.

De Queiroz, Kevin and Michael Donoghue. 1988. Phylogenetic systematics and the species problem. *Cladistics* 4: 317-338.

De Queiroz, Kevin, Michael Donoghue and Jacques Gauthier. 1994. Toward a phylogenetic system of biological nomenclature. *Trends in Ecology and Evolution* 9(1): 27-31. DeRooij, Nelly. 1915. *Reptiles of the Indo-Australian Archipelago*. E. J. Brill, Leiden.

De Roy, Tui. 1995. Where Vulcan lizards prosper. *Natural History* 104(1): 28-39.

Dessauer, H., J. Cadle and R. Lawson. 1986. Patterns of snake evolution suggested by their proteins. *Fieldiana Zoology* (New Series) 34: 1-34.

De Vosjoli, Philippe. 1998. *The Green Iguana Manual*. Advanced Vivarium Systems, Santee, CA.

—, 1997. *The Lizard Keeper's Handbook*. Advanced Vivarium Systems, Santee, CA.

—, 1992. *Green Water Dragons, Sailfin Lizards, and Basilisks*. Advanced Vivarium Systems, Santee, CA.

Diamond, Jared. 1992. The evolution of dragons in the jungles of Indonesia. *Discover* 13(12): 72-80.

Dieter, Christopher. 2000. The Argus monitor. *Reptile & Amphibian Hobbyist* January: 46-47.

—, 1999. Introducing the blue pinspot monitor: *Varanus* sp. *Reptile &Amphibian Hobbyist* November: 29-32.

—, 1999a. Keeping and breeding the Asian water monitor. *Reptile & Amphibian Hobbyist* October: 22-27.

Ditmars, Raymond. 1933. *Reptiles of the World*. Macmillan, New York.

Doles, M. and W. Card. 1995. Delayed fertilization in the monitor lizard *Varanus gouldii*. *Herpetological Review* 26(4): 196.

Dorge, Ray. 1996. A tour of the Grand Cayman blue iguana captive breeding facility. *Reptiles* 4(9): 32-42.

Doria, Giaccomo. 1874. Enumerazione dei rettili raccolti dal Dott. *O. Beccari* in Amboina, alle isole Aru ed alle isole Kei. *Annali Museo Civitas Storia Natural Genova* 6: 330-352.

Duellman, William. 2005. *Cusco Amazónico: the Lives of Amphibians and Reptiles in an Amazonian Rainforest*. Cornell University Press, Ithaca, NY.

—, 1978. The biology of an equatorial herpetofauna in Amazonian Ecuador. *University of Kansas Museum of Natural History, Miscellaneous Publication* 65.

Dwyer, Q., and M. Bayless. 1996. Notes on the husbandry and reproductive behavior of the Argus monitor (*Varanus gouldii horni*). Pp. 81-86. In: Strimple, P. (ed.). *Advances in Herpetoculture. Special Publication of the International Herpetological Symposium* No. 1.

Dwyer, Q., M. Bayless and M. Perez. 2007. Husbandry and reproduction of the black water monitor, *Varanus salvator komaini*. *Biawak* 1(1): 13-20.

Earley, R., O. Attum, and P. Eason. 2002. Varanid combat: perspectives from game theory. *Amphibia–Reptilia* 23: 469-485.

Edmund, A. 1969. Dentition. Pp. 117-200. In: Gans, Carl (ed.). *Biology of the Reptilia*. Volume 1. Morphology A. Academic Press, New York.

Edwards, Ian, A. MacDonald, and J. Proctor (eds.). 1993. *Natural History of Seram, Maluku, Indonesia*. Intercept Ltd., Andover, England.

Ehmann, Harald. 1992. *Encyclopedia of Australian Animals*. Reptiles. Angus and Robertson, Sydney.

Eibl-Eibesfeldt, I. 1962. Neue Unterarten der Meerechse, *Amblyrhynchus cristatus*, nebst weiteren Angaben zur Biologie der Art. *Senckenbergiana Biologica* 43: 177-199.

Eidenmüller, Bernd. 2007. *Monitor Lizards: Natural History, Captive Care & Breeding*. Edition Chimaira, Frankfurt.

—, 1997. *Warane: Lebensweise, Pflege, Zucht*. Herpeton, Offenbach.

—, 1995. The successful breeding of Mertens' monitor lizard, *Varanus mertensi*. *The Vivarium* 7(2):18-20.

—, 1990. Beobachtungen bei der Haltung und Nachzucht von *Varanus* (*Varanus*) mertensi Glauert, 1951. *Salamandra* 26(2/3):132-139.

Eidenmüller, Bernd, and R. Stein, R. 1998. Beobachtungen an *Varanus mertensi*-Gelegen, inkubiert unter verschidenen Bedingungen. *Herpetofauna* 20(116):30-34.

Eidenmüller, Bernd .1991. Zwillingsanlage bei *Varanus* (*Varanus*) mertensi Glauert, 1951. *Salamandra* 27(4):282-283.

Eidenmüller, Bernd, and Rudolf Wicker. 2005. Eine weitere neue Waranart aus dem *Varanus prasinus*-Komplex von der Insel Misol, Indonesia. *Sauria* 27(1): 3-8.

Elias, J., L. McBrayer, and S. Reilly. 2000. Prey transport kinematics in *Tupinambis teguixin* and *Varanus exanthematicus*: conservation of feeding behavior in 'chemosensory-tongued' lizards. *Journal of Experimental Biology* 203: 791-801.

Engle, Kelsey. 2004. Breeding behavior of the canopy goanna (*Varanus keithhornei*). Australia Zoo online publication.

Erickson, G., A. De Ricqles, V. De Buffrénil, R. Molnar and M. Bayless. 2003. Vermiform bones and the evolution of gigantism in *Megalania*—how a reptilian fox became a lion. *Journal of Vertebrate Paleontology* 23(4): 966-970.

Estes, R., and G. Pregill (eds.). 1988. *Phylogenetic Relationships of the Lizard Families*. Stanford Press, CA.

Eyeson, K. N. 1971. Pituitary control of ovarian activity in the lizard, *Agama agama*. *Journal of Zoology* 165: 367-372.

Ferraris, Joan and Stephen Palumbi (eds.). 1996. *Molecular Zoology: Advances, Strategies, and Protocols*. John Wiley, New York.

Fitzgerald, L., J. Cook, and A. Aquino. 1999. Phylogenetics and conservation of *Tupinambis* (Sauria: Teiidae). *Copeia* 1999: 894-905.

Flannery, T., and P. Schouten. 2001. *A Gap in Nature: Discovering the World's Extinct Animals*. Atlantic Monthly Press, New York.

Frank, N., and E. Ramus. 1994. *State, Federal, and CITES Regulations for Herpetologists*. Reptile and Amphibian Magazine, Pottsville, PA.

Freeman, S. and J. Herron. 1998. *Evolutionary Analysis*. Prentice Hall, Upper Saddle River, NJ.

Frost, Darrel and Richard Etheridge. 1989. A phylogenetic analysis and taxonomy of iguanian lizards (Reptilia: Squamata). *University of Kansas Museum of Natural History, Miscellaneous Publication*, 81: 1-65.

Frost, Darrel, Richard Etheridge and David Hillis. 1990. Species in concept and practice: herpetological applications. *Herpetologica* 46(1): 87-104.

Fry, Bryan, N. Vidal, J. Norman, F. Vonk, H. Ramjan, S. Kuruppu, K. Fong, S. Hedges, M. Richardson, W. Hodgson, V. Ignjatovic, R. Summerh, and E. Kochva. 2005. Early evolution of the venom system in lizards and snakes. *Nature doi*: 10.101038/nature04328.

Fuchs, K. and M. Fuchs. 2003. *The Reptile Skin: a Key-Feature in the Identification of Lizards and Snakes*. Edition Chimaira, Frankfurt.

Fuller, S., P. Baverstock, and D. King. 1998. Biogeographic origins of goannas (Varanidae): a molecular perspective. *Molecular Phylogenetics and Evolution* 9(2): 294-307.

Gasc, Jean-Pierre. 1980. *Les Lizards de Guyane*. Chabaud, Paris.

Gaulke, Marin. 1992. Distribution, population density, and exploitation of the water monitor (*Varanus salvator*) in the Philippines. *Hamadryad* 17: 21-27.

—, 1992a. Taxonomy and biology of Philippine water monitors (*Varanus salvator*). *Philippine Journal of Science* 121(4): 345-381.

—, 1989. Zur Biologie des Bindenwaranes, unter Berücksichtigung der paläogeographischen Verbreitung und der phylogenetischen Entwicklung der Varanidae. Courier Forschungsinstitut Senckenberg 112: 1-242.

Gibbons, John. 1984. Discovery of a brand-new-million-year-old iguana. *Animal Kingdom* 87(1): 23-30.

—, 1981. The biogeography of *Brachylophus* (Iguanidae) including a description of a new species, *B. vitiensis*, from Fiji. *Journal of Herpetology* 15(3): 255-274.

Glasby, C., G. Ross, and P. Beesley (eds.). 1993. *Fauna of Australia. Volume 2A Amphibia and Reptilia*. Australian Government Publishing Service, Canberra.

Goodman, Steven, and Jonathan Benstead (eds.). 2004. *The Natural History of Madagascar*. University of Chicago Press, Chicago.

Gotch, A. F. 1986. *Reptiles—Their Latin Names Explained*. Blandford Books, London.

Gould, G. and B. MacFadden. 2004. Gigantism, dwarfism, and Cope's rule: "Nothing in evolution makes sense without a phylogeny." *Bulletin of the American Museum of Natural History* 285: 219-237.

Goulding, Michael. 1989. *Amazon, the Flooded Forest*. BBC Books, London.

Greek, Tom. 2004. Open up and say aaah! *Reptiles* 12(4): 30-37.

Green, B., and D. King. 1993. *Goanna: the Biology of Varanid Lizards*. New South Wales University Press, Kensington, NSW.

Greenberg, N., and P. MacLean (eds.). 1978. *Behavior and Neurology of Lizards: an Interdisciplinary Colloquium*. U.S. Department of Health, Education, and Welfare, Rockville, MD.

Greer, Allen. 1989. *The Biology and Evolution of Australian Lizards*. Surrey Beatty & Sons, Chipping Norton, NSW.

Grismer, Lee. 2002. *Amphibians and Reptiles of Baja California*. University of California Press, Berkeley.

Grzimek, Bernhard (ed.). 1984. *Grzimek's Animal Life Encyclopedia. Volume 6. Reptiles*. Van Nostrand Reinhold Co., NY.

Guilette, Louis, Jr. 1985. The evolution of egg retention in lizards: a physiological model. Pp. 379-386. In: Grigg, G., R. Shine, and H. Ehmann (eds.). *Biology of Australasian Frogs and Reptiles*. Surrey Beatty & Sons, Chipping Norton, NSW.

Häberle, Hermann. 1974. Der Panzerteju, *Dracaena guianensis*. *Die Aquarium und Terrarium Zeitschrift* 22(1): 28-29.

Harlow, P. 1993. Life history attributes of an agamid lizard with temperature dependant sex. Abstract, 2nd World Congress of Herpetology, Sydney.

Harvey, M. and D. Barker. 1998. A new species of blue-tailed monitor lizard (genus *Varanus*) from Halmahera Island, Indonesia. *Herpetologica* 54(1): 34-44.

Hauschild, Andree. 2001. Kenntnisse, Beobachtungen und Nachtzucht des Duméril-Warans, *Varanus dumerili* (Schlegel, 1839). *Draco* 7(2): 76-8.

Hazard, Lisa. 2004. Sodium and potassium secretion by iguana salt glands: acclimation or adaptation? Pp. 84-96. In: Alberts, A., R. Carter, W. Hayes, and E. Martins (eds.). *Iguanas: Biology and Conservation*. University of California Press, Berkeley.

Heatwole, Harold. 1975. Biogeography of reptiles on some of the islands and cays of eastern Papua-New [sic] Guinea. *Atoll Research Bulletin* 180, Smithsonian Institution.

Heatwole, Harold, and J. Taylor. 1987. *Ecology of Reptiles*. Surrey Beatty & Sons, Chipping Norton, NSW.

Henkel, F., and W. Schmidt. 2000. *Amphibians and Reptiles of Madagascar and the Mascarene, Seychelles, and Comoro Islands*. Krieger Publishing, Malabar, FL.

—. 1997. *Agamen im Terrarium*. Landbuch Verlag, Hannover, Germany.

—. 1995. *Geckoes [sic]: Biology, Husbandry, and Reproduction*. Krieger Publishing, Malabar, FL.

Hermes, N. 1981. Mertens' water monitor feeding on trapped fish. *Herpetofauna* 13(1):34, Sydney.

Hillis, David. 1987. Molecular versus morphological approaches to systematics. *Annual Review of Ecology and Systematics* 18: 23-42.

Hillis, David , C. Moritz and B. Mable. 1996. *Molecular Systematics*. Second edition. Sinauer Associates, Sunderland, Mass.

Hoffmann, Christian Karl, and Heinrich Georg Bronn. 1890. *Klassen und Ordnungen des Thier-Reichs. Reptilien. Vols II. Eidechsen und Wasserechsen*. C.F. Winter'sche Verlagshandlung, Leipzig, ii.

Hollingsworth, Bradford. 2004. The evolution of iguanas: an overview of relationships and a checklist of species. Pp. 2-44. In: Alberts, A., R. Carter, W. Hayes, and E. Martins (eds.). *Iguanas: Biology and Conservation*. University of California Press, Berkeley.

Horn, Hans-Georg. 1980. Bisher unbekannte details zur kenntnis von Varanus varius auf grund und feldherpetologischen und terraristischen beobachtungen (Reptilia: Sauria:Varanidae). *Salamandra* 16(1): 1-18.

Horn, Hans-Georg, W. Bohme and U. Krebs (eds.) 2007. *Advances in Monitor Research III*. Edition Chimaira, Frankfurt, viii + 447 p. *Mertensiella* 16.

Horn, Hans-Georg, and R. Sprackland. 1992. The importance of the contributions of amateurs to herpetology. *The Vivarium* 4(1): 36-38.

Horn, Hans-Georg, and G. Visser. 1989. Review of reproduction of monitor lizards *Varanus* spp. in captivity. *International Zoo Yearbook* 28: 140-150.

—.1997. Review of reproduction of monitor lizards, *Varanus* spp. in captivity II. *International Zoo Yearbook* 35: 227-246.

Horn, Hans-Georg, and Raymond Hoser. 2003. Incubation of lace monitor (*Varanus varius*) eggs. *Herpetofauna* (Sydney) 33(1): 26-27.

Hoser, Raymond. 1998. Lace monitors (*Varanus varius*) in the wild and in captivity in Australia, with reference to a collection of seven adults held in captivity for eight years. *Monitor* 10(1): 22-36.

—. 1996. *Smuggled-2: Wildlife Trafficking, Crime and Corruption in Australia.* Kotabi Publications, Doncaster, Victoria.

—. 1993. *Smuggled: the Underground Trade in Australia's Wildlife.* Apollo Books, Mosman, NSW.

—. 1989. *Australian Reptiles and Frogs.* Pierson & Co., Sydney.

Houston, T. 1998. *Dragon lizards and Goannas of South Australia.* Second edition. South Australian Museum, Adelaide.

—. 1978. *Dragon Lizards and Goannas of South Australia.* South Australian Museum, Adelaide.

Hudson, Rick. 2007. Big lizards, big problems. *Reptiles* 15(4): 54-61.

Hudson, R., A. Alberts, S. Ellis, and O. Byers. 1994. *Conservation Assessment and Management Plan for Iguanidae and Varanidae.* IUCN/SSC Conservation Breeding Specialist Group, Apple Valley, MN.

Hurt, C. 1995. The red tegu: notes on captive breeding. *Reptiles* 3(1): 80-89.

Hutchins, Michael and James Murphy (eds.). 2003. *Grzimek's Animal Life Encyclopedia. Second edition. Volume 7: Reptiles.* Thomson Gale, Detroit.

Ibrahim, A.A. 2002. Activity area, movement patterns, and habitat use of the desert monitor, *Varanus griseus*, in the Zaranik Protected Area, north Sinai, Egypt. *African Journal of Herpetology* 51(1): 35-45.

International Commission on Zoological Nomenclature. 2000. Opinion 1948. *Hydrosaurus gouldii* Gray, 1838 (currently *Varanus gouldii*) and *Varanus panoptes* Storr, 1980 (Reptilia: Squamata): specific names conserved by the designation of a neotype for *H. gouldii. Bulletin of Zoological Nomenclature* 57(1): 63-65.

—. 1999. *The International Code of Zoological Nomenclature, 4th Edition.* ICZN, London.

Irwin, Steve. 1997. Courtship, mating and egg deposition by the captive perentie *Varanus giganteus* (Gray, 1845). *The Vivarium* 8(4): 26-56.

Irwin, Steve, Kelsey Engel, and B. Mackness. 1996. Nocturnal nesting by captive varanid lizards. *Herpetological Review* 27(4): 192-194.

Iverson, John, B. Kirsten, N. Hines, and J. Valiulis. 2004. The nesting ecology of the Allen Cays rock iguana, *Cyclura cychlura inornata* in the Bahamas. *Herpetological Monograph* No. 18: 1-36.

Jacobs, Hans. 2004. A further new emerald tree monitor lizard of the *Varanus prasinus* species group from Waigeo, West Irian (Squamata: Sauria: Varanidae). *Salamandra* 39(2): 65-74.

Jacobson, Elliot R. 2007. *Infectious Diseases and Pathology of Reptiles.* CRC Press, Boca Raton, FL.

James, C., J. Losos, and D. King. 1992. Reproductive biology and diets of goannas (Reptilia: Varanidae) from Australia. *Journal of Herpetology* 26(2): 128-136.

Janovy, John. 1985. *On Becoming a Biologist.* Harper & Row, New York.

Joger, Ulrich. 1991. A molecular phylogeny of agamid lizards. *Copeia* 1991(3): 616-622.

—. 1986. Phylogenetic analysis of *Uromastyx* lizards, based on albumin immunological distances. pp. 187-192. In: Roek, Z. *Studies in Herpetology: Proceedings of the European Herpetological Meeting* (3rd ordinary general meeting of the Societas Europaea Herpetologica) Prague 1985. Societas Europaea Herpetologica, Prague.

Joger, Ulrich and M. Lambert. 1996. Analysis of the Herpetofauna of the Republic of Mali, I. Annotated inventory, with description of a new *Uromastyx* (Sauria: Agamidae). *Journal of African Zoology* 110(1): 21-51.

Kardong, Kenneth. 1995. *Vertebrates: Comparative Anatomy, Function, Evolution.* Wm. C. Brown, Dubuque, Iowa.

Kavaliers, M. S. Courtenay, and M. Hirst. Opiates influence behavioral thermoregulation in the curly-tailed lizard, *Leiocephalus carinatus. Physiology and Behavior* 32(2):221-4.

Keogh, S., D. Edwards, R. Fisher, and P. Harlow. 2008. Molecular and morphological analysis of the critically endangered Fijian iguanas reveals cryptic diversity and a complex biogeographic history. *Philosophical Transactions of the Royal Society, series B* 2008 (363) 3413–3426.

Kiat, Chua. 2007. Feral iguana attacks *Varanus salvator* at Sungei Buloh Wetland Reserve. *Biawak* 1(1): 35-36.

Klingenberg, Roger. 1993. *Understanding Reptile Parasites: a Basic Manual for Herpetoculturists & Veterinarians.* Advanced Vivarium Systems, Escondido, CA.

Koch, A., E. Arida, and W. Böhme. 2007. Zwischenbericht über die Herpetofauna Sulawesis unter besonderer Berücksichtigung der Gattung *Varanus*: phylogeographische Beziehungen zu angrenzenden Gebieten. *Elaphe* 15(3): 42-52.

Köhler, Gunther. 2006. *Diseases of Amphibians and Reptiles.* Krieger Publishing, Malabar, FL.

—. 2002. *Schwarzleguane: Lebensweise, Pflege, Zucht.* Herpeton Verlag Elke Köhler, Offenbach.

—. 2000. *Reptilien und Amphibien Mittelamerikas. Band 1: Krokodile, Schildkröten, Echsen.* Herpeton Verlag Elke Köhler, Offenbach.

—. 1997a. *Inkubation von Reptilieneiern: Grundlagen, Anleitungen, Erfahrungen.* Herpeton Verlag Elke Köhler, Offenbach.

—. 1995. Eine neue Art der Gattung *Ctenosaura* (Sauria: Iguanidae) aus dem südlichen Campeche, México. *Salamandra* 31(1): 1-14.

—. 1993a. *Schwarze Leguane: Freilandbeobachtungen, Pflege und Zucht.* Verlag Gunther Köhler, Hanau.

—. 1993b. *Basilisken: Freilandbeobachtungen, Pflege und Zucht.* Verlag Gunther Köhler, Hanau.

Köhler, Gunther and E. Blinn. 2000. Natürliche Bastardierung zwischen *Ctenosaura bakeri* und *Ctenosaura similis* auf Utila, Honduras. *Salamandra* 36:77–79.

Köhler, Gunther and K. Klemmer. 1994. Eine neue Schwarzleguanart der Gattung *Ctenosaura* aus La Paz, Honduras. *Salamandra* 30(3): 197-208.

Köhler, Gunther and B. Langerwerf. 2000. *Tejus; Lebensweise, Pflege, Zucht.* Herpeton Verlag Elke Köhler, Offenbach.

Köhler, Gunther, W. Schroth, and B. Streit. 2000. Systematics of the Ctenosaura group of lizards (Reptilia: Sauria: Iguanidae). *Amphibia-Reptilia* 21(2): 177-191.

Krebs, Uwe. 1979. Der Dumeril-waran (*Varanus dumerilii*), ein spezialistierter krabbenfresser? *Salamandra* 15(3): 146-157.

Kunstaetter, Roger. 2003. *Ecuador and Galápagos handbook.* Footprint Handbooks, Bath, England.

Lamar, William W. 1997. *The World's Most Spectacular Reptiles &Amphibians.* World Publications, Tampa, FL.

Lambertini, Marco. 1992. *A naturalist's guide to the tropics.* University of Chicago, Chicago.

Lang, Mathias. 1989. Phylogenetic and biogeographic patterns of basiliscine iguanians (Reptilia: Squamata: "Iguanidae"). Bonner *Zoologische Monographien* 28: 1-171.

Lange, Jürgen. 1989. Observations on the Komodo monitors *Varanus komodoensis* in the Zoo-Aquarium Berlin. *International Zoo Yearbook* 28: 151-152.

Langerwerf, Bert. 2006. *Water Dragons*. T.F.H. Publications, Inc., Neptune City, NJ.

—. 1998. The Australian Brown Water Dragon and its reproduction in outdoor vivaria. *Reptiles* 6(5): 44-57.

—. 1998a. Einfluss schwankender Temperaturen auf den Schlupf bei zwei Echsenarten. *Elaphe* 3(98): 22-24.

—. 1995. Keeping and breeding the Argentine black and white tegu, *Tupinambis teguixin*. *The Vivarium* 7(3): 24-29.

Langerwerf, Bert and M. Paris. 1998. The Argentine black and white tegu, *Tupinambis teguixin* (Linnaeus, 1758). *Reptile Hobbyist* 13(12): 50-59.

Larson, E. and C. Summers. 2001. Serotonin reverses dominant social status. *Behavioural Brain Research* 121(1-2): 95-102.

Leenders, Twan. 2001. *Amphibians and Reptiles of Costa Rica*. Zona Tropica Publications, Miami.

Lemm, J. 1998. Year of the monitor: a look at some recently discovered varanids. *Reptiles* 6(9): 70-81.

Lemm, J. and A. Alberts. 1997. Guided by nature: conservation research and captive husbandry of the Cuban iguana. *Reptiles* 5(8): 76-87.

Lenk, P., B. Eidenmüller, H. Staudter, R. Wicker, R., and M. Wink. 2005. A parthenogenetic *Varanus*. *Amphibia-Reptilia* 26(4): 507-514.

Lentz, Sigrid. 1995. Zur Biologie und kologie des Nilwarans, *Varanus niloticus* (Linnaeus, 1766) in Gambia, Westafrika. *Mertensiella* 5: 1-256.

Le Poder, J. 2007. Notes on breeding *Varanus exanthematicus*. *Biawak* 1(2): 78-84.

Licht, Paul, and Albert Bennett. 1972. A scaleless snake: tests of the role of reptilian scales in water loss and heat transfer. *Copeia* 1972(4): 702-707.

Losos, J., and H. Greene. 1988. Ecological and evolutionary implications of diet in monitor lizards. *Biological Journal of the Linnean Society* 35: 379-407.

MacDonald, Stewart. 2007. Observations on the stomach contents of a road-killed perentie, *Varanus giganteus* in Western Queensland. *Biawak* 1(1): 21-23.

Mader, Douglas. 2007. Prevention and treatment of gout. *Reptiles* 15(9): 60-65.

Maderson, Paul. 1984. The squamate epidermis: new light has been shed. Pp. 111-126. In: Ferguson, Mark (ed.). *The Structure, Development and Evolution of Reptiles. Symposia of the Zoological Society of London, number 52.*

Maeda, N. and Walter Fitch. 1980. Amino acid sequence of a myoglobin from lace monitor lizard, *Varanus varius*, and its evolutionary implications. *Journal of Biological Chemistry* 256(9): 4301-4309.

Malfatti, Mark. 2007. A look at the genus *Ctenosaura*: meet the world's fastest lizard and its kin. *Reptiles* 15(11): 64-73.

Manthey, U., and N. Schuster. 1996. *Agamid lizards*. TFH Publications, Neptune City, NJ.

Manzani, P. and A. Abe. 1997. A new species of *Tupinambis* Daudin, 1802 (Squamata, Teiidae)from central Brazil. *Boletim do Museu Nacional, Nov. Series Zoology* 382: 1-10.

Martini, Frederic. 1982. *Exploring Tropical Seas: an Introduction for the Traveler and Amateur Naturalist*. Prentice-Hall, NJ.

Martins, Marcio. 2006. Life in the water: ecology of the jacarerana lizard, *Crocodilurus amazonicus*. *Herpetological Journal* 16: 171-177.

Massary, J-C de, and M. Hoogmoed. 2001. *Crocodilurus amazonicus* Spix, 1825: The valid name for *Crocodilurus lacertinus* Auctorum (*nec* Daudin, 1802) (Squamata: Teiidae). *Journal of Herpetology* 35(2): 353-357.

Mayes, Phillip. 2006. The ecology and behaviour of *Varanus mertensi* (Reptilia: Varanidae). Doctoral Thesis, Edith Cowan University, Perth.

Mazorlig, Tom. 2004. *The Simple Guide to Iguanas*. TFH Publications, Neptune City, NJ.

McArthur, Robert and Edward Wilson. 1967. The theory of island biogeography. *Princeton Monographs in Population Biology*, No. 1: 1-203.

McCoy, Michael. 2006. *Reptiles of the Solomon Islands*. Pensoft Publishers, Sofia, Bulgaria.

—. 2000. *Reptiles of the Solomon Islands* (CD-ROM). ZooGraphics, Kuranda, Queensland

—. 1980. *Reptiles of the Solomon Islands*. Wau Ecology Institute Handbook No. 7, Wau, Papua New Guinea.

McDowell, Samuel and Charles Bogert. 1954. The systematic position of *Lanthanotus* and the affinities of the anguinomorphan lizards. *Bulletin of the American Museum of Natural History* 105(1): 1-142.

McNiven, Ian, and Garrick Hitchcock. 2004. Torres Strait Islander marine subsistence specialisation and terrestrial animal translocation. *Memoirs of the Queensland Museum, Cultural Heritage Series* 3(1): 105-162.

Melbourne Aquarium. 2003. A water dragon paradise. *Reptiles Australia* 1(1): 20-23.

Mertens, Robert. 1954. Über die Rassen des Wüstenwarans (*Varanus griseus*). *Senckenberg Biologica* 35(5/6): 353-357.

—. 1942. Die Familie der Warane (Varanidae). *Abhandlungen der Senckenbergischen Naturforschenden Gesellschaft* 462, 465, 466.

—. 1934. Die Inseln-Reptilien, ihre Ausbreitung, Variation und Artbildung. *Zoologica Stuttgart* 32(84): 1-209.

Minton, Sherman, and Madge Minton. 1973. *Giant Reptiles*. Scribners, New York.

Mitchell, Lyndon. 1990. Reproduction of Gould's monitors (*Varanus gouldii*) at the Dallas Zoo. *Bulletin of the Chicago Herpetological Society* 25(1): 8.

Montgomery, J., D. Gillespie, P. Sastrawan, T. Fredeking, and G. Stewart. 2002. Aerobic salivary bacteria in wild and captive Komodo dragons. *Journal of Wildlife Diseases* 38(3): 545-551.

Moody, Scott. 1980. Phylogenetic and historical biogeographical relationships of the genera in the family Agamidae (Reptilia: Lacertilia). Ph.D. Thesis, University of Michigan, Ann Arbor.

Morrison, Clare. 2003. *A Field Guide to the Herpetofauna of Fiji*. University of the South Pacific, Suva, Fiji.

Morris, Rod, and Alison Balance. 2003. *South Sea Islands: a Natural History*. Firefly Books, Buffalo, NY.

Müller, Ulrike, and Sander Kranenbarg. 2004. Power at the tip of the tongue. *Science* 304: 217-219.

Murphy, James. 1972. Notes on Indo-Australian varanids in captivity. *International Zoo Yearbook* 12: 199-202.

Murphy, James, C. Ciofi, C. de la Panouse, and T. Walsh (eds.). 2002. *Komodo dragons: Biology and Conservation*. Smithsonian Institution Press, Washington, D.C.

Murray, B., S. Bradshaw, and D. Edward. 1991. Feeding behavior and the occurrence of caudal luring in Burton's pygopodids *Lialis burtonis* (Sauria: Pygopodidae). *Copeia* 1991(2): 509-516.

Myers, George. 1970. *How to Become an Ichthyologist*. TFH Publications, Neptune City, NJ.

Noegel, Ramon. 1989. Husbandry of West Indian rock iguanas *Cyclura* at Life Fellowship Bird Sanctuary, Seffner. *International Zoo Yearbook* 28: 131-135.

Norman, David. 1994. *Amphibians and Reptiles of the Paraguayan Chaco, Volume I*. Privately published.

Obst, F., K. Richter, and U. Jacob. 1988. *The Completely Illustrated Atlas of Reptiles and Amphibians for the Terrarium*. TFH Publications, Neptune City, NJ.

Owerkowicz, T., C. Farmer, J. Hicks, and E. Brainerd. 1999. Contribution of gular pumping to lung ventilation in monitor lizards. *Science* 284: 1661.

Packard, Gary, and Mary Packard. 1972. Photic exposure of the lizard *Callisaurus draconoides* following shielding of the parietal eye. *Copeia* 1972(4): 695-701.

Pandav, Bivash, and Binod Choudhury. 1996. Diurnal and seasonal activity patterns of watermonitor (*Varanus salvator*) in the Bhitarkanika mangroves, Orissa, India. *Hamadryad* 21: 4-12.

Parsons, Thomas. 1970. The nose and Jacobson's organ. Pp. 99-192. *Biology of the Reptilia. Volume 2. Morphology B*. Academic Press, New York.

Perry, G., R. Habani & H. Mendelssohn. 1993. The first captive reproduction of the desert monitor (*Varanus griseus*) at the research zoo of Tel Aviv University. *International Zoo Yearbook* 32: 188-190.

Peters, James. 1964. *Dictionary of Herpetology*. Hafner Publishing, New York.

Peters, Uwe. 1970. Taronga Zoo hatches Spencer's monitors. *Animal Kingdom* 73(2): 30.

Pfeffer, Pierre. 1965. *Auf den Inseln des Drachen*. Schwabenverlag, Stuttgart.

Philipp, Kai, W. Böhme, and T. Ziegler. 1999. The identity of *Varanus indicus*: redefinition and description of a sibling species coexisting at the type locality. *Spixiana* 22(3): 273-287.

Phillips, John, and Robert Millar. 1998. Reproductive biology of the white-throated savanna monitor, *Varanus albigularis*. *Journal of Herpetology* 32(3): 366-377.

Pianka, Eric. 1995 Evolution of body size: Varanid lizards as a model system. *American Naturalist* 146: 398-414.

—. 1994. Comparative ecology of *Varanus* in the Great Victoria Desert. *Australian Journal of Ecology* 19: 395-408.

—. 1982. Observations on the ecology of *Varanus* in the Great Victoria Desert. *Western Australian Naturalist* 15: 37-44.

—. 1970. Notes on the biology of *Varanus gouldi flavirufus*.

Western Australian Naturalist 11: 141-144.

Pianka, E., D. King, and R. King. 2005. *Varanoid Lizards of the World*. Indiana University Press, Bloomington.

Pietsch, T. and W. Anderson (eds.). 1997. *Collection Building in Ichthyology and Herpetology*. American Society of Ichthyologists and Herpetologists Special Publication 3, Lawrence, KS.

Pike, Lindsay. 2004. Desert delights. *Reptiles USA 2005 Annual*: 100-107.

Polleck, R. 1999. F2-Nachzucht mit Anmerkungen zur Terrarienhaltung des Mertenswarans *Varanus mertensi* Glauert, 1951. *Herpetofauna* 21(119): 19-23, Weinstadt.

Pregill, G., J. Gauthier, and H. Greene. 1986. The evolution of helodermatid squamates, with description of a new taxon and an overview of Varanoidea. *Transactions of the San Diego Society of Natural History* 21(11): 167-202.

Presch, William. 1983. The lizard family Teiidae: is it a monophyletic group? *Zoological Journal of the Linnean Society* 77: 189-197.

—. 1973. A review of the tegus, lizard genus *Tupinambis* (Sauria: Teiidae) from South America. *Copeia* 1973(4): 740-746.

Purcell, Rosamond. 1999. *Swift as a Shadow: Extinct and Endangered Animals*. Houghton Mifflin, Boston.

Quammen, David. 1996. *The Song of the Dodo*. Scribners, New York.

Radford, Larry, and Frederick Paine. 1989. The reproduction and management of the Dumeril's monitor *Varanus dumerilii* at the Buffalo Zoo. *International Zoo Yearbook* 28: 153-154.

Rajan, T. 2001. Would Darwin get a grant today? *Natural History* 110(5): 86.

Rassmann, K., M. Markmann, F. Trillmich, and D. Tautz. 2004. Tracing the evolution of the Galápagos iguanas: a molecular approach. Pp. 71-83. In: Alberts, A., R. Carter, W. Hayes, and E. Martins (eds.). *Iguanas: Biology and Conservation*. University of California Press, Berkeley.

Rassmann, K. and F. Trillmich, and D. Tautz. 1997. Hybridization between Galápagos land and marine iguanas (*Conolophus subcristatus* and *Amblyrhynchus cristatus*) on Plaza Sur. *Journal of Zoology* 242: 729-739.

Rehak, Ivan. 1999. Captive breeding of the caiman lizard, *Dracaena guianensis*. *Herpetofauna* (Sydney) 29(2): 57-60.

Reisinger, M., and D. Reisinger-Raweyai. 2007. *Varanus boehmei* keeping and first breeding in the terrarium. *Reptilia* 50: 20-24.

Rieppel, Olivier. 2000. The braincases of mosasaurs and *Varanus*, and the relationships of snakes. *Zoological Journal of the Linnean Society* 129: 489-514.

Rismiller, P., M. McKelvey, and B. Green. 2007. Life history studies of Rosenberg's goanna (*Varanus rosenbergi*) on Kangaroo Island, South Australia. *Biawak* 1(1): 42-43.

Romer, Alfred. 1956. *The Osteology of the Reptiles*. University of Chicago Press, Chicago.

Romer, Alfred , and T. Parsons. 1986. *The Vertebrate Body*. Sixth edition. Saunders, Philadelphia.

Rosenblum, Erica, H. Hoekstra, and M. Nachman. 2004. Adaptive reptile color variation and the evolution of the Mc1r gene. *Evolution* 58(8): 1794-1808.

Ruibal, Rodolpho. 1952. Revisionary studies of some South American Teiidae. *Bulletin of the Museum of Comparative Zoology* 106(11): 477-529.

Savage, Jay. 2002. *The Amphibians and Reptiles of Costa Rica: a Herpetofauna Between Two Continents, Between Two Seas*. University of Chicago Press, Chicago.

Schmidt, Karl, and Robert Inger. 1957. *Living Reptiles of the World*. Doubleday, New York.

Schürer, U. and H. G. Horn. 1976. Freiland- und Gefangenschaftsbeobachtungen am australischen Wasserwaran, *Varanus mertensi*. *Salamandra* 12(4): 176-188.

Schwartz, Albert, and Robert Henderson. 1991. *Amphibians and Reptiles of the West Indies: Descriptions, Distributions, and Natural History*. University of Florida Press, Gainesville.

Shea, Glenn. 1998. Backyard blue-tongues. *Nature Australia*. Summer 1998-1999: 31-39.

—. 1994. Three species of goanna occur in the Sydney basin. *Herpetofauna* 24(2): 14-18.

Shea, Glenn, and Gary Reddacliff. 1986. Ossification in the hemipenes of varanids. *Journal of Herpetology* 20(4): 566-568.

Shine, Richard. 1986. Food habits and reproductive biology of four sympatric species of varanid lizards in tropical Australia. *Herpetologica* 42(3): 346-360.

Shine, R., P. Harlow, Ambariyanto, Boeadi, Mumpuni, and J.S. Keogh. 1998. Monitoring monitors: a biological perspective on the commercial harvesting of Indonesian reptiles. *Mertensiella* 9: 61-68.

Shnayerson, Michael, and Mark Plotkin. 2002. Supergerm warfare. *Smithsonian* Oct. 114-126.

Slowinski, Joseph, and Jay Savage. 1995. Urotomy in *Scaphiodontophis*: evidence for the multiple tail break hypothesis in snakes. *Herpetologica* 51(3): 338-341.

Solessio, E. and G. Engbretson. 1999. Electroretinogram of the parietal eye of lizards: photoreceptor, glial, and lens cell contributions. *Visual Neuroscience* 16: 895-907.

Spears, Michael. 2004. The wonderful world of water dragons. *Reptiles* 12(6): 44-55.

Sprackland, Robert. 2007a. Neurophysiology and behavioral ramifications in varanid lizards. *Biawak* 1(1): 44.

—. 2007. Peach-throat monitors. *Reptiles* 15(2): 40-47.

—. 2001a. To the parents of a young herpetologist. *Bulletin of the Chicago Herpetological Society* 36(2): 29-30.

—. 2001b. *Guide to the Care and Maintenance of Savannah and Grasslands Monitors*. AVS/Bowtie Press, Mission Viejo, CA.

—. 2000. Magnificent millennial monitor maintenance: a beginner's guide to five easy species. *Reptiles USA*: 54-63.

—. 1999a. Character displacement among sympatric varanid lizards: a study of natural selection and systematics in action (Reptilia: Squamata: Varanidae). *Mertensiella* 11: 113-120.

—. 1999b. It's a bird, it's a plane! It's... a turtle?? *Reptile & Amphibian Hobbyist* 4(12): 18-19.

—. 1999c. Convergence: when parallel lines meet. *Reptile & Amphibian Hobbyist* 4(10): 20-21.

—. 1999d. A new species of monitor (Squamata: Varanidae) from Indonesia. *Reptile Hobbyist* February: 20-27.

—. 1999e. Are sympatric monitors speaking with forked tongues? Sympatry and tongue colour in sibling species of monitor lizards. *Herpetofauna* (Sydney) 29(2): 65-70.

—. 1998. Mangrove monitor lizards. *Reptiles* 5(3):48-63.

—. 1998a. Iguanids, iguanines, and drawing lines. *The Vivarium* 10(1): 24-26.

—. 1995. Evolution, systematics, and variation in Pacific mangrove monitor lizards. Doctoral Thesis, University College, London.

—. 1995a. Duméril's monitor lizard. *Reptiles* 3(7): 56-69.

—. 1995b. *Animals and Fishes in Aquaterrariums*. TFH Publications, Neptune City, NJ.

—. 1994. Rediscovery and taxonomic review of *Varanus indicus spinulosus* Mertens, 1941. *Herpetofauna* (Sydney) 24(2): 33-39.

—. 1994a. Herpetological explorations of New Guinea: discovering new life on the mysterious island. *Reptiles*, 1(3): 60-67.

—. 1993. The taxonomic status of the monitor lizard, *Varanus dumerilii heteropholis* Boulenger, 1892 (Reptilia: Varanidae). *Sarawak Museum Journal* 44(65): 113-121.

—. 1993a. Rediscovery of a Solomon Islands monitor lizard (*Varanus indicus spinulosus*). *The Vivarium* 4(5): 25-27.

—. 1993b. Venomous lizards. *Tropical Fish Hobbyist*, June: 138-145.

—. 1993d. Carnivorous lizards and their diet. *The Vivarium* 5(5): 12-14.

—. 1992. *Giant Lizards*. TFH Publications, Neptune City, NJ.

—. 1991a. Taxonomic review of the *Varanus prasinus* group with descriptions of two new species. *Memoirs of the Queensland Museum* 30(3): 561-576.

—. 1991b. The origin and zoogeography of monitor lizards of the subgenus *Odatria* Gray (Sauria: Varanidae): a re-evaluation. *Mertensiella* 2: 240-252.

—. 1991c. The emerald monitor lizard, *Varanus prasinus*. *Tropical Fish Hobbyist*, April: 110-114.

—. 1991d. A myriad of monitors. *Tropical Fish Hobbyist*, January: 130-138.

—. 1990. College herpetology: is it for you? *Northern California Herpetological Society Newsletter* 9(1): 14-15.

—. 1989a. Mating and waiting: a status report on reproduction in captive monitor lizards (Sauria: Varanidae). In: *Northern California Captive Propagation and Husbandry Conference Proceedings*, 1989: 57-63.

—. 1989c. A preliminary study of food discrimination in monitor lizards (Reptilia: Lacertilia: Varanidae). *Bulletin of the Chicago Herpetological Society*, 25(10): 181-183.

—. 1989d. Endangered species and placing blame: what statistics say about the real causes of animal extinctions. *The Vivarium* 1(4): 40-44.

—. 1982. Feeding and nutrition of monitor lizards in captivity and in the wild. *Bulletin of the Kansas Herpetological Society* 47: 15-18.

—. 1982a. *Varanus* "monitor," an invalid name for *Varanus bengalensis*. *Herpetological Review* 13(4): 117.

—. 1977. Notes on Dumeril's monitor lizard, *Varanus dumerili* (Schlegel). *Sarawak* Museum Journal 24(45): 287-291.

Sprackland, Robert and Hans-Georg Horn. 1992. The importance of the contributions of amateurs to herpetology. *The Vivarium* 4(1): 36-38.

Sprackland, Robert and Sean McKeown. 1997. Herpetology and herpetoculture as a career. *Reptiles* 5(4): 32-47.

Sprackland, Robert and Sean McKeown. 1995. The path to a career in herpetology. *The Vivarium* 6(1):22-34.

Sprackland, Robert , H. Smith, and P. Strimple. 1997. *Hydrosaurus gouldii* Gray, 1838 (currently *Varanus gouldii*) and *Varanus panoptes* Storr, 1980 (Reptilia, Squamata): proposed conservation of the specific names by designation of a neotype for *H. gouldii. Bulletin of Zoological Nomenclature* 54(2): 95-99.

Sprackland, Robert, T. Sprackland, and D. Diessner. 2004. Reptiles and mammals of Fitzroy Island, Queensland. *Memoirs of the Queensland Museum* 49(2): 733-739.

Sprackland, Teri and Robert Sprackland. 1999. A collection of translations of type descriptions of monitor lizards. Part 1, *Varanus indicus* and its allies (Reptilia: Varanidae). *Lizard Biology* (online at www.curator.org). 1(1).

Spawls, S., K. Howell, R. Drewes, and J. Ashe. 2002. *A Field Guide to the Reptiles of East Africa*. Academic Press, San Diego.

SSAR. 1985. *Herpetology as a Career*. Society for the Study of Amphibians and Reptiles, Cleveland.

Stanner, Michael. 1999. Effects of overcrowding on the annual activity cycle and husbandry of *Varanus griseus*. *Mertensiella* 11: 51-62.

Stanner, Michael and H. Mendelssohn. 1991. Activity patterns of the desert monitor (*Varanus griseus*) in the southern coastal plain of Israel. *Mertensiella* 2: 253-262.

Stanner, Michael and H. Mendelssohn. 1987. Sex ratio, population density and home range of the desert monitor (*Varanus griseus*) in the southern coastal plain of Israel. *Amphibia-Reptilia* 8(1987): 153-164.

Storr, G. 1980. The monitor lizards (genus *Varanus* Merrem, 1820) of Western Australia. *Records of the Western Australian Museum* 8(2): 237-250.

Storr, G., L. Smith, and R. Johnstone. 1983. *Lizards of Western Australia: Dragons and Monitors*. Western Australian Museum, Perth.

Summers, Adam. 2003. Monitor marathons: how one group of lizards turns a gasp into a gulp. *Natural History* June: 32-33.

Summers, C. and N. Greenberg. 1995. Activation of central biogenic amines following aggressive interaction in male lizards, *Anolis carolinensis. Brain Behavior and Evolution* 45:339-349.

Swan, Gerry, and Ralph Foster. 2005. The reptiles and amphibians of Mutawintji National Park, western New South Wales. *Australian Zoologist* 33(1): 39-48.

Swan, G., G. Shea, and R. Sadlier. 2004. *A Field Guide to Reptiles of New South Wales*. Second edition. New Holland Publishers, Frenchs Forest, NSW.

Sweet, Samuel. 1999. Spatial ecology of *Varanus glauerti* and *V. glebopalma* in northern Australia. *Mertensiella* 11: 317-366.

Sweet, Samuel, and Eric Pianka. 2003. The lizard kings. *Natural History* 112(9): 40-45.

Switak, Karl. 2002. Field notes for *Varanus albigularis* in Southern Africa. *Bulletin of the Chicago Herpetological Society* 37(6): 98-99.

Tennesen, Michael. 2006. What's your poison? *New Scientist* 191(2571): 51-53.

Thireau, Michel, R. Sprackland, and T. Sprackland. 1998. A report on Seba's specimens in the herpetological collection of the Museum National d'Histoire Naturelle, Paris, and their status as Linnean types. *The Linnean* 13(4): 38-45.

Thomas, C., A. Cameron, R. Green, M. Bakkenes, L. Beaumont, Y. Collingham, B. Erasmus, M. Ferreira de Siqueira, A. Grainger, L. Hannah, L. Hughes, B. Huntley, A. van Jaarsveld, G. Midgley, L. Miles, M. Ortega-Huerta, A. Peterson, O. Phillips, and S. Williams. 2004. Extinction risk from climate change. *Nature* 427(6970): 145-148.

Thompson, G. 1995. Foraging patterns and behaviours, body postures and movement speed for *Varanus gouldii* (Reptilia: Varanidae), in a semi-urban environment. *Journal of the Royal Society of Western Australia* 78:107-114.

Thompson, G. and E. Pianka. 1999. Reproductive ecology of the black-headed goanna *Varanus tristis* (Squamata: Varanidae). *Journal of the Royal Society of Western Australia* 82: 27-31.

Trembath, Dane. 2000. Nocturnal activity by Goulds [sic] monitor (*Varanus gouldii*) at Town Common Environmental Park, Townsville, Queensland. *Herpetofauna* (Sydney) 30(2): 52.

Underwood, Garth. 1970. The eye. Pp. 1-98. In: Gans, Carl, and Thomas Parsons (eds.). *Biology of the reptilia. Volume 2. Morphology B.* Academic Press, NY.

Vance, Thomas. 1980. Sighting of *Dracaena guianensis* (Lacertilia, Teiidae) from the region of the Rio Napo, Ecuador. *Bulletin of the New York Herpetological Society* 16(1): 10-11.

Van Devender, R.W. 1982. Growth and ecology of spiny-tailed and green iguanas in Costa Rica, with comments on the evolution of herbivory and large body size, pp. 162–163. In: G.M. Burghardt and A.S. Rand (eds.). *Iguanas of the World: Their Behavior, Ecology and Conservation.* Noyes Publications, Park Ridge, NJ.

Vanzolini, P., and J. Valencia. 1965. The genus *Dracaena*, with a brief consideration of macroteiid relationships (Sauria: Teiidae). *Arquivos de Zoologia* 13: 7-35.

Vernet, R. 1977. Recherches sur l'écologie de *Varanus griseus* Daudin (Reptilia: Sauria: Varanidae) dans les ecosystems sableaux de Sahara nord-occidental (Algérie). Ph.D. thesis, University of Pierre and Marie Curie, Paris.

Vernet, R., M. Lemire, and C. Grenot. Field studies on activity and water balance of a desert monitor *Varanus griseus* (Reptilia, Varanidae). *Journal of Arid Environments* 1988(15): 81-90.

Vincent, Matt, and Steve Wilson. 1999. *Australian Goannas.* New Holland Publishers, Sydney.

Visser, G. 1985. Notizen zur Brutbiologie des Gelbwarans *Varanus (Empagusia) flavescens* im Zoo Rotterdam. *Salamandra* 21(2/3): 161-168.

Vitt, Laurie, and Eric Pianka (eds.). 1994. *Lizard Ecology: Historical and Experimental Perspectives.* Princeton University Press, NJ.

Vogel, P., R. Nelson, and R. Kerr. 1996. Conservation strategy for the Jamaican iguana, *Cyclura collei.* Pp. 395-406. In: Powell, R., and R. Henderson (eds.). *Contributions to West Indian Herpetology: a Tribute to Albert Schwartz.* SSAR, St. Louis, MO.

Vogel, Zden k. n.d. (1950?) *Reptile Life.* Spring Books, London.

Walsh, T., R. Rosscoe, and G. Birchard. 1993. Dragon tales: the history, husbandry, and breeding of Komodo monitors at the National Zoo. *The Vivarium* 4(6): 23-26.

Wareham, David. 1993. *The Reptile and Amphibian Keeper's Dictionary: an A-Z of Herpetology.* Blandford Books, London.

Waterloo, Brian, and Mark Bayless. 2006. Notes on the breeding behaviour of the crocodile monitor (*Varanus salvadorii*) in captivity. *Herpetological Bulletin* 98: 2-6.

Watts, P.C., K.R. Buley, S. Sanderson, W. Boardman, C. Ciofi, and R. Gibson. 2006. Parthenogenesis in Komodo dragons. *Nature* 444: 1021-1022.

Weigel, John. 1988. *Care of Australian Reptiles in Captivity.* Australian Reptile Keeper's Association, Gosford, NSW.

Weis, Peter. 1996. Husbandry and breeding of the frilled lizard (Chlamydosaurus kingii). Pp. 87-92. In: Strimple, P. (ed.). *Advances in Herpetoculture.* Special Publication of the International Herpetological Symposium No. 1.

Whittier, J., and D. Moeller. 1993. *Varanus prasinus* (the emerald monitor) on Moa Island, Torres Strait, Australia. *Memoirs of the Queensland Museum* 1993:130.

Wiewandt, T. 1979. La gran iguana de Mona. *Natural History* 88(10): 56-65.

—. 1977. Ecology, behavior, and management of the Mona Island ground iguana, *Cyclura stejnegeri*. Unpublished Ph.D. Dissertation, Cornell University.

Wikelski, M., and F. Trillmich. 1997. Body size and sexual dimorphism in marine iguanas fluctuate as a result of opposing natural and sexual selection: an island comparison. *Evolution* 51(3): 922-936.

Williams, Ted. 1984. Game laws weren't writ for fat cats. *Audubon* July: 104-113.

Wilms, Tomas. 2001. *Dornschwanzagamen: Lebensweise, Pflege und Zucht*. Herpeton-Verlag, Offenbach.

Wilson, Steve. 2005. *A Field Guide to Reptiles of Queensland*. New Holland, Frenchs Forest, NSW.

—. 1987. Goanna! *GEO, Australasia's Geographical Magazine* 9(3): 92-107.

Wilson, Steve and D. Knowles. 1988. *Australia's Reptiles: a Photographic Reference to the Terrestrial Reptiles of Australia*. Collins Publishing, Sydney.

Wilson, Steve and G. Swan. 2003. *Reptiles of Australia*. Princeton Field Guides, Princeton University Press, Princeton, NJ.

Winsor, Mary. 1991. *Reading the Shape of Nature: Comparative Zoology at the Agassiz Museum*. University of Chicago Press, Chicago.

Winstel, Al. 1997. It's not the heat, it's the humidity! *Reptile & Amphibian Magazine* 49: 50-55.

Wright, Dan. 2007 (?). Quick to defend: Nile monitors have a reputation for being eager to attack. *Reptile Care* 3(6): 19-21.

Ziegler, Thomas, and Wolfgang Böhme. 1996. Über das Beutespektrum von *Varanus dumerilii* (Schlegel, 1839). *Salamandra* 32(3): 203-210.

Ziegler, Thomas, Wolfgang Böhme, and K. Philipp. 1999. *Varanus caerulivirens* sp. n., a new monitor lizard of the *V. indicus* group from Halmahera, Moluccas, Indonesia (Squamata: Sauria: Varanidae). *Herpetozoa* 12(1/2): 45-56.

Ziegler, Thomas, K. Philipp, and W. Böhme. 1999. Zum Artstatus und zur Genitalmorphologie von *Varanus finschi* Böhme, Horn, und Zaiegler, 1994, mit neuen Verbreitungsangaben für *V. finschi* und *V. doreanus* (A. B. Meyer, 1874)(Reptilia: Sauria: Varanidae). *Zoologisches Abhandlungen Dresden* 50(2): 267-279.

Ziegler, Thomas, A. Schmitz, A. Koch and W. Böhme. 2007. A review of the subgenus *Euprepiosaurus* of *Varanus* (Squamata: Varanidae): morphological and molecular phylogeny, distribution and zoography, with an identification key for the members of the *V. indicus* and *V. prasinus* species groups. *Zootaxa* 1472: 1-28.

Zimmermann, Elke. 1983. *Reptiles and Amphibians: Breeding Terrarium Animals*. TFH Publications, Neptune City, NJ.

Zug, G. 1991. The lizards of Fiji: natural history and systematics. Bishop Museum Bulletin in *Zoology* 2: 1-136.

Zug, G., L. Vitt, and J. Caldwell. 2001. *Herpetology: an Introductory Biology of Amphibians and Reptiles*. Second edition. Academic Press, San Francisco.

Professional Academic Resources

American Society of Ichthyologists and Herpetologists
(publishers of *Copeia*)
Maureen Donnelly, Secretary
Grice Marine Laboratory
Florida International University
Biological Sciences
11200 SW 8th St.
Miami, FL 33199
Telephone: (305) 348-1235
E-mail: asih@fiu.edu
www.asih.org

Association of Reptile and Amphibian Veterinarians (ARAV)
P.O. Box 605
Chester Heights, PA 19017
Phone: 610-358-9530
Fax: 610-892-4813
E-mail: ARAVETS@aol.com
www.arav.org

Association of Zoos and Aquariums
8403 Colesville Rd.
Suite 710
Silver Spring, MD 20910
Telephone: (301) 562-0777
Fax: (301) 562-0888
G.e.n.e.r.a.l.I.n.q.u.i.r.y@aza.org

Australian Herpetological Society
(publisher of *Herpetofauna*)
www.ahs.org.au

Australian Society of Herpetologists
John Wombey, Secretary
c/- CSIRO Wildlife and Ecology
PO Box 84, Lyneham, ACT 2602
Australia.
Email: J.Wombey@dwe.csiro.au

Deutsche Gesellschaft für Herpetologie und Terrarientiere
(publishers of *Salamandra*, *Mertensiella*, and *Elaphe*)
www.dght.de/ag/schlangen/index.html

The Herpetologists' League
(publisher of *Herpetologica*)
/www.herpetologistsleague.org/en/

Society for the Study of Amphibians and Reptiles (SSAR)
(publisher of *Journal of Herpetology* and *Herpetological Review*)
Marion Preest, Secretary
The Claremont Colleges
925 N. Mills Ave.
Claremont, CA 91711
Telephone: 909-607-8014
E-mail: mpreest@jsd.claremont.edu
www.ssarherps.org

Herpetological Societies

British Herpetological Society
11 Strathmore Place
Montrose, Angus
DD10 8LQ
United Kingdom
www.thebhs.org

Center for North American Herpetology
www.cnah.org

Chicago Herpetological Society
Phone: (312) 409-4456
www.chicagoherp.org

Kansas Herpetological Society
Phone: (785) 272-1076)
www.ukans.edu/~khs

League of Florida Herpetological Societies
www.jaxherp.tripod.com/league.htm

Nebraska Herpetological Society
www.nebherp.org

New York Herpetological Society
www.wnyherp.org/index.php

San Diego Herpetological Society
PO Box 503835
San Diego CA 92150
E-mail: sdhs@sdherpsociety.org
www.sdherpsociety.org

Information sources

General Herp Information

Convention on International Trade in Endangered Species (CITES)
www.cites.org

Field Museum of Natural History
request article reprints at:
 www.fmnh.org/research_collections/zoology/aandr_reprints.htm

International Reptile Conservation Foundation
www.IRCF.org

Venomdoc(venom research)
www.venomdoc.com

Virtual Museum of Natural History
www.curator.org

Agamids

Melissa Kaplan's Herp Care Collection: Water Dragons
http://www.anapsid.org/waterdragons.html

Dragon Attack (sailfin dragons)
www.sailfindragon.com

Iguanids

West Coast Iguana research (ctenosaur information)
www.westcoastiguana.com

Cyclura.com
www.cyclura.com

Iguana Specialist Group
www.IUCN-ISG.org

International Iguana Foundation
http://www.iguanafoundation.org/index.php

Utila Iguana Recovery Program
www.utila-iguana.de

Varanids

International Varanid Interest Group, (publishers of *Biawak*)
www.varanidae.org

Monitor-Lizards.net
www.monitor-lizards.net

Varanus albigularis

Note: **Boldfaced** numbers indicate illustrations.

Photo Credits

AliciaHH (courtesy of Shutterstock): 56

Lynsey Allan (courtesy of Shutterstock): 199

Ben Aller and Michaela Manago: 212, 269 (both)

Anastazzo (courtesy of Shutterstock): 94

Olivier Antonini: 80, 136 (both)

Randall D. Babb: 161

Marian Bacon: 1, 8, 41, 52, 72, 118, 126, 198, 201, 202, 227 (right), 235 (left), 244, 252, 253, 266 (right), 283, 291, 292, and front cover

R. D. Bartlett: 10, 24, 59, 62, 108, 120, 131 (right), 150 (left), 162 (right), 168 (both), 172, 174 (left), 178, 255 (right), 304

Norman Bateman (courtesy of Shutterstock): 181

Mark K. Bayless: 22, 50, 60, 65, 76, 95, 100, 115, 217, 222 (left), 223,

John Bell (courtesy of Shutterstock): 6, 12, 57, 186

Allen Both: 67, 197, 218, 243

Marius Burger: 218 (right), 226

Chris Burt (courtesy of Shutterstock): 272

R. E. Carr: 182

Clearviewstock (courtesy of Shutterstock): 20

John Coborn: 179

Norma Cornes (courtesy of Shutterstock): 38

Scott Corning: 54, 134, 137

David Davis (courtesy of Shutterstock): 166

Anthony Del Prete: 162 (left)

Dhoxax (courtesy of Shutterstock): 325

Apostolos Diamantis (courtesy of Shutterstock): 274

Christopher Dieter: 71 (left), 220, 221, 246, 258

Herb Ellerbrock: 61

Evgeniapp (courtesy of Shutterstock): 256

Fivespots (courtesy of Shutterstock): 209, 301

Isabell Francais: 39, 90, 200

Paul Freed: 16, 74, 92 (right), 97, 107, 138, 152, 158, 191 (left) 198, 219, 222 (right), 236 (right), 24 (left), 242, 266 (left), 271 (both), 295 (left)

U. E. Friese: 71 (right)

C. M. Garrett: 231 (right)

Maren Gaulke: 109, 267, 268

James E. Gerholdt: 132 (both), 191 (right), 205

Michael Gilroy: 148 (right)

Chris Graham: 156

Richard Griffin (courtesy of Shutterstock): 83 (top)

Raymond Hoser: 277 (left)

Aron Hsio (courtesy of Shutterstock): 66

Ray Hunziker: 254 (right), 293

Innocent (courtesy of Shutterstock): 14 (right)

Eric Isselee (courtesy of Shutterstock): 282 (bottom)

Javarman (courtesy of Shutterstock): 154, 290

Manoj Jethani (courtesy of Shutterstock): 35

V. T. Jirousek: 189, 249

Wayne Raymond Johnson,: 140

K. Kaplan (courtesy of Shutterstock): 110

Julie Keen (courtesy of Shutterstock): 86

Gunther Köhler: 157, 163, 165

Wayne Labenda: 254 (left)

Bert Langerwerf: 139, 141, 194, 195, 196 (both)

Michael Ledray (courtesy of Shutterstock): 294

Luis Louro (courtesy of Shutterstock): 84

Erik Loza: 43, 83 (bottom), 210, 211

Ken Lucas: 28 (right)

Michaela Manago: 261 (both), 262, 263, 264 (both), 265

Barry Mansell: 159 (left)

W. P. Mara: 227 (left)

Martin Maun (courtesy of Shutterstock): 190

Sean McKeown: 55, 122, 176, 184, 280

G. and C. Merker: 68 (left), 69 (both)

Holger Mette (courtesy of Shutterstock): 289

L. A. Mitchell: 112, 236 (left)

Phil Morley (courtesy of Shutterstock): 102

Tatiana Morozova (courtesy of Shutterstock): 75

John C. Murphy: 33

Aaron Norman: 235, 257

Opis (courtesy of Shutterstock): 207

Carol Polich: 58

R. Powell: 173

Jason Prime: 81, 183

Wayne Rogers: 28 (left and center), 32, 93, 99

Ivan Savima: 192

Ian Scott (courtesy of Shutterstock): 7

Helen Shorman (courtesy of Shutterstock): 213

Ilya Shulman (courtesy of Shutterstock): 117

Mark Smith: 174 (right), 245 (right)

Juha Sompinmäki (courtesy of Shutterstock): 18

Adi Soon (courtesy of Shutterstock): 26

Robert G. Sprackland: 9, 30 (all), 40 (all), 77, 98, 104, 116, 123, 124, 160, 170, 180, 187 (both), 188, 224, 228, 229, 231 (left), 233 (right), 234, 237, 238, 239, 240 (right), 241, 245 (left), 247, 250, 251, 255 (left), 273 (left), 281, 282 (top), 284, 285 (both), 295 (right), 335

James Steidl (courtesy of Shutterstock): 47 and back cover

Stan Sung: 64

Karl H. Switak: 14 (left), 17, 36, 92 (left), 128, 131 (left), 145, 146, 153 (both), 155, 159 177, 204, 225, 273 (right), 275 (both), 277 (right), 278, 279, 296, 298

Zoltan Takacs: 150 (right)

Morozova Tatyana (courtesy of Shutterstock): 288

John Tyson: 96

Maleta M. Walls: 68 (right), 88, 91

Jeremy Wee (courtesy of Shutterstock): 216

Brooke Whatnall (courtesy of Shutterstock): 37

Ashley Whitworth (courtesy of Shutterstock): 286

David Zoffer: 148 (left)

Michael Zysman (courtesy of Shutterstock): 4,

About The Contributors

Ben Aller and **Michaela Manago** have been breeding large monitors for nearly two decades, and have had particularly spectacular success propagating *Varanus dumerilii*. Ben also designs and builds zoo and museum exhibits.

Chad Brown and **Robyn Markland** own ProExotics in Denver, a well-known retail outlet where they specialize in producing captive bred pythons, monitors, and venomous lizards.

Dr. Gunther Köhler is curator of herpetology at Frankfurt's prestigious Senckenberg Museum, where he specializes in the study of large iguanids, particularly those of Central America. He has published several German books on the lizards of that region. He is also the describer of several ctenosaur species and heads the international effort to save the Utila iguana.

Bert Langerwerf was the founder of Agama International in Alabama. He became a recognized authority on the breeding of large iguanids, agamids, and tegus. His extensive field observations of wild populations in South America gave him considerable insight into developing captive breeding techniques that he shared through writing and lectures. Bert passed away in 2008.

Paul Rodriguez is a private herpetoculturist who has been keeping and breeding water monitors for many years.

About the Author

Robert George Sprackland, Ph.D., is Director of The Virtual Museum of Natural History at www.curator.org and is a world-recognized authority on monitor lizards who has studied herpetology and paleontology for more than four decades. He holds degrees in zoology from the University of Kansas (B.A.), San José State University (M.A.), and University College London (Ph.D.), where he conducted the bulk of his research at the Natural History Museum, London. This was followed by postdoctoral work in the herpetology section of the National Museums of Scotland, Edinburgh.

Robert conducts tropical biodiversity surveys, principally in Australia and New Guinea; taught biology, ecology, and anatomy and physiology for nearly three decades; and is a Research Associate in Zoology at the National Museums of Scotland and the University of Papua New Guinea. His earlier books include *All About Lizards*, *Giant Lizards*, *Aquaterrariums*, and *Care of Savannah and Grasslands Monitors*, and he wrote the CD-ROM *Key to the Sharks and Rays of the World*. Robert is a regular contributor to *Reptiles* magazine, and he has been published frequently in *Tropical Fish Hobbyist* (for which he won a Peninsula Press Club Award for nature journalism), *Natural History*, *Military History Quarterly*, *American School Board Journal*, *Nikkei Electronics Asia*, and *High Technology Careers* magazines.

Robert has served as a zoological consultant to BBC, the Discovery Channel producers, and the television show *O'Shea's Big Adventure*. In addition to his interest in herpetology, he conducts research on neurobiology and behavior, military history, and education policy and methods.